Welsh Journal

Jeremy Hooker
Welsh Journal

seren

Seren is the book imprint of
Poetry Wales Press Ltd
Nolton Street, Bridgend, CF31 1EF, Wales
www.seren-books.com

© Jeremy Hooker 2001

The right of Jeremy Hooker to be identified as the
Author of this Work has been asserted in accordance with
the Copyright, Designs and Patents Act, 1988.

ISBN 1-85411-301-1

A CIP record for this title is available from
the British Library

Cover painting: *A Welsh Stream* (Beidog) by Aubrey W. Hooker

*The publisher works with the financial assistance of the
Arts Council of Wales*

Printed in Plantin by Bell and Bain Ltd, Glasgow

Foreword

This book has been shaped from extracts from my journal for the period from October 1969 to December 1980, together with a selection from my poetry written during the same period. The factual background is as follows.

In the autumn of 1969, my then wife, Sue, and I moved out of Aberystwyth, where I was a lecturer in the English department at the University College, and went to live at 'Brynbeidog', a cottage we had bought in the parish of Llangwyryfon some nine miles south-east of the town, in the hill country under Mynydd Bach. From there, we made periodic visits to my wife's parents, Charles and Winifrid, in Pulborough, Sussex, and to my parents who lived in the house where I had grown up, 'Hayford', in Pennington, a village situated near the Solent and on the edge of the New Forest, in Hampshire. My relationship with my elder brother, Tony, and certain friendships, especially with Jim Insole, were an integral part of my life during this period, as they are to the present. The years at Brynbeidog saw the births of my son and daughter, Joe and Emily.

The journal from which I have drawn simultaneously records my gradual 'discovery' of Wales, through the life of a particular Welsh neighbourhood, and through my involvement as a critic in what was then commonly referred to as Anglo-Welsh literature, and a phase of my self-discovery as a poet. It is a book of meetings across cultural and geographical boundaries, and a chapter of intellectual and spiritual autobiography. While I have placed some poems at the times when they were written, I have not done so with all of them. In any case, the 'materials' that went to the making of poems were frequently laid down over a period of years. Instead of an exact temporal 'placing', my aim has been to relate poems to the imaginative and experiential grounding – the life – from which they evolved.

The Poems

The poems have been taken from the following collections:

The Elements (The Triskel Poets Six, Christopher Davies, 1972): 'Earth Poems'.

Soliloquies of a Chalk Giant (Enitharmon Press, 1972): 'Matrix'; 'The Giant's Shadow'; 'The Chalk Pebble'; 'The Giant's Boast'.

Landscape of the Daylight Moon (Enitharmon Press 1978): from 'A Hambledon Sequence'; 'Landscape of the Daylight Moon'; 'Friend with a Mandolin'; 'Birthday'.

Solent Shore (Carcanet, 1980): 'Birth'; 'Floating Bridge'; 'Paintings'; 'Rat Island'; 'Gull on a Post'; 'Prospect of Boulder Church'.

Englishman's Road (Carcanet, 1980): 'A Neighbour'; 'Dragons in the Snow'; from 'Englishman's Road'; 'Brynbeidog'; 'As a Thousand Years'; 'Hill Country Rhythms'; 'In a Welsh Primary School'; 'Curlew'; 'Sarisbury Green'; 'Beidog'; 'Wind Blew Once'; 'Shepherd'; 'Behind the Lights'; 'Wind and Shadow'; 'Emily'.

Common Ground: Poets in a Welsh Landscape (Poetry Wales Press, 1985): 'Leaving'.

1969

Brynbeidog

One of my fingers and one leg above the ankle tingle with nettle-burn and my right thumb is split from honing a scythe. This is what I have to show for work in the garden, cutting down tall dead thistles in a shower of white seeds, masses of dark-green nettles bristling with poison hairs, and long rank grass. Indoors we have cut pine and made bookshelves & a table, where I now write. A sense of belonging has already come to us here. When we arrived, a neighbouring farmer, who has the right to drive his cows through our gate and into his field, called, and refusing the offer of a drink, stood in the doorway and welcomed us. Later his stepson, lithe with sharp features & dark eyes, brought the scythe.

Life is now, it is here, in October afternoon sunlight falling through the sycamores as I sweat.

•

One note: the queer soft call of an owl at dusk.

•

Dr Leavis held his first seminar in college this morning. I left at the end feeling an anger that even now I find difficult to moderate. Sunk in his chair, with his small brown head appearing over the desk and his lean bony fingers flexing and unflexing expressively, he was the image of a man I felt compelled to revere, both for what his presence suggests him to be and for his best writings. Listening to his convoluted ramblings about T.S. Eliot in his peeved, autobiographical style, I framed in my mind a serious question to ask: whether, as one who began his critical career championing writers such as Eliot, D.H. Lawrence and T.F. Powys, it was not a principle with him that the young critic, wherever his centre of interest might lie, should be concerned primarily with the best literature of his own day. But it soon became clear that any question would be lost on him, as he went on and on in a tiresome monologue, running down Eliot as a man; and it seemed to me that whatever slights he had received from Eliot, and however just his contention about the decadence of Bloomsbury, he was jealous. What I was listening to, and longed to interrupt, was the culmination of a mind turned in upon itself, which, despite his nominal championship of wholeness, was dedicated to self-justification alone. Most of my colleagues, more charitable in this than I am, forgive excesses they can't help noticing by invoking the scandalous unfairness of his treatment at Cambridge. To hell with that! How hollow his claim to be isolated sounds when one numbers his admirers & disciples! I found myself more convinced than ever of the danger for a critic of his specialization, leading as it often does to the conditioning of his soul. Here was the death of all generosity, of all humility, of mystery & the sense of wonder; the apotheosis of the dying ego quick to resent slights, indeed *quicker* in its pride than in its moribund humanity. He has long since ceased to recreate himself in the way that real poets & critics must do until death; the bigot in Lawrence did not have the hard shell of this man. And it was all so banal, so boring, lacking the play of intelligence, even cleverness. I could gain nothing from the experience but the conviction that we need to make our minds more flexible; that this cannot be achieved by reading alone, but principally by gaining a critical perspective on oneself, and by releasing one's unconscious powers, the appetite for living & loving, so that one has both an inwardness, where the spirit is buoyant on the powers of the unconscious, and an outwardness, where the mind can range sympathetically, and understand, as a first principle, that there are a thousand ways to wisdom & millions of egos each supreme to itself in its narrow world.

There are moments in reading John Cowper Powys's *Autobiography* when I laugh aloud, moved by the recognition of a man living fully, being fully human. However, despite JCP's confession of his kind of lust, I find it by no means as sordid & savage as mine. There is an idealism in his that contrasts with my burning itch to devour and violate the earth mother's gigantic tits; to move as it were in the freedom of a dream from house to house, throwing down their women. The erotic savagery my dreams have often expressed strikes me as being more inhuman than the peculiarities Powys admits in himself. Surely

the barbaric ancients knew it when they cut Helith into the chalk at
Cerne Abbas, creating an image of man as all penis – but calling it by
its crudest names. The elegiac is of the same world, and the magnet-
ism of wet leaves or grass; the feeling that wells up when dark soil spills
through my fingers or when I hear the owl cry. All these things are of
the earth & the nature we share with Nature: beast & ineffectual angel
rise up from the enchained earth; the whole man integrates both.

•

The hills are mist, unnaturally white from a big moon whose aura
dissolves and reforms faster than shadows on water as low-flying
clouds are driven quickly across.

My feeling for the Cerne Giant takes on a deeper significance as I
learn of J.C. Powys's preoccupation with the figure; my sense of the
earth is fortified. I have been stony ground; now my mind grows
roots, which tap unconscious forces. I feel more resourceful, more
powerful, as if I were drawing strength from a deeper level.

•

Cut a hazel stick from a clump above the waterfall and walked for the
first time towards the uplands above Llangwyryfon. Up at Trefenter
there are enormous views across a lowland plain, patched & pieced
with miniature fields up-thrust & down-sloping irregularly, and
ranging in colour from fertile green to buff & ochre moorland, so that
the first impression of space is immediately followed by a sense of the
piecemeal, enclosed nature of the country. But spacious it is, reaching to a dark-blue horizon edged with hills that vanished in a
cloud-bank, rounded like a child's drawing of clouds, and falling
westward into what looked, to my myopic sight, like the sea, but may
have been an ocean of sky.

Enthralled by this spaciousness, and by feeling Brynbeidog below
me in a fold of the land, I also had gates to lean on, wooded fields to
look at, birds in small flocks – buntings, finches, tits – and above all a
'ride' between high banks under hazel wood, mounting mysteriously
to the ridge. But it's the landscape above Trefenter that's enchanted
– country of the *Mabinogion*'s Arthur – where hills rise in curious

mounds, like misshapen barrows, and into quaint sugar-loaves & conical eminences. To me it was new and strange, a fairyland invented by an imaginative child, and a place of labour & community, where I'm foreign, a place whose tracks carry farmers to their fields.

•

An image: beaters in the mind, thrashing steadily day after day till the terror breaks cover in a soundless panic scream.

November
A broad step of the waterfall, washed black ... I saw Cardiganshire as a huge stone slanting to the Atlantic and on it the cover of fields was held back from the power of the wind to rip it off, like grasses straining in a hedgetop, caught by twigs, only by a few trees rooted in rock.

Our stream is a brown torrent, but where it empties into the waterfall, a continuous surge, no longer falling but rushing in a headlong slide from the field into the bridge's tunnel. Only at the pool's outer edges is there a thin rim of peaceful water; the rest in its forward rush is too powerful for an eddy, carrying the fields down to the sea.

•

Depression this weekend following hints during the week. Then when it comes, really unexpectedly, though I know too well what produces it, no defences & no gathered wisdom can dissipate it. It is as if I have put off three layers of skin so that the quick is exposed. Not suffering or pain, but the impulse to scream for no apparent reason. I have allayed it to some extent by working in the garden, gathering cut grass in a compost heap, feeling hazel boughs vibrate in the wind, letting the stream carry it from me.

It is as if the space I fall through, in the terror of vertigo, is within. I become ghostlike, transparent.

•

A succession of cold nights, at first with the moon running fast through broken clouds, then perfectly clear: a cold full moon – the purity of white frost & moonlight.

December

The somnolence is in blood-warmth, not fatigue – many ideas have been passing around my mind; many ideas but few sensations.

•

The sheer common sense of humility. Balls to all fleshy godlings! Welcome again to the flux of bright days, with melting frost on windows concentrating bursts of white sunlight. Welcome release of the rage that destroys me from within.

1970

January

Moist emerald moss padding the base of a beech trunk; above it, seven feet of whitish bark with signatures cut into it, some blurred by healing growth, others still incisive; above that, colonies of ivy, a single strand growing down to the moss, leaves sharply outlined against bark – pale veins rimmed with pale green and thrown into relief by the dark green of the outer edges. This was an individual life emphatic in its identity.

The search is of course within as well as without; it is inside oneself that the self stands in the place of the other. Again, it is as if the eye were a mirror, apparently transparent but in fact opaque. In a far off, misty dimension other forms swim by.... Yes, yes, my images fail where the old ones ring true: 'in a glass darkly', that's it. And it applies to all relationships in this world. Love, and love alone, can dissipate that opacity so that sunshafts, sunpaths, illuminate the other.

•

Crumbs of frost; crumbled earth. The delicious sensation of treading down yielding ground. Spasmodic tinkling note of a coal tit pecking lichen on the bough of a young oak.

No well is deeper than the sick mind, yet it isn't darkness that surrounds it, sharp with stars, but the same daylight illuminating the same objects that the whole mind sees, but tainted by a miasma that is far more horrifying than darkness. At night, dark bereft of its purity; by day, light without clarity.

•

As I move into the caravan which is to be my study, mild blue sky clear from horizon to horizon sharpens the upland ridge; white light from the setting sun is concentrated by yellowish moor grass, and trees are etched black against it.

March

Arriving at Dartington Hall to give a poetry reading, I came close to running off in panic when I heard that Hugo Williams and David Harsent were the other poets due to read. Williams read his poems quickly, one after the other; Harsent read more slowly, with a little introductory matter. Poetry readings seemed everyday to them: they wanted it to be over before a Godard film on TV; it was all rather off hand. I expect they found my intensity peculiar & crude. They brought a breath of the metropolis – not out of place at Dartington – talking about films, and Ian Hamilton.

Meeting Roland Mathias at his home in Brecon on the way back confirmed the impression made by his letters. With him, edge is totally absent. It is easy to talk to him, listen to him, and thus discover his intelligence & openness. This is due in part to absence of the warping assumption of centrality, and of competitiveness; to generosity of spirit, warm interest in other people & in ideas.

•

Paul Nash's 'equation' of sun & sunflower, of mushroom & moon; of the near & the far, the small & the large. *That's* what I've been looking for – and found for myself the day I saw the relationship of a leaf to a landscape seen through leaves.

Metaphor connects; when connections are made something haunts the picture or poem, some spirit moving in & among things. The connections are functional. But why beautiful? Nature could have been functional alone like certain things we make. But it is brother to our senses: moon's rondure & mushroom's curves speak to us of a relationship between them, and with our senses. How it heals the eye! How it breaks the dead waters of depression and makes the living spirit rejoice and flow! Is it man alone who can make disharmony, and who has a sense of beauty?

•

Rain on the tin roof; water blurring the windows – how I love it!

April

Hell's edge again. Since the bout of severe depression early in the month I've been at the mercy of extreme vicissitudes of feeling. Last Thursday I had to force myself to go to the conference of English teachers at Alexandra Hall, and was shaking when I went in. And I met some friendly people: Raymond Garlick, Wyn Binding, Randal Jenkins, with the result that I enjoyed the social side of the conference. So that was one hurdle jumped. Then, yesterday, we had a marvellous day with Bryan Johnson at Gregynog. I was right outside myself and the beginning of term no longer seemed terrible. This morning, I had a generous letter from Raymond Garlick containing a facsimile of John Cowper Powys's last letter to him. Then, in the meeting in college, dissociation started. I rode it, escaped back here and over lunchtime worked myself up to a screaming tension, almost prostrate. Then I took an axe to the logs, and now feel much better. But I learn so little; my mind is demonic, like another man inside me who wishes me harm. It initiates a tightening spiral of panic, which feels, literally, like a spring in my head. And this is largely due to teaching again, seminars, taking coffee with colleagues (or running away from them) – at any moment I am liable to become that tense spiral.

The problem is largely dissociation between inner and outer: between me and my role; between my voice speaking and my inner voice concerned with other things; between myself as teacher and poet, perhaps. It is terrible to come back and fall away again. How much stronger I have seemed to myself during this last year! I have so much in which to rejoice, and yet the demon persists in me. Philosophy, logic, common sense, all are useless when the crisis reduces me to a mask of terror, a tense face desperately trying to withold the scream.

•

Days of tension, dread & emptiness.

To be at the extreme of solipsism shows the true nature of Christ. How could any man but God-made-man take upon himself the infernal depths we are capable of falling into? To take from me even my kind of pain, which is comparatively slight, would require superhuman courage & powers of endurance.

May

Yesterday it was as if spring broke on us in one sudden impulse, winter over, summer close at hand. A yellowhammer crossing the garden was a flash of colour and birds sang lustily all round. One sycamore in leaf. The sky was blue all day, the grass intensely green. Towards evening, the cuckoo was calling; without it spring would have no heart.

•

Reddish-brown of young sycamore leaves – the trees have filled out rapidly in the last ten days or so and are now full-bodied, globe-shaped.

Seeing a spider scuttle over dry earth I remembered how I resolved to observe minutely the life of this place. My connection with it now is not as real as it was in the autumn, so much work & talk draws me away. Spring finds out a person's inner harmony, or lack of it. Health, life delighting in life with abundant energy, rejoices in the profusion & growth of green things, or inner withering becomes conscious of itself.

•

After experiencing David Jones's sense of language the poverty of all but the greatest modern poetry is clear to me. He opens up the history-paths, which lead back to the earth mother & the man of power, she for ever comforting while he violates. He brings to life the male & female archetypes and shows them in & through the actual: myth makes sense of history, yet without history, no myth.

I have to discover the feeling man: the voice alone & the object made of words are not enough.

Can a poet help listening to hear how, at the moment of most selfless searching, of nearest colloquy with God, his voice sounds?

> That man on his knees was no saint.
> Even as he wept to God in broken phrases,
> Deep in his skull in a place yet private
> He was adoring
> The music of their brokenness.

Underparts of a caterpillar, brown fur like healthy chestnut-colour hair. Underparts black & covered with long hairs – like a porcupine. Man and caterpillar are made of the same basic stuff.

June
The best of the year; life fresh and in full vigour before the dusty fullness of midsummer. In a corner of the garden, where the stream passes under the path, beside the purple lilac, sunlight green through grass, dark-green shadow, among meadowsweet, ferns & long grass, where tiny speedwell are – peace, fresh-scented, calm to the eye, perfect peace. Beauty in itself so dazzling that at any moment the door of life might swing open and the mystery be revealed.

Not balance lost but rhythm found: a water-drop falling from leaf to river, carried along without loss of individuality.

•

Watering the garden at dusk, ground dry & cracking after weeks of drought. Now all the young birds are singing in the trees until nightfall, the cuckoo is still calling deep in the greyness, sap is on the air. Earth & air are rich, voluptuous to all the senses, a warm darkness for the mind to bathe in, renewing all its energies.

•

A few drops of rain, dark on whitish-grey stones, then a steady fall. Afterwards, silence. I sit at the edge of myself, unable to concentrate on anything, expecting the thin rain to become a deluge, thunder to crash overhead; but the rain stops, starts, stops again.

No singleness, no integrity, no centre hard & true. The creative effort pushes tongues of water into a dozen creeks, and everywhere evaporates. I am like the men Bonhoeffer describes, at one moment all greed, the next all fear, then all relief.

•

It is the silence in silence
That stifles your heart.

This is love's other face.
At night when the wild tree thrashes
The storm in the storm
Bangs open the gate
Locked years ago on your terrified cry.

•

Here & there I can hear my own voice and it awakens in me, in this period of marking exam scripts, the knowledge that I am still a poet. At root, I can speak most truly & seriously only as a poet. It is what moves in me. As a person carried by lust & appetite, with about as much religion as a prismatic soap bubble or mayfly, I'm nothing; but there, at root, it is life with its needs that speaks.

•

Through nature Wordsworth journeyed to man, and he could do so, I believe, because man was part of nature – the society Wordsworth loved was founded on nature. But if Edward Thomas found, at the end of the journey, man's absence, what have I to find? Childhood, the past, death.

The fields are empty except for grass, the community I look for is there no longer except for ghosts. And it is this constant discovery of death – in this respect, the use of landscape imagery – that is so enervating to me & to my writing.

I cannot *will* my images, by thrashing violence out of them, to pretend to discover what is not there.

I do not want to write of my own life alone – in the profoundest sense, in its uniqueness, it is not sufficiently interesting – but in writing of it to find man. But if I am not part of a community I cannot find man, except in my emptiness, in loss of foundations. Sylvia Plath's poems cry. 'Look! There's nothing, nothing, nothing here! Look!' Terror feeds on the emptiness of the self-enclosed psyche. And David Jones? The present & the future leave him blank; life is rich only in the past. The regenerative powers which he sees are locked in locality, in place & site, in the earth. How can these relate to a now & hereafter?

I respond with excitement to certain things in Charles Olson, in Gary Snyder. Yet they encompass so little of the world as it is now. If only we could go with, but beyond nature, by carrying it into the heart of the modern experience at its most uncompromisingly *un*natural. What I do not want is to journey via despair to a Christ of the elements or a medieval sanctuary. But as a wise man might say: First find Christ. Poetry, belief, the future; the search for one involves the others.

•

What do I *know* before the wheels of rationalization begin to turn? Only that I miss the past when I was at home, and sometimes all Wales seems to surround me with an emptiness in which all I do, think and say rings hollow.

•

Maybe it was because the chalk is so feminine, such a dominating, all-embracing, Willendorf Venus of a rock, that men had to carve Helith at Cerne. The male principle had to be asserted, and in that place. Man has to assert his cockyness, if only to avoid being smothered.

It's no good being too solemn about the erect penis; if one couldn't raise (at least) a smile, or giant laughter, all the Madonnas would weep man out of existence, all the earth mothers crush him to death.

So Helith had to be carved in the heartland of the mothers. Of course, since he is the mate of the Willendorf Venus, they are as gross as each other. They are life at root, and manifestations of the human urge for power & significance in the scale of nature: the creation of exaggerated maleness & femaleness – Gogmagog no less, man & woman deified but in terms of Nature, before the egress of spirit.

There is also something flippant about Helith – so much feminine seriousness has to be challenged. He is the knave. How else could man stay sane in face of woman's natural superiority? How else defy the witch, especially when she exploits her motherhood & her gentleness?

•

Branches of dog-roses curved sensitively into delicate bows. Honeysuckle overrunning the hedges.

•

A sense of history may connect one to the people of the past, but connection to the past alone is essentially morbid. One begins to live vicariously in the imaginative apprehension of past orders & realities: life is a river which, confronted by the mountains of the present, turns back upon its course and wanders among ruins it once passed through with a strong forward movement, when they were living habitations.

July

Campagnano, Italy
Now, dissociated somewhat from the others – partly sheer selfishness, partly something I can't help – I think again of the disastrous holiday at Durdle Door with the Pentz family, when I was about ten. David, who had known me for only a short time, asked me to go with them when the friend who usually went had fallen out. From the start, it was a disaster. Swimming, sailing, climbing cliffs, he was an agile, adventurous boy. I was a starer into deep water, over the side of the boat, down to the weedy bottom, and happy to fish from the rocks all day. So I was persecuted, mainly by him, also by the grown-ups who were (I knew) repelled by my quiet, 'unnatural', introverted nature. Our one moment of intimacy was when I farted, very loudly, involuntarily, in the dark toilet at night; even then I went on laughing too long for his taste. One night our tent fell about our ears in a storm. The holiday went on for three weeks and long before the end I wanted only to get home, to be out in the fields with Boxer.

Now too I feel withdrawn, at moments participating fully, with enjoyment, conscious of peace & well-being, but often withdrawn, rather unhappy, guilty of casting a shadow on the others.

•

Foxgloves in the hedgerow, buzzards, remind me of the day I climbed from Talybont to Bedd Taliesin, a burial mound – stones fallen in, an open grave – with a view over the Dovey estuary. The day was warm & still, the foxgloves had survived into a bright autumn, and as I stood there a buzzard circled overhead, mewing. No need to remind myself to what all this was dedicated, of what it was a sign.

How perfect the autumn was when I first moved into the mill at

Talybont, brook gravel of the path yellow in sunlight, vivid blood-reds of cherry leaves, the brook 'immaculate'. The quality of sunlight & air can only have been perfected by my feeling alive to the woman to whom all seemed to belong. I sat in sunlight beside the stream with a book; I began a first rough draft of 'At Steep', token of another marvellous day when we sat together against Edward Thomas's memorial stone and the south was mine to give.

Then February, twilight with a solitary thrush singing whole-heartedly from the top of an alder by the stream.

Winter, and months of listening for something other than the wind to rattle the gate. Even on days of fullness & peace like today, I cannot walk in the narrow Cardiganshire lanes, under banks of hazel & mountain-ash, with grass growing through tarmac in the middle, without a feeling made permanently part of all this by the past, by Cwm Morgan in autumn, the lanes round Newcastle Emlyn, stone milk steps on which we've sat. Then the end of it, mist in the valley, clouds of willow-herb seed on the air, swallows on wires, Wales a torrent of red leaves – the end I thought a beginning.

By this Wales has been permanently marked for me – the pain mellowed to tenderness, no longer focused on a person but on the place itself.

•

In the shallows of second sleep, lewd & lurid imaginings melt into each other, lust-fever creates image after image. Not far under the skin, in some sense allayed by idealized love, the sex-nerve is promiscuous & wolfish. This is not the shared darkness, the cauldron of rebirth, but the pornographic itch; self against world; man against woman; degrading her, mad for visual experience of degradation. The streets of St Mary's at night, in orange neon, in dark corners, over soiled silver-grey, moon-coloured pavements, symbolize for me this state of lust. Now too I get the burning urge to hurl myself into the corruption of a city in the small hours, live for weeks in a brothel; to be like Faust and make a compact with the devil for no power but the demoniac mating with Helen.

•

Evening, the darkening green. July is going out this year with skies of broken cloud, mild blue intervals. From the rough moorland field beside the house the noise of the waterfall is distanced; no longer unheard background to all my thoughts, it becomes local, defining the place by sound. Seen over treetops, the house soon becomes a single white chimney, and I think of myself in the caravan, self-absorbed, taking the importance of what I think and write for granted. At the centre of wider & wider circles through space & time, it dwindles to nothing. A spray of tiny grasshoppers jets up from my feet. Spikes of orangy-red bog asphodel stick up unopened beside grey ghosts of last year's dead flowers.

August
Quite suddenly, everything that doesn't touch the dimension of mystery through its earth nature loses my interest. I turn again to John Cowper Powys, to *Maiden Castle,* and often think of Llewelyn Powys, wishing I knew someone in the south who could make the place live from its vital centre.

.

Hiroshima Day. Here, under a mild blue sky, there is a fine blue haze in the hollows. Harebells & Herb Robert, my favourite flowers, are not annulled, nor is our life, by that blinding fact. For these too are facts. Yet if I do not know what happened then, what it meant for those people, what it means for all of us, then I am nothing and my work is nothing.

.

Taliesin is in & out of my mind these days. The legend & the poems have a numinous quality, revealing the mysteries of life in a way one can't quite grasp – hence the power of the thing, akin to *The Tempest.* Certainly, the working of the imagination – even man's corporate imagination, part creator, part recipient of the great religious truths – finds stirring symbolism in this legend, which can throw consider-able light on what Keats glimpsed in his idea of Negative Capability.

Towards evening the sky clouded, breaking into the tarnished, disturbed lights & half-lights of a storm. Yet the sun's light, diminished by haze, was beautiful, finding a corner of the waterfall in the field south east of the house.

•

Arriving in Llandeilo in the quiet of early evening, I parked the car by the church wall, with the small town falling away on a slope down to the river & a magnificent bridge. The reception for the new magazine, *Planet*, edited by Ned Thomas, was held in The King's Head, just below the church. In the ensuing hubbub I met Bryn Griffiths, who came on at once with the sensitive-but-down-to-earth-poet-meets-academic bullshit. The topic of David Jones got us on to a few minutes of amicable talk. Otherwise his attitude blew me up into a huge bladder of hurt pride, splitting at the seam ('I'm a poet, a poet, a poet' – puff, puff, puff ...)

The best of the evening for me was getting lost on the way back among haunted lanes between Tregaron and Llangwyryfon, where I saw a white owl silent in the darkness.

•

Walked in the morning along the road to Lledrod and round through the village, needing to get out in the air and sweat up a hill after 'finishing' 'A Hambledon Sequence'. I wanted it out of my blood & nerves. As it is, there's too much death in it, too little of the affirmative experience.

from **A Hambledon Sequence**

i
But slowly, slowly once,
On slow feet down a flinty track –

Dig here, delve, mole,

Into an index of the dead.

Birth, Marriage, Death,
A soft response between two darknesses.

In candlelight,
Her hand on his hand's weathered map,
Our blood's branched source,
Receives the ring.
                    And it contains them,
Perfect as unbitten fruit.

The candle through its halo flares.

ii
Birth, marriage, death:
Words patient as a ploughing team
That rounds its narrow field
From dawn to night.
Yet *natus et renatus* meant,
For one who wrote it in a clerkly hand,
That life's two waters meet
To flow as one.
Jack-in-the-green might have to die
To push the sap along his veins,
But this clear stream went on its way,
No winter bourne, no drying wheel
Turned by the year whose leaves must fall,
Nor poisoned by the yew,
But flowing straight through all, without an end.

Struggling out of my intense mental coil, by a stream that welled up among dark-green ferns before again disappearing underground, I had a fleeting sense of the cosmos outside my narrow mind. The sun was a pale yellow disc through cloud, swirling above a jagged range of cloud mountains and boring down upon the rocky, mountainous earth – was it the unknowable power of the sun's furnace in the beginning, bringing life out of vast seas? Afterwards, still conscious of the unique particularity of leaves & flowers, I saw them as inter-dependent parts of the life-stream connected to the sun, which generates it. This is the only sane way to see things: each in its uniqueness yet borne on a river connecting each to each, and all to the forces of sun, wind, rain & earth, while the eye that sees is no less part of the river seen.

At times one can become conscious of Earth as a great ball spin-ning away from under one's feet, spinning in enormous space with other bodies, and all in the magnificent formal dance of the laws of the universe.

•

Night, large dazzling moon over the ridge, with dark clouds coming & going across its face. The sky, a mass of cloud-banks with seams of clear space between them, appeared to be converging on the moon as if drawn by the power blazing from its centre. Elsewhere all was breaking, dissolving, drawn down the sky towards that pole of posi-tive force. A falling star with a head of green fire – a match struck cleanly in a single stroke against the sky – went down in an arc across the clouds.

At 8 in the evening at this time of year the sun, today a ghost in broken, smoke-grey drifts of cloud & bars of silver, sinks over the sea while the moon is coming up behind the ridge – as one rim of the great wheel – I mean one point on the rim, for the image is inexact – must always go down on the ground as the point above it rises. At times I have a chilling, exhilarating sense of being a minute observer within the movement of this giant wheel; fanciful associations flock round the experience, but the feeling of awe is paramount. I am within this great sweep of motion, all personal attributes are a grain of dust in the whirl of lights.

•

Morning light is a fine dust settling on the field above the caravan, a delicate smoke in the hollow between field & ridge. Everything is touched by kindness, as life itself seems opening to me with a welcome. Autumn, the dying begins, and makes now a season between. Already I think with pleasure of frost & cold, the sharp stars of winter. And for the time being I find it difficult to settle to any work, though on mornings like this it seems to require no more than waiting. This is the best part of creation, when the mind sleeps at the heart of things and the nerves are still.

•

Completed typing *A View from the Source* for submission to Faber.

September
There's madness sure enough in trying to remake the present in the image of the past.

October
The mind is capable of making for itself such a small world, with no goodness in it. Then it may confuse the real world with the world it has made – a small parched thing – and so despair, the universe a grey thought. Or the mind may become conscious of what it is doing, and seek ways out. Sometimes the harder one tries the tighter the small world becomes.

I have lived too much for the ambition to write. It is the sickness in the ego I have to drop, just drop and walk away from. The day moves, the light moves, the blood flows and a man comes awake to destroy. When I walk on Mynydd Bach and am set free by sky & rock & great earth shapes, I look down on Aberystwyth and it is no more than a molehill in the mass of Wales & the sea. Then my tension seems crazy, and I think of myself in the small room down there reducing the whole world to the size of my fear.

•

The more hopeless I become in myself the greater the unattainable outer world becomes: all that is not me, and, in contrast, dynamic, mysterious, the river's massive body, moving, moving.... No, not hopeless, only excessively nervous, because, for some reason, I lose the capacity for becoming what I do – it is the old I, I, I against the world. Loss of faith, loss of impetus, as the wave thrusting forward might become conscious of itself only in retreat.

The habit of projecting our terrors onto nature, as I think Ted Hughes does in his 'Crow' poems, must end by exacerbating them when we have forgotten what their source really is and come to think of it as outside ourselves. For primitive man, fear is probably the threat outside him, eyes in the dark where the fire's glow ends, movement in the bushes. But for most of us now fear is failure in the I/thou relationship, and derives from many things that can go wrong inside ourselves & in relation to others. No landscape I know is as bleak as a room in which people drift round each other without real contact; no beast, no aspect of the wilderness, is so desolate. The exultation I feel on Mynydd Bach is the same as that I have felt among friends: freedom to acknowledge the depths; the peace of belonging. But a room full of people is, for some, a place in which false images hurtle from all directions. *What am I expected to be? What am I? How can I be what I am with your eyes on me?*

•

A burning sycamore log fills the room with a honey-sweet smell, heavy, as if it were a potent, but delicate, tropical flower.

At the age of eleven or twelve, for about a year, I underwent the internal bleeding, the suffocating experience of guilt. I told no one and thought repeatedly of suicide. Sitting in class, I felt tears bursting to flood out; the only peace was at night, in endless conversations with what I took for God. After a time the feeling drained away, and for another long period I seemed to feel nothing. And after an early experience like that it would seem inevitable, from a psychological point of view, that some inadequacy in me, in my human relationships, should engender religious torments. But just because of the intimate connection between a semi-sexual illness and abrupt flight to the supposed comforter, I do not see that the latter can be explained as an aberrant answer to the former.

Anguish or depression is a single sensation but one word belongs to the terrible emptiness of God's absence, and the other to a psychologist's world. It is the hole in the world that God alone can fill. Yet the psychologist's language disturbs the line of my search; as if he might be right in proposing an entirely secular sphere for man's struggle.

•

Walking in mist on Hafod Ithel, sheets of mist driving against me, myriad tiny particles smacking into my face. A lovely sensation of getting wet, water-drops flying off my nose. To imagine oneself a rock: impossible, a pleasant, healthy self-indulgence. In the high wind, with mist around me, I feel the opposite of loneliness & fear.

Belonging: that is the key.

November

Even the word 'existentialist' makes me feel dizzy, like all grandiloquent terms applied to inner experience; but still, in Pascal & Kierkegaard, I find a note that speaks directly to me – a cry uttered from the depth I am terrified by but have to recognise as one fundamental reality in a world that is, too often, like a Chinese lantern of lurid papiermache, torn paper flapping round a wire skeleton ...

Intensity disturbs, and people turn away.

We turn again & again to the common world for protection, and find it in body-warmth & laughter. But when the common world is infected and we feel dizzy even looking into the eyes of a friend, there is nowhere to turn but the source. We have to look into the emptiness; and there some will find God and only thus be able to face any world without vertigo. From a single crack rifts open in life until even in crossing a room we walk among canyons. I have to cry aloud on the God of emptiness.

How far is W.H. Auden's 'Pascal' from embodying the spiritual intensity of the great passages on 'Man's disproportion'! Pascal's 'FIRE' is a word from 70,000 fathoms, Auden's poem is skin-deep. Some passages in Eliot are fed by the black gulf under him; so he remains one of the few genuine poets among perhaps more social versifiers than any other century has to show. I find the experience in poems by David Gascoyne. It has to be in the poem's texture; many may have felt it, but it is in the poems of few. At his best, Ted Hughes writes in the white-heat of an equivalent intensity – in poems where his inner quarrel is between frozen consciousness and animal lust for survival. But he backs away too quickly into simplification & rhetoric. A poet who celebrates & commemorates, like David Jones, has to acknowledge from what depths the ecstasy arises. J.C. Powys in his best prose contains many pressures, but I sometimes sense an emptiness just where he fails to face the void. Between celebration and the void most modern English poets compromise with the depressed note – as in Philip Larkin – or with irony & evasion.

I am frightened by my intensity, as though a cry were being ripped from me, yet to know that others have suffered more and held on to win meaning out of the plunge through emptiness is to know myself not a 'case', but a man in whom one of the deepest roots strikes up through personal limitations from the ground of which real men have been made.

•

Some days I want to make love to almost every woman I meet, envelope her in the warmth & physical tenderness that seem to be bursting out of me. And the impulse seems good.

True sexual love *concentrates*; cerebral lust *dissipates*. From concentration comes renewal; from dissipation, despair. My Helith doesn't sweat over pornography; he wants to make love to the woman in every woman, and in the end he must discover that she can only be found at the uttermost in one. Hence his sad, rather baffled look, and still the penis stands constantly erect only for one.

•

Sustenance, the act of sustaining, is the fundamental creative principle of the universe, and only by recognising it can we learn to live. This is quite clear: our 'community' does not sustain; there are many fine people dedicated to those who have slipped away, but we should all be trying to live so that none can slip away, into suicide or disintegration or isolation.

But what about reticence? What power it gives Thomas Hardy! That sense of contained power, putting on 'a brave face' – 'my punishment is not more than I can bear'. But Hardy, like Henchard, is bound by his pride and lack of religious belief to try to carry *more* than a Christian is required to carry. Almost, he is more than a man. And what in him is more, in others is *less*. Doesn't his courageous reticence resemble the upper-class motif – the stiffness – which has left too many armoured men 'hollow at the core'? Besides, Hardy in his poetry expresses, intimately & passionately, the personal element he was keen to deny in the novels. Reticence, sometimes a noble quality, is at other times a dangerous shell.

I feel that I have to be personal and at the same time objectify, find a form, a structure, an object for the personal to use.

•

Grey morning light, ridge half eaten by mist. Rooks circle the field in & out of swirls of grey-white cloud. A big circle of birds, cawing loudly, turns, breaks the circle, crosses it, reforms in an intense ritual. The circle is broken by birds flying away, singly or in small groups, to different points of the compass. After the ritual has been performed, a purposeful, ritualistic leave-taking.

A grey day for the second rejection; indifference; inner resources functioning. How many more? They are wrong, in comparison with what is being published; right, in terms of my critical sense, which knows I have yet to give my best. Most people, including critics, don't know a poem when they see one unless someone else has told them it is a poem.

December

Dafydd's smile from his car window as I passed him on the way into town; joy, the world grey from self-absorbed depression, was broken by a great crack of light. Others require us only to be ourselves, and by being themselves set us free to set free in turn.

Such a smile, such a sky. There are experiences that fill words, break false eloquence, and teach far more than self-analysis does. Seeing Billy Davies handle wood as he works in our house, an absorbed craftsman, modest, open, kind, and talking to him every day, I have learnt what most of my writings force me to forget: the humanity, the filled moment, the word made palpable.

•

Dawn pure as an icicle. Later, white sun in blue sky; flashing beads in the grass; a slow-moving finger traces a straight white line in the sky.

On these bright winter days even the sunlight is white, and the moon is in the sky all day. The warmth brings out a bluebottle, midges dance in clearings by the stream, but all is under the influence of the moon, which, during the short afternoon, brightens until all is concentrated in & upon it. Nothing is as we think it! One drop of this solution turns all to strangeness.

Landscape of the Daylight Moon

I first saw it inland.
Suddenly, round white sides
Rose through the thin grass
And for an instant, in the heat,
It was dazzling; but afterwards
I thought mainly of darkness,
Imagining the relics of an original
Sea under the chalk, with fishes
Beneath the fields. Later,
Everywhere upon its surface
I saw the life of the dead;
Circle within circle of earthen
Shells, and in retraced curves
Like finger marks in pale sand,
The print of a primaeval lover.
Once, climbing a dusty track,
I found a sunshaped urchin,
With the sun's rays, white
With the dusts of the moon.
Fetish, flesh become stone,
I keep it near me. It is
A mouth on darkness, the one
Inexhaustible source of re-creation.

1971

January

This year I must heave more of the iceberg into sight; recalcitrant as it is to the kind of technique imprisoning me, which must be shattered by pressure of the life it excludes.

•

Very soon there will not be one of my poems that doesn't bore me and seem worthless. Not one. And then to go on; to begin clean & free. As life is – the huge full moon slowly rising as the sun sets and fields of grass & reeds shine golden brown.

Yesterday I woke up early, the writings I could have done buzzing in my head. Begin, begin, begin. I was amazed that none had found expression.

•

Early morning, the full moon sinks, burning white, behind the sycamores, becomes yellow just above the horizon. Early evening, the full moon rises, yellow, through branches of the solitary sycamore. The sun goes down *at the end of the road.*

No step is lost on this path, and no dangers are found. And even a little progress is freedom from fear.

The follower of this path has one thought, and this is the End of his determination. But many-branched and endless are the thoughts of the man who lacks determination.

Set thy heart upon thy work, but never on its reward. Work not for a reward; but never cease to do thy work.

★   ★   ★   ★   ★

Greater is thine own work, even if this be humble, than the work of another, even if this be great. When a man does the work God gives him, no sin can touch this man.

And a man should not abandon his work, even if he cannot
achieve it in full perfection; because in all work there
may be imperfection, even as in all fire there is smoke.

(*The Bhagavad Gita*, translated by Juan Mascaro)

•

February

For me, Emyr Humphreys's reading was the outstanding event of the
weekend at Gregynog. I have rarely been so impressed by or drawn
to a man. There is a brightness about him, and he is a charitable,
modest and wise man, whose responsiveness is perhaps tempera-
mental, but is also the outcome of an active religious philosophy. His
writing bears this out. Deep insight into human experience was what
I most admired in his poems. It is there in the man and in his novels,
in which I am discovering a real Wales, perceived by one who is part
of what he sees, yet retains the intelligence to see all in the perspective of a wide-awake religious belief. Asked about his work as
literature, he said: 'I don't know if it is literature. All I can do is have
a go.' He also said he wrote about the past 'because I was born in it'.

R.S. Thomas introduced himself as if totally without confidence,
apologizing in advance for boring us. As he read, the vibrancy of his
emotive undertone increased; the new poems had great power. A
poetry near to despair, a religious questioning that underlined the
futility of the following discussion. When he finished reading and the
windows were opened, long quavering notes of an owl came in from
the Gregynog oakwoods.

He answered questions monosyllabically and most of the time
refused to say anything, sitting with his feet on a desk and occasionally
casting a searchlight look on the face of the questioner.

Some Welsh people feel he is exploiting the country, writing as it
were for the English, and they tend to question the worth of his poetry
on a shallow political level. I found him powerful, disturbing, but
impossible to love. No love was given, none received.

Roland Mathias asked me to be reviews editor of *The Anglo-Welsh
Review*. At the end of the weekend, I declined the invitation. As I
explained to him, so much talk about Wales made me conscious of
where my basic commitments lie. I shall continue to be more than
interested in Wales, but I do not belong here. Perhaps I came most alive

when Roland told me how much the southern chalk landscape awed him. Life could take me anywhere, but I carry the south inside me.

•

When I was a child I saw what Paul Nash saw in the dump of wrecked German planes near Witney, when he painted *Totes Meer* – not of course his image, but the awe. This was something more than natural – vivid demonic crosses on twisted fuselages – an image of romance and horror. On the way to visit Ralph & Connie in Wiltshire we passed Silbury Hill, and it transfixed me, a child in the back of the car. This too was awe: the very old, the more than natural. And I felt the same about big, hand-shaped flints from gravel pits near Warsash; at the tale that along the small river Roman boats had once come; at bones of woolly mammoth dredged from Southampton Water, and dug-out canoes where the ocean liners came in. These things excited in me a feeling of strangeness & something like fear.

To feel in childhood a deep affinity with the beginnings of place, with the formation of chalk, the laying down of gravels, changing relations of water & land! For the child to be drawn by a sense of origins in the world it is born into!

For a native to return he has to discover a means of returning. Some ways are closed. Opening other ways alters both his self- image & his image of the place.

•

Curlew first heard at night, then at dusk in the marshy field, with a long, bubbling call. Icicles, glassy cylinders with brambles inside them, over the waterfall. Mynydd Bach coated with snow on the first of March.

April
At Cerne Abbas, white violets & a loud noise of nesting rooks. Climbing Giant Hill we were above them and they could no longer be heard, though the knocking of a milk churn on the other side of the valley was clearly audible.

Bats Head. The sudden view stunned me: chalk headlands projecting into space, a broken wing of chalk. Between White Nose and

Bats Head, green spears of young wheat were thrusting up in cliff top fields round Llewellyn Powys's memorial stone.

The Living the Living he shall praise thee.

Fear is an element in the thrill the chalk cliffs give me. The great rounded downs dash straight down hundreds of feet. The body wants to go on walking right on out into all that air.

May

This afternoon, cutting hazels for bean sticks, the old question: who taught you betrayal? A face, a gesture, a few words; the whole of the past in every detail is always within. If the self is a submerged country I bring up one headland, and forget the rest to which it is joined.

I have felt since childhood that this life is the dream one will wake out of into a completely different reality, and may perhaps wake oneself.

'I have mistaken my life. I was not that person but another.'

•

Spring brings back the shadows, cool, deep tunnels, passages & caves, where little more than a month ago were open ground & naked spaces. As if the stitchwort were not enough, there has to be Herb Robert too; yet each is a miracle. Bluebells in the woods at Cwm Mabws, a blue haze, an excess of delicacy & loveliness. Even a single blade of grass is more beautiful than anyone has a right to expect. This abundance, the wastefulness with which seeds are spent, a horn of plenty overflowing in every corner & ditch. And still the richness pours on.

That return to nature which is genuine in Gary Snyder cannot happen here *in that way*. Snyder's strength is that he is in contact with both myth and rural society. In this respect we are a colder ember than America; but the individual mind still craves relationship with nature through contact and myth. The eye alone sets us apart, detaches us and puts us outside, at a distance. It is by bodily movement and imagination that we know ourselves whole.

I have been disappointed for my own good.

How can there be attention to anything either within or without when the eye is on success and the ear is listening for applause? The truth of this is proved in another way by my relief since the book was turned down and I decided to withdraw from further attempts.

What I feel is the beginning of freedom.

•

Walking home late at night, I see two lighthouses flashing, one far to the north off Bardsey, the other south off Pembrokeshire. In a negative state of mind I forget that it is only necessary for me to walk a hundred yards or so to see the sea & the mountains of north Wales.

•

Morning, looking up at the ridge of Mynydd Bach: there is a limit to the images we can impose upon this place. This is a country belonging to its people, and subjective impressions come up against their reality – just as the figure of Glyn Davies striding with his long crook through the fields contrasts with my musing progress over the hill.

Last year, visiting the 'commune' at Ynyslas, I met a student walking down the lane playing a guitar hanging from a cord round his neck and dressed in beads and a colourful smock. An exotic figure against the deep green lanes, dungy farm entrances and concrete milk churn stands, he advanced dreamily, rather selfconsciously, in his 'own world'.

To drift here is to see nothing.

It is necessary to live here – else stay away.

Here the individual is one of a community with work to do.

June

All April curlews surround us with bubbling springs of sound, but in May cuckoos take their place, calling alternately, and sometimes curlews & cuckoos call together. Two or three blackbirds sing in the evening – last night, under a three-quarters moon, at first frail, leaf-like then blazing white.

Sweetness of lilac & hawthorn: the same air rich with sweet sounds of blackbird & thrush.

After dark, the continuous reel-on-ratchet note of a grasshopper warbler.

Gwenallt, the deep-rooted man: a poet drawing life from family &

communal experience in industrial Wales, and from farmyard & neighbourhood in the Welsh countryside; from an old, threatened culture & from personal struggle – political & religious – in the modern world; from language & nation. At a time when I knew almost nothing of his life, and before I had read translations of his poems, I used to pass him in the corridor of the English Department, where, ironically, he had his room: a small, composed man, the bones of the skull showing in his face. I felt he was on more than the other side of a language. Now I know he was on the far side of life from isolated individualism, consciousness as fine sensibility, poetry as self-promotion. To suck life from a great depth in the human community – all that is worthwhile, all that is capable of deepening one's sense of participation, is alien to bourgeois artistic ideals.

•

A torrential midsummer. One night it rained so hard the stream overflowed the drive, swirling over the tunnel that carries it under the path. An old woman to whom we gave a lift predicted rain all summer, because May had been dry and there was thunder then. The stream is still high, but runs cleanly, a pure quick transparency. Yesterday the high ground was slowly swallowed by greyish vapour; then, late in the evening, a reddish glow seeped through in the west, the wet sycamore leaves broke into points of red fire. Trees and the hill's outline emerged hard & clear as the mist thinned and retreated, pale rainbows shining in misty light. Today great broken rainclouds are moving across from west to east, their shadows sliding quickly over the fields, darkening then clearing the vivid green.

•

Life at its most intense is made up of moments that for ever elude our understanding. The individual consciousness is so complex that none of our literary or psychological analogies for it can get close. The attempt to record a perception is hopelessly approximate, so much of the pattern changes and dissolves and only a fleeting, partial impression can be put into words. And this is only the beginning of difficulties. A writer such as Virginia Woolf may attempt to capture the web-like texture of consciousness, yet our total experience is of material objects & events, of the affect of other people, and of the multitude of causes that constitute 'the age'. Life in our experience is both consciousness & the starkest materialism. So Virginia Woolf only supplies the half which she finds missing ('life escapes') in Arnold Bennett, and both are equally inadequate.

One of my deepest impulses has always been to record the living moment – to give another kind of life to experience – and to set it in the perspective of time. This may be a singularly unoriginal impulse, fundamental to most writers. Curiously, if one succeeds in giving the particular moment the life of words, it is as elusive as ever. The unique moment cannot be held in this way; the very fact that the sense of life is conveyed annuls the moment, whose character *is* its uniqueness. I cannot believe that some things will never happen again. But is it a real faith or mere self-indulgence to feel that intense moments will be relived *and* understood?

July

When term had ended I would probably have written anyway, but Glyn Jones's few words at Gregynog helped me, and showed me what I must do. After my reading, he took exception to the way in which I was answering questions by using a kind of critical language to explain the springs of my writing. He stated with feeling that this was releasing the creative valve and bringing out into the open what should be kept hidden and used creatively. I saw immediately that I had been doing this for a long time. What he could not know, perhaps, was that this had been due to lack of confidence. After that weekend, and partly as a result of it, I have found confidence, and the poems have confirmed it. I have had to learn the hard way that confidence is not a condition one can expect external circumstances or other people to provide; it has to be created by going on with one's work despite everything that can happen to discourage it. And it has to be one's own work, as the *Gita* says; to be obsessed by what other people are doing is merely a hindrance. One can be buried by too much reverence, too.

Misty half-moon not quite there in deep blue sky, a young raven laconically circling round & round, folding its wings and tumbling as if pretending to be dead, then flying on, each time with a deep croak of satisfaction. Hardly any birdsong now except the *tic-tic-tic-tzee* of the yellowhammer.

August

What really matters is my growing frustration at not being part of anything I can share with others. Even in my writing I tend to create a sense of shared life rather than write out of it. This is the tragedy of our impoverishment, mine & many others, and this is what we'll be remembered for, if anything, our pale faces at the edge of life.

Earth Poems

1. *Song of the Earth*

Bring or do not bring your mind's distress.
The seas it foundered in
Are none of mine.
My words are flint, cold to your touch.
They tell I am
What you become.
No tree bore the branch
From which your sick thoughts spin.
There is no vertigo in falling leaves.
Along brain's empty dancing-floor
My small blades creep.
The grass's flood-tide bears you home.

2. *At the Edge*

You will haunt the edges
Becoming more shadowy the more
This world streams past.
Now there is nothing but grassblade
Running into grassblade,
Each a separate wave where the colours flux
Orange into brown. The field is going out
With the autumn tide,
And where you were there is now
Only a cry.

3. *The Elements*

Even a poor eye
Can see clear through the globe
To its Antipodes. All, all,
Like a frail door banging in the wind,
A leaky raft through which the sea springs,
Cannot keep out the other elements.
With faculties so weak
You can reach out to touch the other side of death.

Heavy curtains of rain on all sides blot out the landscape. I look up at long grass straggling along the bank, at the wire fence strung out, & the black & white cattle, sodden, cropping the field, and everything farther away fades into greyish atmosphere. Rain on the tin roof. What am I doing here? What am I giving to anyone, sitting here writing?

Lightning, thunder. A sudden blast of fear. After more than ten years self-consciousness still encloses me.

•

Grass, stones, water, earth.

Wasps swarming in the plum tree.

Butterflies flying over the sycamores, almost as fast as bats, as if a sudden delight had been released in them.

Summer again. Renewal. Another chance. This is how it must always be. Bursts of creative energy. Excitement at what I have written. Staleness. Disappointment. Self-doubt. New energy. A sense of being closer to the object, which is always ahead. All that matters is to continue the pursuit with all one's powers.

No word for a wet stone *is* a wet stone. But without words there is no wet stone either. How our world depends upon our language yet is always beyond or aside from it! The world does exist outside consciousness; sometimes we catch a glimpse of it at the edge, the world contemplating the world outside all our schemes and concepts. Chaos, but also the very opposite. Only the hopeless pursuit can give me glimpses of the wonder in which my life comes fully alive.

Acute appreciation of nature does not make a poet. There is an area of disturbance where words and things touch – I mean in the mind aware of this frontier. So the life of words and my sense of things are part of a single process when I write. There is at least the comfort of knowing that no one knows exactly what constitutes this act, or indeed what language is, or poetry.

Bring speech to the inanimate.

Hear what the thing has to say – in you, but never for itself.

•

Midnight, sky clear overhead but obscure all round the horizon. Flashes of lightning behind the ridge to the south, and, in the same area, a sharp probing searchlight turned on the dark sky. Startled, it took me several seconds to realise it was the headlights of a distant car climbing the other side of the hill. I remembered Idris Morgan's story. When there were few cars on the roads, his mother knew of his father's return from north Wales when she saw, from the house on Mynydd Bach, the headlights of his car as far away as Dolgellau! Spaces at night. Two solitary people communicating with lights at a distance of 30-40 miles.

•

I gave Dai Morris, the old shepherd, a lift up the hill. He has rheumatism now, and finds walking increasingly difficult ('the beginning of the end,' he said, rubbing his legs). When we reached his home he sat in the car and talked for a long time, mainly about people's sentimentality towards 'killer' dogs, & dogs that should be hunters or gun dogs, about 'frustrated old women' who 'talk through their hearts'. He spoke with feeling, uncompromisingly, directly, seldom turning to look at me. A strong face, with the familiar weathered redness of the Welsh farmer, with a protruding underlip & powerful, clear blue eyes, his teeth set apart, brown at the roots, cap pulled over his forehead at a slight angle. A man with powerful convictions about nature and our proper relationship to it; hard but not unkind, 'soft' & 'sentimental' his fiercest terms of criticism. Just in passing he spoke of 'strangers', in contrast to local people. Seeing the misty blue bulk of Mynydd Bach today, I feel again its essential Welshness, the uncompromising but elusive kernel of its difference.

•

Overcast, muggy weather has brought on a plague of insects, wasps in the caravan, small moths in the bedroom at night. We're frequently jerked back from the edge of sleep by a moth blundering into the pillow or a daddy longlegs tickling us under the sheets. The way a philosopher lives with minor irritations is a guide to the soundness of his philosophy! I can't imagine any of the Chinese or Indian thinkers thrashing the air like a deranged windmill when a stinging insect came near. Similarly I've realised the vacuity of a meditation in which I've stubbed my toe on a rock and been painfully reminded that intractable hardness and sensitive nerves really do exist! Thus readiness for all things in & out of their seasons seems to me true wisdom – or to be surprised by nothing and everything, but never, never, to indulge a spoilt child's tantrum with the universe.

I was born and grew up in a village. I have lived for a few years in a relatively small city (Southampton) surrounded by rich countryside. I am most free from any mental obsession when walking in fields with no one to see me. This disposition determines the things I love/the things I have grown up to love determine my disposition. I have been forced to acknowledge my need to live close to nature, and have tried to acknowledge the need without sentimentalizing the present condition of nature or man's relationship with it. At times my situation makes me feel irrelevant to the lives of most other people, especially in so far as my writing is the work I live to do. At times I feel certain that the 'nature poet', who is close to the life and death mysteries, and whose instinct is to embrace the body of the earth, is more important today than at any other time.

What we need above all is to experience 'the pleasure that there is in life itself'; it is this alone that can heal the open wounds. It is in this respect that J.C. Powys was a 'magician': his 'magic' made me want to live more fully. Isn't it vital now to remind people of the life force within them? Not to ignore pain, or corruption, or cruelty, but to show that there is one force alone that can fight the greatest evil of all, the will to destroy.

Seeking my bearings I can't help but be preoccupied with coming to terms with the earth my immediate ancestors worked. The necessity is a deep-rooted inner experience. And I hate the literary image if only because, in other respects, I am threatened by it.

It is only by moving away from England – and in Wales one is much farther from England than many people know – that I have come increasingly to value the experience of belonging. Again, I know that if one does belong to a place the strength derived from it becomes part of the self, and thus one carries it into other places. In the end, if one is 'at home' in oneself no place is alien.

September

Last brief freedom before term begins. The negative and destructive relationships within the college, which give an air of backstage jealousies & futility to the gloomy rooms off King Street, still affect me strongly when I go there. At worst, going back to this life is like forcing an ill-fitting iron helmet onto my head, with spikes that cut into my temples. Why have I remained here so long? The most negative reason is the element of defeatism in my temperament, that awful spoilt child's feeling of irritable hopelessness I experience when even the smallest details – like trying to erect a tent in a stiffish breeze – seem intractable. Arian Kiriloff once observed, when I had spoken of going abroad, that our destiny had to be worked out in this place.

Brynbeidog is another world. So is Wales. Returning, I felt the green grass & trees, all the reds, yellows & browns of autumn & the damp earth-smells drench me through & through. It was like a journey from the earth's surface into the earth's interior. The sun went down fiery red through the sycamores and twigs were black across the red disc. At such times, when the grass is wet with dew, the earth gives off a heavy odour and it is as if we participate in its breathing. Mounds of cut reeds were lying in the fields, a large machine was vibrating somewhere on the hill. Stream a thin trickle between dry stones. I submit instinctively to the atmosphere, as if to life itself outside the anxieties, evasions, and roles in which one lives with a crippling sense of time: time to be got through, time to be used, hours of endurance followed by hours of endurance.

We are obsessed by our 'modern' position; we are not part of a continuity that makes us content simply to live from day to day, but are preoccupied by the fact that it is *1971*. The Fifties, the Sixties, the Seventies – fashions and trends change rapidly so that periods of ten years, five years, two years, seem far apart, hastening on with a heightening sense of crisis, leaving the quaint and outmoded behind. The Seventies it appears are a box opening into the Eighties, which pundits are already attempting to unlatch. The modern version of reality encourages us to live in and for time, and time is interpreted as fashion, taste, style, the new and the outdated, political and economic crises, as if there were no other reality one could live in and for. The continuity of personal experience is assaulted, just as the continuity of human life itself is no longer an element in which people can live without a massive effort of reconstruction. But I resist this tendency, instinctively. I know that my life has continuity, which comprehends its changes, and extends behind my birth into the lives of others, and after my death. All the vivid transformations of a changing society, a technology with built-in obsolescence, are essentially superficial as far as the human spirit and emotions are concerned. The social and pseudo-scientific awareness that is advertised as contemporary reality limits our grasp of human potential to the point of madness, and thus makes anxiety its natural mode of consciousness.

It should be possible to feel the same kinship with people of the twenty-first century, or the thirtieth century, that we can feel with seventeenth-century or even primitive man. Naturally, the experience of living with crisis – the planet poisoned or laid waste – intensifies our consciousness of time. But this is a vicious circle since that intense consciousness is the very element that must destroy sources of self-renewal. A particular form of consciousness is the cruellest trap, and the imagery of boxes and containers that is so precious to our technology is its material manifestation.

Knocking holes in this consciousness – holes through which a larger life can enter – is the occupation of every serious artist today. Kindness, tenderness, generosity, warmth of a concentrated integrity diffused through the whole body and spirit – these are the qualities real art needs.

•

The pretentions to security of a whole way of life are rent asunder by bombs exploding in the heart of cities. These are 'holes', but not of the kind the responsible revolutionary, in art or in any creative activity, can fail to resist totally with his spirit. Such holes represent a destructive and negative principle which is far worse than the rottenness of the system they are aimed at destroying. Dafydd Iwan, speaking on television recently, said that he *could not* deplore the bomb outrages in Belfast because they were part of a total situation of violence that included our acceptance of militarism and colonialism. I sympathise with his sense of the total situation, but not to deplore, not to see the *difference*, is unforgivable. When children are filled with hatred; when men without pity plant bombs whose victims may be arbitrary; then all values are negated in a way that no system, militarist and capitalist, comes near to achieving.

When in the past, how often, and in what circumstances, have poets felt guilty, as if their work were parasitic and luxurious activity? In the Thirties, certainly; and look how false much of that concern seems now, often unfairly, considering the dangers to which men like Auden subjected themselves. Yet the important writers were often at a tangent to the political and social events which to the others were a knife's edge on which they balanced. The great writers draw their criticism of society (and it is usually implicit rather than explicit in their work) from their awareness of man and civilisation as a whole. And this is often a religious awareness, which forces upon the individual, as an inner necessity, the need to live with utter seriousness of moral and creative purpose – the very opposite of luxuriousness and parasitism. The meaning of life is being challenged all the time in every single individual; so that what each one *does*, and *is*, is as important as what happens in the major disaster areas of the time.

•

Quite often, my thoughts betray me. They start into life through sensation and emotion but then develop a life of their own. Hence some of the demands I make on myself are in excess of what it is actually possible for me to do or be. Attempting to push myself in a wrong direction, what I should be doing, as a necessity of my nature, gets left undone.

J.C. Powys is very alert to the way in which a person can live for years mistakenly believing his real life is *this* not *that*. For example, a man lives for a sense of duty, but discovers at a late stage that he has really lived *for* certain kinds of sensation. So I discover, as my words unfold, that the source of my essential insights is particular sensuous experience, whether mine or others'. There is a subtle chemistry by which sense impressions, through the medium of the imagination, become thoughts, ideas, images. But in my ignorance I think the process can be stimulated by reading books or by abstract thinking, whereas it is often a single sense impression, sometimes fleeting, a mere ghost, that brings it about.

•

Golden tint deepening where I walk with Brutus in the field of rushes & reeds. Almost twenty years ago I walked with Boxer enjoying the same sensations that give me an ecstasy of well-being, sunlight warming my neck & back & the backs of my legs, until I am completely thoughtless, like a cool flame. How easily one forgets these essential things in pursuing an image of oneself as cultured & moral & sensitive! Yet this simple basking in warmth and trampling through grass with a dog make me complete.

October
Began the Giant poems last Friday. I am concentrating at last.

•

Walking across the Beidog, as the water's sudden pleasant chill reaches through my boots and I step into a patchwork of bright sunshine & shade, the first pool below me is greenish-gold and like a quivering hide.

Last night, the comfort of a good fire and the primal satisfaction of four stout walls with rough weather hammering against them; this afternoon, the serene pleasure of breathing deeply as I walked slowly about the fields. This way of life does suit me much better, now I see many people and talk with them of different things, then come back here to my writing, and all the time, quietly, at the back of my mind,

I'm active with a single preoccupation. No wordy dissipation, no senseless fretting at a dozen things I might or ought to be; just the act of doing what I can.

Matrix

A memorial of its origins, chalk in barns and churches
moulders in rain and damp; petrified creatures swim in
its depths.

It is domestic, with the homeliness of an ancient
hearth exposed to the weather, pale with the ash of
countless primeval fires. Here the plough grates on an
urnfield, the green plover stands with crest erect on a
royal mound.

Chalk is the moon's stone; the skeleton is native to its
soil. It looks anaemic, but has submerged the type-sites
of successive cultures. Stone, bronze, iron: all are assimilated
to its nature; and the hill-forts follow its curves.

These, surely, are the work of giants: temples
re-dedicated to the sky god, spires fashioned for the
lords of bowmen:

Spoils of the worn idol, squat Venus of the mines.

Druids leave their shops at the midsummer solstice;
neophytes tread an antic measure to the antlered god.
Men who trespass are soon absorbed, horns laid beside
them in the ground. The burnt-out tank waits beside
the barrow.

The god is a graffito carved on the belly of the chalk,
his savage gesture subdued by the stuff of his creation.

He is taken up like a gaunt white doll by the round hills,
wrapped around by the long pale hair of the fields.

A rough cold wind before dawn, its primeval noise in the trees, then
cold that sends a shiver right through the skeleton. At this hour, in
this weather, I feel totally discounted and made nothing in a way that
is eerie & awe-inspiring. All the houses are swept away; they do not
exist, nothing exists but a man or a small group alone, naked of all
superior comforts & glad of a little protection, feeling the elements in
their complete indifference. It is what a child feels, perhaps before he
is conscious; we recall such feelings from the border with consciousness, when the protective mechanisms were only a thin covering. I
remember my cot being shaken by thumps of the AA gun in the field
beside Fairacre; and the experience of the wind was like that – where
opposite feelings meet, vulnerability and fear, shelter and protection.

November
In the morning we drove to Prestatyn where I gave a talk on R.S.
Thomas to John Davies's sixth form at the High School. The talk was
held in the library, all the students rising as we entered, and I sat on
a hard wooden yellow chair facing them and they sat on hard wooden
yellow chairs staring back. It was okay, though questions were slow in
coming afterwards and most were provided by staff. The head master
is an old boy from Aberystwyth and it is the glory of his life that he
played rugby for the college. Apparently, in Professor Atkins's time
no one was accepted to study English who couldn't make the first
team.

Arriving at the school, almost the first words we heard were
addressed by a young teacher to a boy: 'Why were you running? ...
Stand up straight ... not responsible for your actions ... Take your
hands out of your pockets ...' The old familiar atmosphere which I
had forgotten; veiled by formality, a sense of the battlefield. It was
present even in the library, and I tried to ignore it by talking naturally
– my readings of the poems interrupted by prolonged harsh jangles
of the school bell.

On a bright rather chilly morning we called on Phyllis Playter at 1

Waterloo Terrace, Blaenau Ffestiniog. A frail old lady, she was dressed entirely in black with a large silver cross around her neck. An ascetic face with red-rimmed eyes. But she was warm and welcoming as the house itself, the single downstairs room austere and beautiful. After a hesitant beginning, once we were drinking coffee and smoking (she lit woodbine after woodbine) the reminiscences and warm enthusiastic exchanges made us feel very much at home. Later she showed us her fine collection of books by the Powys brothers, and also some of the books dear to JCP. There was a deep quietness and tranquillity of spirit about the whole atmosphere of the place with its views of high mountains through the windows. She said how much JCP would have liked to meet us. Underneath this frail exterior I could imagine the girl she was, and how she had released him to become more fully himself through her total acceptance and love. In a way I learnt little that I did not already know, except about her and the serenity he has left behind. But she did confirm my suspicion that his dislike of Robert Graves stemmed partly from the fact that they were both working in the same area; and he did read *The White Goddess*, painfully slowly.

December
Beidog a cold dark blue, the colour of wet slates forming the garden path. Seen close-to, the clear water has a faint greenish tint, which is the colour of all the local mountain streams. I can't dissociate the water's colour from its texture, feel & taste: a wet stone held to the lips is the stream's living body.

Often, lying awake at night, I feel utterly self-sick. In my writing, unconscious though the process is when I am attending to work in hand, I have been striving to create, not a singleness that excludes new discoveries, but a world that is my own and at the same time an image and an exploration of the worlds we share. But my oblique approach seems at times to exclude so much experience, personal and common, that it is reduced almost to the level of the naked chalk. Like the Giant, the juices are locked in me ... all the rich disorder, the moment when life is, the changes & contradictions – all that should pound against the shape of the work, which the order should barely contain ... it's this that, all too often, fails to move.

My present work has revived never-long-dormant anxieties about my sparsely peopled archaic landscape. The same image, or the same anxiety in different images, keeps swimming to the surface of my mind and I see myself making structures out of a heap of white bones. In all the self-sick phases the sense of awe presents itself as the one positive: feelings aroused in me, discoveries I can't quite get through to, not the dead earth seen in the image of the moon. And awe plunges me deep into history, into the rich many-layered life of a people in which I try to express something of my living experience – finding myself, finding others: the single act.

The lonely being finding in nature only images of its own isolation – this is what I now resist: the sensitive-face-in-the-crowd of many English contemporaries. The one contemplating the many and finding the many are but a mirror reflecting its aloneness: in a deep sense, this is *finished*. Wordsworth's love and relationship, perhaps a new love, certainly a new relationship, are what I must hang onto, wed to my nature, despite many temptations to the contrary. The Giant must be worked through.

•

Not in the least like a Breughel Christmas. No crispness, no clarity, only unnaturally warm, with low grey skies deadening the senses. I am now in bed with 'flu, in Pulborough, watching a warm sun white on the Downs, and reading, with considerable impatience, one of Powys's empty late romances, *Atlantis*. The more of his later work I read, the more I feel inclined to expose his charlatanism, which he, with Odyssean cunning, confesses to in *Autobiography*. He strikes me as a writer entirely lacking in spiritual sincerity – another charge against which he has covered himself by being the first to bring it! There's no affirmation, no exploration, no discoveries in these late books, only pretentious wordy repetitions of all the old tricks and habits of bookish thought. How different is the case with Hardy, with Yeats, with Eliot! Powys takes life's substance and reduces it to sticky streamers of coloured candyfloss.

I shall be glad now when this year is over. If only a hard frost and cleansing snow would write *finis* to the unnatural atmosphere. For me this Christmas there has been no germ of nativity, and Christ seems as remote as the pharaohs or Horus.

•

Snow falling on the last two mornings in Sussex. Returning to Brynbeidog on a cold day, we found a heap of Christmas cards & a rejection of my book by Macmillan.

1972

January

Winter, winter. Mynydd Bach, like a rock by which I drag myself up from illusion. One morning the mountains of north Wales were unbroken, perfect white. One night we lay awake for hours talking with great excitement of going back to Southampton. Some days the Giant's reality has contained me. And sometimes I wake up to, or dream, a state of total indifference. Yesterday Sue brought in some catkins already shedding pollen.... Accept the work and live in the world, there's no alternative but cold pride or madness.

•

Fine snow grains on the air yesterday morning. Two robins in territorial combat seemed to be everywhere in the garden, skirmishing, uttering short angry challenges, pursuing each other. Bullfinches in small groups, exotic against the winter landscape. Great tits, almost as brilliant, their characteristic unmusical notes, like a squeaking see-saw, only faster.

Earth stayed frozen all day, ice on the roads did not melt. Coming home in the early evening, under a bright star in clear sky, we saw the orange full moon rising.

Feeling, thinking, being driven by exasperation to assert that the unconscious is merely a convenient fiction, this is despair. Tearing at the mind's walls with broken nails, this is the self-image that drives the despairing on to exhaustion. And in exhaustion there is no access to the energy that comes from – where? By bodily action, by the accompanying sensations & perceptions, by letting part of the mind sleep, I gather creative energy, and then feel that consciousness is resting upon something else: a darkness carrying me and feeding what I do.

Let the darkness alone, be content with the image of earth or water, fertile elements.

Farther out, deeper in.

February

How rarely is a person conscious that he is living *his* life! At

Christmas, Dad showed me a photograph of his father as a boy, a young lad among older agricultural workers, grouped around a donkey, each posed with the tools of his or her trade. I was conscious of more than time; and he, did he know who he was? He lived such a long life.

•

Sodden fields & hedgerows, reddish-brown sticks above ochre-coloured dead grass on the banks. Winter clarities, the landscape's bone structure laid bare.

For some time the air has been full of talk of impending disaster. The danger of man exhausting his resources is evident, yet some of this talk is a revelling in the idea of death. In a few centuries, if things get better instead of worse, people will see this century in terms of an astonishing contrast between sophisticated and ingenious thought and crass political systems that supplied our social reality. I find it impossible to believe we are near the end because there are so many ways in which we seem to be scarcely at the beginning.

•

Slender orange boat of the moon seen through sycamore branches.
    Frogspawn in the shallow pool in the old gateway between hedge-banks in the marshy field, where small waterplants with clover-shaped leaves have been tender, living green all winter.
    The difference between imposing an image on nature and allowing an image to form in the mind through long transactions between mind and nature.
    We must not be afraid. It is fear that creates the chasm between mind and world, which is only a ghastly appearance.
    Misunderstanding of life is a continual downpour of lava which turns the mind into a statue, a small collection of rigid gestures. Then there's an image, a moment, and the statue falls apart, the cramped life suddenly unbends.

•

At about 1 in the morning, we caught a polecat in the car headlights, trapping it in a narrow lane between tall hedgebanks which it was unable to scale. It looked black in the lights, with glittering eyes, and was the size of a full-grown cat but with an elongated body that made its sinuous, twisting movements more like an otter's. As we slowly drove past, I thought of its relief to be left alone in the dark.

•

Why did Joyce have Stephen write a diary at the end of *A Portrait*? As further evidence of his self-concern, according to one critic. Too moralistic. The diary entries have a confidence in his judgments and feelings that nothing he has previously done or said shows. How long can Narcissus rule in a writer's life? How long anti-Narcissus (the same in a new disguise?), scrutinising feelings and ideas, tracing motives, lambasting backslidings into self-concern? If both stages are necessary, their too-long continuance obstructs full use of resources.

A certain kind of reflection prevents creation; hives off energy needed for the free play of thought and the integrity and force of emotion.

So it is: I return to myself as the subject experiencing and the wholeness of experience falls into mouldy tatters. Life rent in this way will inevitably appear to be a flimsy curtain with a staring face behind it. The reflection is a confidence trick, proving the subject's isolation on every occasion, the alien nature of the world set over against him. True writing is action, not reflection. In consequence it can never be *about* the self. Without experience there is no self to reflect upon. Identity cannot be laid bare by concentrating upon it: it just vanishes like an hallucination examined with clear eyes.

Outside relationships, nothing exists. But what about the 'I am I' feeling that persists through all stages of life, through change and enormous variety? Freud called it the ego and ascribed it to the inter-action between instinct and society. Christians call it the soul and derive it from the breath of God. My thought about identity oscillates uneasily between extremes of social construct and God-given essence, to which I add the ideas I find most attractive in Jung. The result is a proper botch, a rare eclectic fuddle. Naturally, I take the 'I' for granted, but when I try to reflect upon it, outside the field of experience, it dissolves in a mist: there is only the experience, only 'my life', a web of relationships with this 'I'-feeling the spider at the centre – a spider that vanishes when the web is pulled to pieces!

Belief in the soul requires an act of faith; reduction of soul to ego is science's attempt to extend its realm into an area that is by its nature mysterious. I have made myself giddy by peering into a chasm that does not exist. The attempt to know oneself in isolation makes the self horribly anxious: so one holds back from life, everything seems far off. Experience mirrors the illusion, becomes the mist. The non-existent chasm deepens, the breech between self and world seems to extend for ever. The mind spins on its axis, alienated from its true nature which lies in action, in relationship. The vertigo is all the worse for being induced by an illusion.

March

In the studio at HTV, Cardiff: a plunge into an overwhelming atmosphere of affability. Men greet you as if you were the one person they have always wanted to meet, question you closely and greet another in the same tone just as you have begun to answer. An evening swimming in drink and jocularity in the cradle of the ego. No doubt buffets to the ego are correspondingly rough in a world where personality is almost all. In fact everyone I met was amiable, and several friends were there, Roland, Glyn Jones and Emyr Humphreys, who made the evening worthwhile. Meic Stephens was eloquent about the artificiality of the studio, which appeared to be composed of a substance like blue and white kitchen formica, and occupied a small corner of a vast building, which I first likened to a converted aircraft hanger, then to the boiler room of an enormous ship. Wynford Vaughan-Thomas was kind to me, flattering. There's part of me that could swim in this element, after three or four whiskies, like a dolphin.

On the way down I was in a state of near panic, creating obsessive dramas of flight or collapse. When the programme began I soon lost all self-consciousness, all awareness of camera and occasion, in the heat of what I was actually saying about Anglo-Welsh literature.

•

A smell of spring from the earth, in the morning & again at evening: slightly sweet, slightly acrid – earth & wet stones, water & crocuses.

A smell of seaweed by the college. A full-grown herring-gull, contemplatively: *huk-huk-huk*. The gulls are everywhere, I love to see them. Dove-grey above, with an orange spot, like a blood-drop, on the cruel tough beak, they sit hunched, with cunning eye & cocked head, or sidle awkwardly along the white rails, then launch gracefully into the air. A ruthless squabbling gang plucks at something in the water. Town of herring-gulls: that is how I shall remember Aberystwyth. The grey back is the same delicate soft colour as the smooth pebbles.

On such a mild warm day the beach vanishes into sun-mist and the sea breaks gently, leaving the sky mirrored in a narrow band of water on the sand, which vanishes so that the reflected sky drains away, absorbed into fine grey particles. I watch the gulls until my eye is still. Outside, all is so calm & clear; nothing vibrates and twangs like stretched nerves. When I can see them, things hold me steady.

•

Warm fresh days of growth & birdsong, nights of the waxing moon, chill with a little frost.

The Giant falters at present, but not the curlews. I watch them flying round Brynbeidog in a large circle, uttering short shrill whistles or a long bubbling call, which rises almost hysterically as they settle, then dies away. I see long necks & curved beaks rising above a ridge in the field, and the cries are *shaped*, curving, like a Palaeolithic hunter's delicate carving in reindeer bone.

Buzzards are nesting near the top of a birch tree about 200 yards above the house, at the far end of Glyn's field. We can see the bulk of one of the parent birds sitting in the lower branches, or the two birds flying in a graceful spiral over the tree.

•

Giant thriving. Terrific hailstones battering the caravan roof.

April
Days & nights of heavy rain till the river runs down fast & brown carrying away brambles & twigs hacked from the old hedge. In the evening mist lifts suddenly from Mynydd Bach, blows away in trailing

wisps from the ridge and a pale blue sky brings out fresh greens &
browns of the high ground.

•

Got our letters from the postman in the village on our way to Sussex.
A letter from Diana telling me Chatto turned down the book in
January and it has been with Oxford for two months; and it will
almost certainly be rejected there. I felt tired and depressed.

I think I shall ride this rebuff fairly easily, though it seems as if 'the
writing is on the wall' as far as the next year or so is concerned. What
chiefly puzzles and depresses me is the amount of mediocre verse
Chatto publishes. When I think of 'Elegy for the Labouring Poor' &
'Landscape' & of passages in 'Hambledon' I'm staggered by the
rejection. I know well enough the inadequacies of my early work, and
of the later work too, and I don't feel that I've yet written anything
with my full power & conviction, but even so ...

•

Spring flowers in Stopham Woods. Daffodils fading as bluebells
unfold. Stitchwort. Milk maids. Celandines. Primroses. Herb Robert.
Flowering wild cherry trees. Sunlight among the trees and sudden
unexpected gusts of wind that made dead leaves fly. Keats is the poet
of luxuriant growth. More often than consummation, English poetry
expresses the sadness of seasonal rhythms. After so much awareness
of ruined nature, as if permanent winter were our season, and in my
concern with the chalk's bleak bed-rock, it is almost a surprise to find
spring lusty & delicate as ever. After beginning the Giant poems at
the start of winter, I need this awareness to complete them.

•

When I visited him again at Southampton University, F.T. Prince
talked kindly to me about his own isolation & disappointments and
assured me that the only way to have a book of poems published was
by making contacts. He promised to arrange some introductions for
me. Chiefly, though, it was his animation & openness that I found
heartening and his readiness to talk to me in that way, on equal terms

& on the basis of a common problem. I was able to tell him about our desire to come back to Southampton, and though his appointments are frozen for the time being, it was possible to make my feelings known because he understood them, and there was no need to elaborate and say too much.

Is it wise to go back rather than forward? Even now I'm not sure. But I would not be going back. A rather dream-like state accompanies me in my visits to the south, but I think of coming *back* to make something, not to idealize. Where to? Deeper into one's footsteps. The return must be the beginning of a period of discovery, not the end of anything.

The Giant's Shadow

I am the giant who carries a giant
On his back.
This is my comrade.
Is he alive or dead?

I stoop and cry out
Let go, let go.
When I look up
The shadow hangs over me
With crossed wings ...
Impure fancies, how they breed
In the sludge
Of a standing mind!

Do you imagine the dead stop in their graves?
Stones of the abbey that vanished
Are mounted on my spine.
This is history,
When the mind is an open grave.

You are sunlight,
You are darkness,
Green god.
The rest is illusion.
Illusion with talons hooked through my bones.
It is an anchor
From the bottom of the sea,
It is fixed in the floor of the sea
Like an axe-head fast in a skull.
If I could move it, the world would shift.

How heavy the shadows are!
I wrestle with them all day long,
Fingers clutched round my cold stave.

At Cerne Abbas. As I stood at the Giant's head a Wessex helicopter circled us. In the burial ground a child had scrawled a face in charcoal on the flat top of a tomb. Naturally, it was rather like the Giant's face. In 'the field called Bevoir' where some of the abbey ruins may be, I picked up several Poole oyster shells, fragments of pottery, and what looks like a piece of Kimmeridge shale. Blackbirds' songs counterpointed the noise of rooks and I saw St Augustine's Well for the first time, with clear water flowing from it. A couple of boys were swinging on a rope from a tree on the lower slopes of the hill; noisy, rough and happy.

•

Calvary Guest House (the Little House of Mary), Sudbury Hill, is a large red brick house, probably Victorian, surrounded by peaceful, rather wild gardens.

David Jones is living in Room 1, as the nun who lets me in tells me, with a significant look. In this long narrow room he is sitting between a table and a chest of drawers covered in books, and with two small tables in front of him, with papers and a tray full of biros and pens on them. He is very frail and moves about with difficulty and only with a support. He smiles often, with the characteristic boyish look, grey hair combed forward over his forehead, and talks slowly, sometimes becoming quick and animated, sometimes losing the thread and sitting forward with his head in his hands, or sideways, until he picks it up again or takes up another line of thought or reminiscence.

He talks a great deal about the First World War, which he says he remembers much more clearly than the Second, and about his early life, especially about his grandfather who was ultimately responsible for preventing him from learning Welsh, which he bitterly regrets. He speaks of his breakdowns, too, though only in passing, and of his lack of 'education', and he shows me the drawings of Welsh soldiers in an old copy of J.R. Green's *History of the English People* that inspired him as a child: the fact that they wear only one sandal accounts for the same detail in some of his paintings.

He speaks of his love of words, and of how he might have become a philologist instead of a painter and writer if he had had the appropriate education so that he is glad he did not! He speaks with love of *Gawain and the Green Knight* and of Langland, both of which he prefers to Chaucer. He surprises me by speaking with admiration of John Cowper Powys's *Owen Glendower* and *Porius*; he believes there is more of 'the real thing', of the spirit of ancient Welsh tradition, in them than in any other Anglo-Welsh writing, and he dislikes Robert Graves for his 'Teutonic' attitudes, which Graves applies to the White Goddess; but he is anxious to be fair, and speaks of the exciting effect Graves had on his students as Professor of Poetry at Oxford.

After I have been with him for more than an hour, I suggest he should tell me when he wants me to go, so as not to tire him too much, but he says, 'Go! we haven't started yet!' When I mention, rather naively, that Saunders Lewis is deeply respected in Wales, he says, abruptly and fiercely, 'So he should be'.

While he talks he either draws on a sheet of paper with a biro – for instance, to show me the position of Portslade – or smokes or plays with a cigarette in his fingers, which are heavily stained with nicotine.

After about two hours Douglas Cleverdon arrives to visit him and I think it time for me to leave. But he is very unwilling to let me go: 'there are so many things I want to talk to you about'. Towards the end of my visit he tells me about his broken hip and speaks with nostalgia of his 'dugout' in Harrow which he is still hoping to go back to. He insists I should come again whenever I am in London. As I am leaving he accuses me, humorously, with a twinkle, of being 'one of those people who visit me and leave their wives outside'.

On the journey back to Wales, when I go into Hereford Cathedral to look at the Mappa Mundi, I think of the vast difference between that cosmology and ours, and wonder what a modern map, analogous to the old one with its fabulous and mythic dimensions, would look like. It seems to me that, in a sense, David Jones's work, especially *The Anathemata*, is a kind of *Mappa Mundi* and what the medieval cartographer could do with ink on vellum David Jones has done with images and words.

•

The expected rejection from Oxford was awaiting our return. They suggest I should 'prune' the book in some places, 'expand' it in others and send it back in six months or a year but they don't say where I should prune it. They express admiration for 'Elegy for the Labouring Poor', 'Landscape' and 'Friend with a Mandolin'. It is all very bewildering but I suppose I may present another version of the book at some time. What they really mean, I feel, is 'we don't know you'.

•

As I sit here in the caravan I can hear a willow warbler singing in a blackthorn beside the stream. Earlier, I saw it close-to, elusive among the flowers and picking at twigs with quick, deft movements, then opening its beak wide till I could see the pale interior of its throat. Close by, two grasshopper warblers hid in gorse and I saw the warm red of a bullfinch as it flew rapidly away.

Yesterday evening Emyr Humphreys came to read to the English Society. He was a student at Aberystwyth in the Thirties and he remembers Alun Lewis giving an impassioned address on the Spanish Civil War. Very few came to the reading and I was disappointed and embarrassed but Emyr took it all in good part and read from his novels and work-in-progress with characteristic nervousness and self-deprecation, which are so engaging and do not diminish the worth or interest of his work. He spoke afterwards of the novel as a dying form and said he believes poetry and television are the contemporary forms of communication. But for all that, and despite his advice to young writers to think twice before writing novels, it is clear that he is dedicated.

•

How often I have looked up and seen shadows in the fold under the hill, and mild blue sky above it. A crow, glossy black in sunlight, lands in the field where lambs lie down, jump in the air or feed with long tails wriggling. Sheep feed just a few yards from where I work, heads moving with rapid jerks and I can see the long primeval skulls that are so earthy, and the delicate red interior of lambs' ears with sun shining through them, as Hardy saw the ears of rabbits. And I forget this is not common experience, nor my happiness & peace.

•

A week of fine days & evenings when the daylight moon, nearing full, rises behind the ridge long before the sun sinks. At evening, when I see the sun through branches, the sky's colours are etherialized, with the radiance of transfiguration.

I walk in the field with long blond grasses and its irregularity makes me happy & calm ... the high bank where gorse & willows grow, the overgrown ditch beside it & the pool in the gateway ... the foreground stretches a long way to the north-west then vanishes into the Dovey estuary and the faint blue, barren mountains seem to adjoin the landscape yet be in another world from the small green fields. The personality of this landscape has absorbed my attention only very slowly, and now begins to be part of me and stir in my imagination.

Brynbeidog & the surrounding fields are like a small, known estate in a vast alien territory; but here, too, I feel we belong and do not belong so that I still make discoveries about the place when, seeing it from a new angle, it thrills me with a sense of wonder.

•

First cuckoo calling in grey, misty before-dawn light on the 28th, a muffled vibrant throbbing somewhere under the mountain. Song of

the risen sap, of the fullness that overflows ... but as if from a mysterious crack in the material world. Marriage of childhood & spring.

•

In bed at 2 am listening to a high wind, spasmodic rattle of raindrops
against the window, brought to mind the pill-box with spray breaking
over it & the great submerged jungle of seaweed, just off the shingle
spit near Hurst Castle. A broken concrete box half buried in shingle.

I thought of Rat Island, on the estuary side of the spit, where, with
a float made from a gull's quill, I went fishing for flounder & checker
bass Sunday after Sunday as a boy. One day in particular, lying on
salt grass and looking up at the summer sky, I knew myself to be perfectly happy and could see an endless succession of similar days.

I am so childishly possessive that when I think of dying and
having my ashes scattered I want a handful to be sprinkled in a
hundred different places; on the Solent & the Lymington river, at
Boldre & at many sites in the Forest, on Pennington Common & at
Wainsford. What a weird thought, as if one could make love to the
earth but only in dissolution, whereas it is only a living mind that
experiences this love and at the same time, by its very nature, cannot
get enough of it, cannot sink deep enough or remain long enough in
the body of its love!

The trend of modern thought reflects little of my actual experience, yet has an advocate in part of my mind when I pretend that this
attachment to place is not at the very root of my experience, and
therefore, beyond the ability of my conscious mind to change it, the
matrix of my imagination. The first problem is to know what one
loves, what one cannot help loving, and to acknowledge it; the
second, to express it confidently, without apologetic irony, but in a
way that implies necessary perspectives on the circumstances
shaping one's place in place. There is a point beyond which irony
becomes the enemy of love.

May
Reading *Wolf Solent* again, I take heart. *There* is a writing from the
emotions & a rendering of 'powers of earth' that makes use of a self-
consciousness at least as extreme as mine. In this novel JCP combines
intense inner conflict with a wonderful evocation of nature; earth-

powers are mind-powers feeding imagination & the strength to live through sensation, and he renders levels and, more importantly, *kinds* of psychological experience in a way that enables a reader to feel accepted, understood. It is for me as if an animal that looks like the other animals of its species but contains a strange inner world that makes it feel separate discovers one much like itself in this respect. I am convinced that Powys unfolds realms of inner experience that are much more like the real thing, which all share to some degree, than any other novelist, and shows up the absurdity of reductive psychologies.

A Chalk Pebble

This is perfect:
A chalk pebble,
Smooth and round,
Like an egg
With the foetus
Of a giant
Curled inside.

When I touch it,
My hand crumbles.
The hill is a fine cloud
Whitening the Cretaceous sea.

Starfish, urchin, spunge,
I have become many:
We do not trespass here,
Composed on the white floor.
We are not foreign to this ground.

Who is the saurian
Tyrannizing the shallows,
Smashing a trackway
Through the new green trees?

His familiar,
Disproportionate head
Is small and mean.

The giant turtle is in its element,
Housed on the summit
Of low white hills.
The dead spunge mingles
With alchemic water
For the slow formation
Of a perfect stone.

A leisurely heron flies over, the ends of its wings slowly turning down, like flaps. I watch it go over near Rhos-y-garreg, in a direction between Cnwc-y-barcut and Felin Cwm, towards the Wyre.

Thrush in a flowering blackthorn, breast among the freckles as white as the flowers. A bird that knows it's being watched, but not from where.

Now the grass shoots up, and there is an impalpable mist over the fields & in the trees, a just perceptible thickening of the air. Stopping to dash water from a stream in my face, when the coolness reaches through to my hot feet, my mind too is refreshed and set free from its interminable, skull-enclosed monologues.

Last night, looking again at pictures of Henry Moore's sculptures, I realised once more that my instinctive feeling for things and for land-scapes is closer to the feeling of sculptors like Moore and Barbara Hepworth, and of certain painters, than to that of most writers. Reading Herbert Read on Moore's symbolism and organic form, I was moved by the kind of language he used, and the perception it conveyed; and I can see now that the only really hopeful, new rela-tionship between man and nature has been expressed in stone rather than words, and effected through a return to origins and the renewal of archaic forms. Even so, it is work like *Atom Piece* which most arrests and excites me. This compounds the expressionless expression of a brutal idol, Yeats's 'blank and pitiless' beast, and the smooth, purposeful cranium of a machine-head, the helmeted skull of a high altitude jet-fighter pilot, but with a rudimentary, bestial trunk. It is a 'deep image', which also suggests the domed cloud of a nuclear explosion. This is the closest visual approximation I know to what I think of as the 'new god', as opposed to Helith, Cernunnos, or Jehovah and it is an image of what man has made of himself, according to the mechanical principle.

•

Broken white cloud & blue sky over the ridge. The gaunt bony structure of these hills corresponds to irregular cloud shapes above them, the white of the farms to the whiteness of the clouds, their gaunt, solid forms to the hills.

Blackbirds' songs rise from hedgerows, a solitary cuckoo's muffled note, a curlew's distant cry.

How elusive this countryside is! That is its secret: elusiveness, quick, delicate changes of light playing on a foundation of solid, hard hill-shapes, softening them. A landscape inseparable from its changing skies and at once harsh and soft but in degrees that are always changing, impression swallowed by impression – as if this were the 'baseless fabric' of Prospero's vision.

•

At Dyffryn House, near Cardiff, with Cardiff Writers' Circle. A breathless programme of talks, readings, discussions, which Roland chaired admirably, with energy, kindness, humour and tact, especially when the talk returned again and again to the commercial aspects of writing and to the details, such as the need to enclose a SAE with one's contributions! I got very dispirited on several occasions and it was all too much for Meic Stephens, who was blunt, vehement, huffy and departed in a silent thundercloud.

Inevitably, there tended to be a segregation of 'professionals', as we were called, Ned, Aled Vaughan, John Tripp, Gillian Clarke and John Ormond (who were in the audience), Meic, Glyn Jones and me, from 'amateurs'. But I learn some things over and over again, especially *never to judge*.

For instance, during the session before my reading on Sunday morning I became gloomier and gloomier at the low level of discussion, then frightened and tense in anticipation of a blank response to what I was going to do. At the break I had got worked up to a pitch that made me unable to drink my coffee, and I walked out in the grounds, over to the round pond with reddish lily leaves floating on clear water. This calmed me a little, and I went back into the lecture room to place copies of poems on the desks. One of the organisers joined me. I asked him whether he had ever written any poetry and he told me that he had, once. Six lines, when his daughter was killed in Greece and he had come away from seeing her body, sat down on a wall and, near to collapse, written these six lines. He answered my question naturally, completely without self-consciousness. A few minutes later I was reading from the Giant for the first time. I became absorbed, and cast a spell, but wasn't aware of it at the time. Afterwards Roland was so moved that he suggested there should be no questions but that they should go away in silence to absorb the experience. John Ormond shook my hand, pressing into my palm a half-stick of chalk, a chalk phallus!

A true poet has nothing to do with market values, but he wants to speak and must be heard. Has he, then, to create his own market, as many important writers at some time do by creating their own outlets? Let me spell this out: the criteria of taste by which my work is being judged by the inner circle in London, criteria laid down principally by Alvarez and Ian Hamilton and operated by their satellites, revolt my intelligence. I have only myself ... Patience, patience ... I cannot take Prince's advice; I will not go on my belly to people I despise. My place as a poet is not here, in Wales, though there is a place for me here, and I am grateful for it.

•

Through the dirty window of my room in college, through black arrow-headed iron bars and over parked cars, I look out on the pier, broken off in mid-reach, with some of its remaining supports buckled and twisted under it, where a few cormorants always rest at the very end, often with outstretched wings held crooked, hanging out to dry, like men with their elbows awkwardly thrust out. It is only on certain days, in certain conditions of sunlight or storm, that I realize the presence of the sea.

The college building with turret and pinnacles, biscuit-coloured brick and violet tiles, must be one of the oddest in the world. It is part fairy-tale palace, part palace of medieval romance, or castle on the Rhine. The quadrangle and the side facing the sea are dominated by heavy statues of Victorian worthies, academics and the Prince of Wales, which heavily express the Welsh reverence for men of substance in the spheres of religion and learning.

•

Deep green recesses under trees and hedgerows and in ditches. Evening. The sycamores in full leaf are like giant green mushrooms – there is a dank fungoid *look* about the darkness under trunk and among the leaves. Stooping by the hedge, I smell the grass, but not intentionally; its smell invades me, filling me with happiness. To be alive in the present *and* to have memories! When I experience this feeling most intensely I cannot believe in death: the experience is of this world, yet seems to reveal that dull normal consciousness conceals other dimensions that are more real.

The grass is full of sunlight, which it absorbs, and becomes the lovely yellow-green I was not conscious of until we lived here. Now I have only to look up to feel growth advancing, surrounding me. In her seventh month of pregnancy Sue is lovelier than ever. For a few minutes, thinking of being present at the birth, I felt frightened, with a twinge of panic; then I said to myself, 'that's the wrong way to think about it,' and immediately there was no fear, only complete peace.

•

Wind suddenly rocks the caravan as if it would hurl it into the air, and blasts against the sycamores with brute violence so that we lie in bed at night thinking it may tear the roof off. In the evening livid clouds against a purplish background sail rapidly over the ridge.

Grass in the blond marshy field is whiter now than at any other time of year. Lousewort growing in large colonies show their small pink ears with beads of rainwater clinging to them. We used as children on Pennington Common to pluck out handfuls of the flowerheads and suck honey from them. Bog beans flower in wet

places, white stars furry with a tangle of small white hairs, and petty
whin is flowering close to the ground, prickly and yellow as broom.
Cuckoo-flowers are everywhere.

Lying in bed this morning we watched a big hare in the field. It came
close to the fence and sat up, face twitching over a mouthful of grass.
Later, another one appeared and they worked the field, meditatively.

The bullocks have long white eyelashes over soft bulbous eyes.
Looking at them for a long time makes me think of mind – there's a
look in their faces, as if aspiring to the moment when consciousness
floods in, but held back, inexorably ... Nature seeking intelligence; for
ever thwarted.

If my Giant is a god, he is Herakles, too, champion of the
common man.

The Giant's Boast

I was before Christ, and I remember
The saurian head of my begetter.
I conceived these words at my creation,
When you traced your shadow on the stone.

I was before Moses, and his fury
Returned me to the elements,
From which I am remade.

I have walked with my ribcage naked,
When the strong man dug his grave.
I have contemplated the skeleton
Under the flesh of all things,
And I gave to the holy waters
A natural potency.

The smoke from a wicker basket
Was sweetest to my nose;
For I have levelled and engendered

Multitudes, and I do not answer
To a single name.

No man understood me
Who called me brutal, and no woman
Who called me kind.
Mothers and daughters worshipped me.
I worshipped with my body
The naked ground.

Pencwmbeidog was auctioned yesterday afternoon. We stood or
walked about with quite a crowd in the fields, and, in sunshine and
high winds, looked down across the Wyre valley. The place was sold
for £6500 to an English buyer who already has several similar farms.
When the geese were driven out to be auctioned the parent birds
wedged the goslings between them and hissed, long snake necks
weaving. One parent bird had a bright blue eye. John Jones, our shy,
silent neighbour, who has lived with his old mother, walked about on
the edge of the crowd, speaking to no one, and watching his posses-
sions fall under the hammer.

June
Giant sleeping. Everything asleep but spasms of lechery, my jaded
eye swimming over inky scrawls.

Every morning I read a page or two of Kilvert. How much better
if it had been he, rather than Kierkegaard and St Augustine, who set
me scribbling. I love the man who can go out of himself, be discovered unconsciously in the life he submits himself to.

•

Earth full of moisture and fragrant when broken.

Looking through the window at a fence post I did not see it as a
flat surface, but felt it with my mind. Existing for a period in a world
of mental images, all is a flat screen.

Put aside exam marking for an hour and worked in the garden, shirt off, smelling cut grass, feeling my hands harden. What disgusting objects hands are when adapted for holding only a pen.

•

Dark rainclouds, almost the colour of wet slate, over the mountain to the south east. A vast cave of dark clouds with the fine arch of a rainbow vanishing into the roof. The whole sky overhead washed blue, pressing on the dark mass as if forcing it to retreat, low sun flashing red through sycamore branches. Briefly the night sky is perfectly clear but rainclouds from the west keep coming on.

Wettest June since records began, 100 years ago.

The Americans are reported to have created rain artificaly in Vietnam, to ruin agriculture.

The French detonate their vile bomb over the Pacific. How eloquent the passage in the old parish register where, in time of civil war, the clerk has written, to explain his ellipses: 'The times were such ...'

Anger and sick loathing diminish fear. When physical power over the universe is in the hands of men with the brains of computers, one is forced back on spiritual power and the joy that love and contact with the earth give. The meaning of life is invested in man the creator; destroyers can kill everyone's body but only their own spirit. The creator must assert spirit, must not participate subtly in the crude work of destruction.

•

Yr Academi Gymreig conference at University Hall, Cardiff. Roland – with apologies to his friends – on the background of Anglo-Welsh literature. Gwyn Williams on Welsh poetry. Belinda Humfrey on the landscape of Anglo-Welsh poets. Gwyn Thomas on the Welsh theatre – himself! I spoke on 'Rites of Passage', developing some thoughts about mythology and history in literature.

Gwyn Thomas, especially, was memorable, though some who have heard him before, think he has begun to parody himself. But to me he was the very embodiment of the Valleys, their tragedy, pathos and humour. A pudgy man in a dark suit, with the stance of a young bull, his face coarse-featured yet also peculiarly sensitive and expressive, as if moulded out of heavy, whitish clay, he spoke without notes, enacting his stories with dramatic gestures. *A man who is more than himself.* His taproot, like Gwenallt's, deep in the spirit of a people.

July
In Brighton. A man shouting in the streets, 'Listen to me you fucking sadists. This is the most fucking sadistic society in the world.' On and on, the same words over and over in a voice vibrant with hatred, and beneath the hatred, nerve-racked despair.

•

Jim sang in the Bugle all evening with the same old zest and expressiveness, filling the bar with students but taking nothing for it except free drinks. It was the same ten years ago, and now he sings for another generation, as no one else could. Still the same wonderful voice, the same generosity and deep, wide-ranging talk, the same problems.

Friend with a Mandolin

Singer with a mandolin,
Pluck from the smoke
Of a humdrum bar
The raw defiant strings
Of Mountjoy and Van Dieman's Land,

Let the bland south
Hear the blues.

From the cradle
Twanging in your hands,
Pick Cafe Mozart.

At closing time, we'll sit out

On the shingle drunkenly
Amazed to think of France,
So far away, still serving wine.

In Winchester to meet Graham Fawcett at Southern Arts and talk about possible funding for a literary magazine. Winchester – the song of money. It is the same throughout the south. Even many of those Jim sings for put aside their rags, cut their hair and join the smart crowds. More cars, more luxury flats, more yachtsmen. No one who does not know the place could be blamed for finding it dead and rotten. Yet we want to come back.

•

A family secret was revealed to me a few days ago. Grandad Hooker was illegitimate, as I knew, but his father, it seems, was a Welshman called Evans. Dad was evasive on the subject but why the whole thing should be considered such a dark mystery I can't imagine, unless the secretiveness has been handed down from Victorian times. I wonder what difference it will make, now I can think of the Welshman Evans and the Irish woman O'Brien as ancestors.

•

Sue was woken at 3 am by the first weak contractions. We drank tea, slept and lay awake until 8. After breakfast, set out for Rustington in a heavy atmosphere, Downs hidden in whitish mist. I watched as the head was crowned, at first a small dome of wet inhuman hair, then, quite suddenly, the whole head and the body coming in a rush and lying still like a drowned animal. Then the tiny purplish hands moved and the boy cried softly, undemonstratively, as if a little surprised. Joseph Llewelyn was born just before 1.30pm after a quick labour. I've never felt calmer or more at peace in my whole life.

I kept thinking of this birth as an initiation. I did not share the pain or become part of it, but remained detached throughout while giving my full support. Once or twice I saw myself as a monster, cold-blooded, detached, looking on with a clinical eye.

Birth

I held your mother, child.
She was beyond me.

The shout forced from deep inside
Came shrill: shout
Of a body hurt and labouring
To an end: of a self lost,
Willing unwilled, giving
Delivered.

         I was not afraid
Though a storm's blue light
Flickered on steel, made the room
Tropical, dangerous.
One of the masked attendants.
I held her, beyond myself.

Hair more like seaweed on a stone
Stuck to the crown; then
A creased and slippery form
Came in a gush of blood,
More naked
Than a mussel eased from its shell,
Stranger, more ancient,
Than a creature long-drowned.

Breath came with a cry,
Earthly unearthly cry.
The knot was cut, and tied.

Outside, I watched rain drip
From railings of a balcony,
Form pools on the roof below.

Still on my wrist I feel
The reddish fluid
Where the waters breaking fell.

August
A month away and the garden disappears. Grasses, nettles, thistles, all
kinds of weeds surround the house with dense undergrowth, almost
as it was when we first moved in. Long, snake-headed foxgloves rear
out of hedgerows, and the almost total silence at night, which the faint
trickle of the stream emphasises, is at first rather oppressive. Half-
awake, I heard Sue say, 'Is that Joe crying or a sheep?'

•

This morning, I gave little old Louisa from Cefin Coch a lift into
town. (She always claims to have missed the bus which everyone
knows she hasn't tried to catch.) She launched into a long, incoher-
ent story about some Joe I'd never heard of, perhaps thinking ours
was named after him. When I told her Glyn had wanted to rent the
fields of Pencwmbeidog she said, 'He wants the whole world'.

Everyone around here is thrilled by our news, which has travelled
wide and fast. Heart-felt congratulations on all sides. Jenny Morgan,
who keeps the dog for us, gave me 50p 'for the baby'.

Writing almost every day since we came back. Sometimes one or two
blank days, when I feel wretched, then two poems in a day. What I
realize more and more is how little the will can effect. One or two
nights after we had returned my head suddenly filled with word and
rhythm, and the next morning, in little more than two hours before
lunch, I wrote two poems which needed little working over. Then
nothing, accompanied by mounting frustration, mind shallow and

stale, until I began another sequence – 'Southampton Images' – wrote two more poems without much strain; then again nothing. Afterwards ten to twelve Giant poems, some false starts and failures, in not much more than a fortnight.

All the time the weather, with one or two breaks, has been beautiful. Joe has slept in the shade of the sycamore while Sue and I have gardened in the heat, sweat from scything, back bare to the sun, washing away my tensions and frustrations. Almost overnight the yellowish rowan berries became vivid orange-red. The moon moved towards full in clear skies, and on several nights the whole outline of the mynydd was visible in milky light. A few nights ago the wind got up, rising from deep oppressive stillness, and blew great gusts of moonlight through the flapping curtains.

Several neighbours have come in with gifts for Joe. I understand now what Louisa was talking about. The man who built Brynbeidog was called Joe – many local people are delighted that there is now another in the place.

•

Evening with John Ormond and Gwyn and Daisy Williams at The Ship, Pennant, a single room family pub adjoining a farm and farmyard. John's book of poems has been accepted immediately, with enthusiasm, by OUP. I've never seen him so excited, although he is always so warm and excitable, it was a matter of degree ... Aye, but this was a lovely noisy boozy evening. We left Joe outside in the car and kept an eye on him, but John couldn't resist bringing him in in the end, and everyone was delighted – there were other children in the small bar and the two elderly ladies and their ancient mother who run the place were overjoyed. One of them put a coin in his little fist and he clung onto it for a long time, thus fulfilling an old Cardiganshire custom. A lot of the talk was in Welsh but its spirit included us.

September
Hot afternoon with Gillian and the children at Blaen Cwrt in the shade of a horse-chestnut tree full of cats. Little Max (Macsen Wledig), the sausage dog blind in one eye, saw off Brutus and the

young cats Twm and Caio and their mother Shanny went hump-
backed and spitting at the sight of him. It is dark inside the cottage,
with a wood fire burning and a view of daylight through blue smoke
up the chimney. We walked in the fields nearby, carrying Joe, in warm
mellow sunlight, and looked down on acres of moorland broken up
by cultivated patches, a few yellow fields and a red harvester; in the
foreground, a small round pond. Peter drives up from Cardiff every
evening and Gillian and the children take a torch and go up to a high
bank to watch for him. His car lights appear on a ridge several miles
away and they signal to each other. Seven minutes later he appears
on the other side of the valley and is soon at the cottage. We had a
stew and drank two large bottles of wine after he arrived, then drove
back towards midnight.

The old moon was dark red, only just visible against the sky, then
orange, and finally yellow as we reached home.

•

During one talk at the J.C. Powys Centenary Conference at Churchill
College, Cambridge, a man came in late and sat down next to me at
the back. I noticed that his hair was like curls of black moss close to
his head, and he had the Powys nose and was large and strongly built.
This was Peter Grey, one of the nephews. Later he told me how,
when clearing out his mother's papers after her death, he'd come
across sermons by his grandfather, C.F. Powys. One of these took as
its theme the wheat and tares. It said very little about the tares.

I also met Gerard Casey and his wife Mary, a niece of Powys, who
live at Mappowder. Gerard, too, is a large man, a slow-spoken South
Walian. I gave him a copy of my pamphlet of poems, and he later told
me how moved he was by my poem dedicated to Powys, 'Song of the
Ashes'. Gerard had scattered his old friend's ashes at Abbotsbury.

These big, slow-spoken, deep-voiced Powys men – for Gerard
Casey seemed so much like a Powys – conveyed the spirit of the man
more than did anything else about the weekend.

Once or twice, I had the feeling that JCP himself had engineered
the conference and everything that happened at it. He's so much the
god of his fiction, and, if one considers *Autobiography*, the god of his
own life too, that I sometimes think of him as a supreme actor, and
even as a 'charlatan' of almost supernatural cunning. I imagine him

living, and presenting himself, in such a way that just these images, these words and no others, should be used about him after his death. It is as if he has created one image for the scholar, another for the eccentric, another for the working man, but each *deliberately*, thus shaping his reputation as well as his life. At moments I had a fleeting glimpse of all of us as puppets manipulated by JCP.

Perhaps the Giant is finished now and I can begin to enter into the present of our life here. Perhaps I too can begin to live my life.

•

The day before yesterday I found a small hedgehog on the field between the ruins of Glan-llyn and Glan-Eiddwen, by the lake, and watched it contracting and expanding as it breathed. Then, yesterday evening, Brutus's barking drew our attention to a large hedgehog on the grass under the kitchen window. Perhaps they are preparing to hibernate, now that it is autumn.

•

Climbing the wooden fence and pressing my hands into soft mosses on a sycamore, I cross the Beidog from stone to stone. Below me the stream vanishes into the darkness of the barrel bridge. Sun on the back of my neck, on my back and legs, warmth and slow movement through the fields. Tits tinkle, invisible in thick foliage. A silk thread hanging in the air between bushes gleams along a few inches, then disappears in a slight movement of the eye.

As Powys often says, sanity depends on feeling the earth under one's feet and boundless space surrounding one. Last night, seeing stars in a clear sky, I realized again that this place has returned me to that sense of a vast world outside my mind, and to the experience of a multiverse of other lives, especially in all the minute particulars and differences in nature. I felt this yesterday, beside a warm hedgerow with bees in the sheep's-bit and brambles – how even a few square feet of flowers & insects & leaves were so much richer and more various than my mental impression of them.

•

Season of brilliant white sunlight & spider-webs, the mynydd composed of fine blue mist. Nothing is more beautiful than the
unsymmetrical patterns of the webs; looking through them, they are one
of those margins, in Celtic myth, between nature and the supernatural.

•

At times my instincts seem to say, If only each day were a few fine
clear-cut images – a heron rising from the Beidog, the sun going
down orange over Stoney Cross, the moon, the smell of chilly earth!

October
Walking through deep lanes, in and out of shadow, through odours
of decay, seeing the last few pale, washed-out flowers – campion,
Herb Robert, harebells – all were like snatches of another people's
reality. This is Wales, not just a piece of the earth.

I have lately been more than usually conscious of limitations. It is
a physical sensation: water running out from under my thoughts,
jarring drag of the shingle. The afterglow of a finished work gives way
to coldness & emptiness, before the next can be begun.

•

I have looked for the permanent at the expense of living moments.
Yesterday, as the family sat round the fire, each filling the room with
his or her unique personality, with the presence in and beyond that
of what being together creates, I felt how we fill this place with our
reality and then, what becomes of it when it goes and others fill the
place with theirs? For this is what happens all the time: our feelings
in a derelict building are mostly self-indulgent, since we are always,
wherever we are, walking through spaces others have left, as if
through impressions of their bodies on the air.

At times I want so much to depict life as I see it, in praise of the
people I love. In praise even of their faults. But I am overwhelmed by
detail, by gesture and expression, by the essential livingness of
people, and so lose all. I lack the gift of caricature, the greater gift for
creating an extended image of the living. It is all memory or imita-
tion. I will not allow life to dissolve into the elements from which
'fiction' is made.

Without self-consciousness, no journal. Only images, notes, silence. One has to pass through self-consciousness – and if no one is ever complete, a writer cannot be. Yet he may aspire to completeness and seek what would destroy him – as a writer. Who wants to be complete? I want all the creative imperfection of living.

•

Drifts of falling leaves on the wind. When the hedges are still, a single leaf will flutter down, then another. I think of them letting go, one by one.

One mood above all stands out in connection with my first response to Edward Thomas, when I was 18 or 19: brown fields seen through bare hedges, rooks cawing, stick-like winter branches and a quiet, sad expectancy under grey skies. It's only part of Edward Thomas; it may be more of me – when I cycled out through deserted countryside on Wednesday afternoons, and saw fieldfares and turnips among frozen clods. I was then writing nature sketches, melancholy mood-pieces – the feeling was real to me, though I first found it expressed in some of Jefferies's essays. But when I reread Edward Thomas's poems I realised even more strongly the limitations of this sensibility. The quarrel is with myself not him. In this respect, the Giant too is only a beginning: I have to break out altogether from certain moods implanted in me by the English countryside and its writers.

•

Sue working under the sycamores with a dead leaf in her hair and another in the hood of her duffle coat. Joe wrapped up like a little polar explorer. Brynbeidog against the mountain, stark simplicity of white walls and slate roof against hard, humped-up rock thinly covered in darkening green.

Yellow and brown leaves clog the Beidog. The marshy fields are again dark gold.

•

To the HTV studios in Cardiff, where Ned was guest editor of a programme in which he had invited me to participate with Tony

Harrison, Shiva Naipaul and himself.

From 11.30 until lunch we sat round drinking whisky and discussing our topic: the writer's search for identity in relation to place. This was the best of the day and also the best of the discussion.

After lunch and a few glasses of wine I felt like going to sleep for the rest of the day. Then the recording was postponed until 3.30 and the others went on drinking while we talked and generally made ourselves at home, in a warm, fuggy atmosphere. In fact I contributed little now but concentrated on staying awake and looking interested, glancing through the windows at the park and autumn sunlight outside and imagining the fresh air.

The discussion when eventually recorded was in two parts, interrupted by a commercial break, but we lost the first recording of the second part when a microphone broke down, and had to do it again. In fact, we lost the best of the recorded discussion.

Afterwards, more whisky. Then Ned and I called at the BBC to see Lorraine Davies, and spent a pleasant hour talking with her about writing for radio. I drove Ned home, and in narrow lanes near Tregaron we caught two hares in the headlights, mesmerizing them, and a rabbit scuttled away.

When I got back just before the programme was due to begin, a high, brilliantly cold moon was shining in a clear sky. I felt too embarrassed to watch the programme but succumbed towards the end. It was fairly convincing as such things go. But what an exhausting and artificial way to spend a day, and all for a few fleeting images and perhaps a touch of 'culture' between the commercials. Today, though, it's as if the moon has burned all greyness out of the sky and left it shining and the air sharp and clean.

I respect Ned's belief in the necessity of communicating, and many things that were said during the day or during our drive home were valuable to me and generally important. But in the atmosphere of a television studio, there is so much to which one has to become oblivious before real communication is possible.

November
End of the Faber romance. Giant rejected.

•

White frost. Blue sky, almost cloudless. Dazzling white sun balanced against a chalky moon, a transparent wafer. A few curled up black-thorn leaves, edges iced with frost. Fieldfares in frosty grass. Ponies sunning themselves with eyes closed, thawed coats steaming.

•

Sunday night: reading at the Casson Theatre, Cardiff, with John Ormond and Dannie Abse, whom I liked very much.

Felt very tense out front on a bare wooden stage, but was told it didn't show. We stayed with Peter & Gillian. Belinda Humfrey, too, was staying with them, having come down the previous day for a reading of Powys. Much praise afterwards, which I discounted with gloomy humour, playing on my defeatism. All right at the time, but later I felt ashamed. Also rather desperate & tense, due partly to the knowledge that we had to rush back to Aberystwyth in the morning for a lecture at 11 & a dental appointment at 12. Morbid dread of local anaesthetic. Slings & arrows!

December
It isn't that I'm incapable of ever losing and finding myself, but that in doing so I see the contrast between my normal preoccupations and the life that is possible. Jim lives from week to week, and in every moment. I live in the past, nostalgically; anxiously, in the future. Jim broke down completely, and was reborn. I have lived in a state of partial breakdown, partial renewal.

•

Idris Morgan came in a few nights ago to look at Sue's youngest foal, which is sickly.

He sat in a corner of the sofa with a beer, his greasy brown suede hat tilted rakishly over one eye. Told us that most of his uncles had fought in the Great War, serving with the mules that were used to pull guns & munitions. Often, at night, they would be illuminated by a flare, but at some distance from the lines so that if all stood perfectly still they would be taken for a group of trees.

The mules seemed to know this and were usually motionless. But if one as much as twitched an ear the men ran for the trenches, knowing they would be under fire. The mules also knew where the trenches were, and made a dash for them dragging the heavy equipment and often crushing the men as they fell into the trenches with the guns behind them.

Idris is considering alternative ways of making a living, now the Common Market looks like having a severe effect on farming in the area. He is thinking of caravan sites & mountain centres. Talking about his uncles in the Great War recalled his own memories of the Second World War, and especially of the coachloads of evacuee children arriving without lights in the darkness after crawling nose to tail along then unmade-up roads. The kids entered households where hardly any English was spoken, as was largely the case in this part of Wales until the Forties. He spoke feelingly about the children waiting at stations with just a label describing their particulars pinned on them.

Then we fell to talking about 'the next war'.

When Idris talks, I often glimpse this area as it was, when the men carted stones from the mountain to fill in potholes in the roads and no horse was kept that didn't work for its living. And this was only 25-30 years ago, little English spoken and the men with their memories of the War working on the land.

Everything he says reveals love and admiration for 'the old men', the tough ones. 'Hear them talking together,' he said, 'after they've had a few of these' (tapping his beer glass); 'it's better than anything you see on that' (pointing at our television set). Yet he is friendly & hospitable to us, though we represent one of the elements of change.

•

Depression & fatigue. Days tainted with self-pity.

Got out into sun & wind, sawing logs, digging manure into the garden. Clear blue sky & brilliant white sun, half-moon visible from early afternoon. I watch the loose dark cords of the stream winding & unwinding, and try to hear words in the sound: *therooull, thew, thew, therooull*. A great tit vivid with black & white head & fresh moss-green back swings on a bag of nuts.

Mrs Davies came in last night and brought Elizabeth. Glyn came to fetch them later. She told us about all the things lost when their farmhouse burnt down and how the loss of her books, many of them family books, was worst. She spoke feelingly, but not embarrassingly or with embarrassment. Shortly before Joe was born her daughter-in-law had a stillborn, hydrocephalic child and the nurses in the hospital gave it to her for burial, unwashed, tied up in a package. She observed that there are kinder ways of doing things.

Jeff Wainwright has now left Aberystwyth to take up his post at Manchester Polytechnic. I shall miss him. Now Ken Smith too has got the job he wanted, at Bradford, and will leave in April.

Whatever happens, this must be my last year of teaching here.

Late afternoon: feeding the ponies in the cowshed at Pencwmbeidog, as the setting sun casts the shape of the doorway in a red oblong on the wall.

•

To Cardiff, where I gave the lunchtime lecture on David Jones in the Exhibition room at the National Museum. Gillian was there to meet us as we went in through the revolving glass doors. Very tense beforehand, and tired but happy and relieved afterwards. This tiredness has developed during a strenuous term, and has been augmented by disappointment & failing confidence. Even Gillian set-to, when we went back to Cyncoed for a cup of tea, to convince me that I need to make contacts. I now feel one reason for her hesitation to send her poems to London may be her unwillingness to publish before me; but she has a good chance of being accepted, and I must encourage her to try. Her poems are beautiful, and it has been a privilege for me to help her by offering positive criticism.

•

Looked after Joe all day, feeding & changing him. Managed to do some reviewing in the intervals. He's such a cheerful, good, lovely little boy. One needs no gift except natural love to entertain little children. Their laughter redeems all manner of ordinariness, even my banal humour.

Woke just before dawn when an owl shrieked repeatedly in a sycamore by the stream. Then the moon went down yellow. At night again the moon, now nearly full, was burning, the luminous pale blue sky had a wash of white cloud. I walked a little way up the road, like moving in a dream.

When I look at the moon I think without fully realizing it that a few days ago men were walking there. I think too, without full consciousness of the brutal facts, of Vietnam and Northern Ireland. I am ashamed now of my deadened response to the latter. It is one response among artists, even in Belfast, to fall back on the regenerative powers of nature, to try, in a destructive time, to speak for the continuance of life; another is to render the harrowing detail in order to make people aware. But what, now, do we most need to be aware of?

Even as I write, the patently insane & murderous Nixon has B52s, each carrying 30 tons of bombs, blasting Hanoi and Haiphong.

•

Up early to feed Joe.

Dawn with an old moon. Red-barred sky over the mountain. Ever the new life.

1973

January

Members of the Welsh Language Society have occupied Pencwmbeidog in protest against the buying up of such places as holiday homes by 'wealthy Englishmen' who receive renovation grants. When I went to feed the ponies I saw the front of the house brightly covered with protest messages and posters bearing the Society's symbol, and glimpsed a face at an upstairs window. The place was suddenly quite colourful and we could hear cars coming and going, and talk and laughter on and off all day. Dilwyn was the first to tell us, solemnly and rather angrily, calling the occupiers 'nin-compoops'. Then the Welsh postman held me in the drive for ten minutes with a bitter tirade because I wouldn't condemn the action. I think he was raising his voice so that the protesters could hear him. I told him I didn't intend to be caught in the crossfire.

•

This morning, watching over a bonfire of cardboard boxes, I won-dered whether it would make the slightest difference if it were my poems that were burning.

Does it make any difference at all to speak to the living?

The ashes of the boxes and the ashes of the poems would be much the same, and if no one was to know that I have existed and written poems it would make no difference.

No doubt this is also an argument for fighting for one's hand, since what matters so little to strangers, matters to oneself.

February

Posted the typescript of my Powys study to Meic yesterday. Very tired today so worked outdoors all afternoon, snuffing up the smell of manure that I dug into the earth and seeking to relax my mind. Except for a few scattered days of frost & sunlight, this has been a horribly oppressive winter, overcast & too warm. I keep wondering whether pollution & bomb tests have done something terrible to the atmosphere so that the seasons have been altered. Thoughts of famine & drought & my recurrent half-humorous speculation as to whether it wouldn't be wise to buy up thousands of tins of food and bury them in the garden!

•

Fierce squalls of hailstones, vast movements of cloud, darkness & spasmodic light, then the moon in its first quarter ...

Two or three things have coincided to make me more conscious of a fundamental impulse. First, my study of Powys brought out his concern with the non-human constituents of human nature as well as his elementalism; then two reviews of *The Elements* dwelt on the implications of its title. I have also been lecturing on Lawrence's cosmic awareness and his habit of thinking and feeling in terms of archaic identifications, of man and woman with sun and moon.

Curiously, though, what has long been a personal obsession has become conscious only through these coincidences. True, I have sometimes written, rather portentously, of cosmic awareness, but I have also been torn between criticism and acceptance of my preoccupation with the non-human.

Now I suddenly see it as a reaction to the tyranny of superficial human consciousness – the air loud with distractions; the crush of frictional contacts in place of a few deep relationships. Even sex, one of the last places of darkness, is subjected to the spotlight.

I no longer believe our violence and terror come from the darkness, from unconsciousness. I believe them to be products of a social reality, a climate of thought and feeling, which divorces us from the cosmos.

What we do and what we are accords with what we are part of. I think persistently of 'a world scraped from the top of the brain', which is how I see the terrors of this century and the stultifying features of a civilization – as the outcome of man being cut off from the deep resources of his nature, from his roots in the non-human and creaturely universe.

•

At least once a week I give Mrs Morgan a lift into town and sometimes bring her back again in the evening. The trouble is, she rather expects it, gives me 10p for each journey and exerts a degree of emotional blackmail if I'm not going in at a convenient time. We also feel that the Morgans don't like us, because we're English but make use of us all the same. Yesterday I carted in their old broken-down television set, and brought it back with Mrs Morgan from the shop in the evening. I double-parked for a few minutes in town, and in opening the car door she just touched the side of another car. At once a smart, rather attractive lady leapt out of the other car and with a steely, piercing 'Excuse me!' went down on her knees to see if we'd made a scratch. I replied with some warmth that the door had hardly touched. 'That's not the point,' she said, with another high-pitched metallic thrust and got back in the car, sitting bolt upright in bitter antagonism. All the way home this absurd episode drilled in my mind. Another word might have sparked off an explosion, and I might have stood in the road, white and shaking, denouncing the whole system of petty ownerships and mutual hostilities.

March
First lamb in the field yesterday. A thrush sang on and off all day in the rain. But even now the snowdrops are not quite out, though those in the village, on lower ground, have been for a week or so.

•

Curlews faint & spasmodic through rain on the 5th.

•

Three jackdaws fighting for possession of our vacant chimney, or, more likely, two males fighting for a female *and* the chimney. I heard a loud scuffling noise and looked up to see them all apparently trying to force their way into the chimney-pot. Then one fell with a painful thud on the kitchen roof, and flew off leaving the others in occupation.

Struggled most of the day with the 'Grandfather' poem – poor stuff as yet, but with what seems like a promising beginning made over the weekend.

•

Two cloudless days with frost in the early morning. The weather led

Mrs Morgan to talk about God. She has gathered from watching television that nowadays there are people who hold He does not exist.
But they are wrong. She then told me a story about her aunt's
funeral. The weather had been terrible until the day of the burial,
which was fine and calm. The preacher said she must indeed have
been 'a child of God to quiet all the storm'.

Each week she set aside from her pension £1 for charity.

•

Yesterday afternoon, after a morning rigid with tension, I came home
to find Sue planting seeds in dry earth under a warm cloudless sky (it
had been chilly in Aberystwyth, with an occasional ghostly sun visible
through sea mist). I lay down by the stream, watching bubbles rapidly
float out from the shadow of the stone slab that bridges it, and the
queer, darting dance of water insects against the current ... Sometimes
there is an ecstasy, sometimes a terror, that might destroy one. It is the
same with love. Most of the time we are lucky to live in an atmosphere
of natural warmth and humorous affection, yet there are moments
when it seems something overpowering might break through ...
Perhaps what I am trying to intimate is no more than the wholeness
of life lived in the present, how we eke it out or dwell upon aspects,
and can seek images of its totality only in retrospect, but never be
aware, now, of the force we are part of. In love, in youth, in health, life
is a great force by which we are lived, but with only fleeting awareness
– the self is divorced from it, the mind is set apart. I remember
Thoreau's saying that he had never met a man who was fully alive,
and wouldn't be able to bear looking in his face if he did. With partial
awareness, it seems as if to be wholly alive would destroy with an
ecstasy that is the same as terror. But it would be a state in which such
partial awareness would cease, and it would be beyond words.

On these still nights when I walk out into the garden and see the
many stars with their changing colours and the sycamores' shapes
distinct against the sky, and now when the earth, after the heat of the
day, releases its smells and there is a cold smell of water from the
streams, it is the same feeling of being at the edge of complete ecstasy
that comes during the day. But at night it is more concentrated,
perhaps simpler, because there is a simpler music, only running
water without birdsong, and less for the eye to see, no light on water

or distracting movement from thing to thing. Perhaps this helps to account for the moon's preeminence as an object of worship, for, unlike the sun, it has little competition from the things it illuminates, which are subsumed by its nature. It is the supreme focus for a concentrated worship of life and death, a symbol of the force that is in and outside us, the unobtainable ecstasy which we are nevertheless part of.

·

My thirty-second birthday.

Birthday

When I wake, you are standing
Beside me. In the icy Victorian vase
Decorated with glass-cut fern,
You bring catkins, silver-grey

Pussy willow, and snowdrops.
A fine yellow powders your hand.
It is late March, the cold earth
Is broken and out of darkness

You bear a gift. I marvel, love.
To have been born for this.

Hot sun in a cloudless sky. A whistling breeze stirring the grasses, somehow malevolent with a muted violence.
    Depression has been building up during the last few weeks.
    I had an appointment with the dentist this morning, forced myself

as far as the waiting room but could not endure the thought of being captive, as if I would simply break down and cry at the first question. Pleaded a migraine and was excused.

Sue is depressed too, but has gone to work.

Acute tension has contributed to this: for the last fortnight at least, and in a lesser degree before that, I have conducted tutorials with a frozen mask, sitting rigid and scarcely being able to look anyone in the eye for more than a few seconds, with my head strained round staring out the window. The disappointments are the root of it, dragging me back to the same stale obsessions from things in which I have tried to lose myself.

Even in the morning, walking in the fields, I have had to remind myself to look at things, constantly to remind myself.

The academic 'career' has died in me: I have lost all will and desire to pursue it, and all conviction and confidence in my teaching. Yet a living has to be made.

I am now considering the alternatives, and this brings some relief. But nothing relieves the total indifferent silence surrounding my poems. Even a rejection – and one is now due – would be better than this. But the deepest problem is still that I should again internalise the rejections, and thus lose all confidence in the work I have already done and also the capacity to continue.

It is all right, though. I shall survive this, and I will continue.

April
Last week a letter from John Haynes, with some wise comments on vanity and becoming consumed with resentment, made me see sense. It was the word *vanity*, I think: how long since I've applied that to myself! Sue's depression, my depression – seepage of black rainwater from the same rotten stump. Then term ended, and that had something to do with the relief; but it is mainly because I can begin to be free, with a future to make.

•

Early April: a light grey doorway opens out of darker grey hanging heavily over the ridge. There's a mystical quality in April rain-light, in the fine mist of light clinging to the lower slopes. And then the smells released by a warm shower.

Yesterday a strong, gusty wind; a short flurry of snow, then fine columns of hailstones slanting across the open fields and slopes, hailstones hopping like miniature white frogs as they bounced off the garden. This morning I found small clutches of hailstones in hollows in the ground. Now the bog is like a huge spunge covered with tufts of burnt grass, reeds sticking up like porcupine quills. Ravens were pursuing each other as I walked across it.

Awe and tenderness: these are the great qualities we are afraid to own. And today, in England, a sense of wonder. But for me there is also the toil of not looking back in the wrong way.

•

As Maskull says, in *A Voyage to Arcturus*: 'We are each of us living in a false, private world of our own, a world of dreams and appetites and distorted perceptions'. The great teachers have told us the same.

What I have begun to see is that I do not see clearly. Destructive feeling can be an energy in the poem only when it is used, not when it is brooded on. When its root is in self-pity or personal disappointment, it must be transformed into something else. I have already done this to some extent in the Giant, and must now seek another ground that will make it possible in another way.

•

Two days of full spring when it is almost possible to see things growing. In the sun, the hot faces of dandelions are almost too bright to look at, and I keep wanting to say the grasses are bluish-green, but it is the glow of life in them. How they prick up and assert themselves in hedgerows spiky with life! Tiny spiders scuttle across dry earth; at night the smell of earth mingles with the damp smell of water.

I feel that I know nothing and have never known anything.

Towards evening, the first cuckoo. At first distant so that I could scarcely hear it, then closer and closer the unmistakable echoing call.

•

Is the sadness or deep melancholy associated with feeling for the English countryside – Edward Thomas's 'sad passion' – something of the last two centuries alone? And is it perhaps a longing to lapse back into the apparent security of a gentle matrix?

It is present in Keats; it is an impulse in Wordsworth, which he controlled with his robust nature; it is in Jefferies and in J.C. Powys. Lawrence felt it, as something to be resisted. Just as, in *Sons and Lovers*, Paul and Miriam's love begins as a mutual response to 'something in nature', so I was first compelled to write by a similar feeling. As an energy, in Hardy, the passion is valuable, but as an end in itself, debilitating. It can sap life-energy; it is outside culture and all human relationships; it can be the death-instinct in one of its guises, the instinct which, held in balance with life-instincts, is a creative power.

May
One evening early in the week the moon rising on Mynydd Bach balanced the setting sun at the other horizon. On clear evenings the sycamore in leaf is a tree of light.

All I can see now is the oppressive atmosphere through which I look, the frosted air beyond which all is distorted and blurred.

June
A goldfinch, face scarlet, as if dipped in blood. After weeks of rain, mist & low skies grass is too green, patches of sky too blue: I have tired 'the eyes of the mind'.

•

After writing yesterday, I hoed among the blackcurrants, blistering my hands, smelling the bushes' sharp smell. Then clipped the hedge in a fury of dutiful emotion, destructive & refreshing, so that my hands shook, and still have a slight tremor this morning. In the evening all my awareness was in my hands, blistered, trembling, stinging with nettle-burn.

This morning, as I walked down the muddy path at Pencwmbeidog to feed the ponies, I thought: the future will judge us for our obsession with sex, for the superficiality with which we divorce it from the whole of human experience and concentrate upon it, analytically, destructively, making ourselves wretched because of our stupidity, because we have arrested the life-flow, broken it up into a chain of shallow muddy pools.

•

Half-strangled hiccuping note of the June cuckoo, piercing shrieks of hawking swifts, then long bubbling calls of curlews flying with rapid wing beats over the house. A heavy smell of hawthorn replaces the smell of gorse in the lanes. Clots of flowers on rowans, orchids in the marsh & buttercups everywhere. Once more under the sycamores, deep, dark-green caverns.

Again I look up from marking exam scripts, wincing & almost delirious from sinusitis & from concentration, to find June almost half-way through and passing more quickly than any other month, because it is the most perfect. I am always promising myself to prepare for life, but this is how it is, looking up, seeing things beautiful in their passing, because they pass.

•

Two snails, one on a stone in the middle of the Beidog: broad reddish-brown bands separated by thin dark-brown bands; the other with a yellow bobble at the apex, broad yellowish-green and narrow brown bands. 'Whorl', like the shape: like 'clump' and 'clot', a word shaped to its meaning.

•

Lazing in the garden, drinking the cider Jim and Lin had brought from Dorset, we talked a great deal about the south, our feelings much the same. The difficulty of distinguishing our sense of identity from what the area has become, from images of it only in terms of that – reactionary, privileged, effete. Among ourselves identity is no problem; problems arise only from imposed stereotypes.

•

This is the first summer for at least two years with no schedule of work. A time of possibilities. After all these dead months I feel life stirring in me again.

This is sometimes the best part of writing, sometimes the most frustrating: to feel the ability and the need for expression but without

knowing what form it will take. Where the Giant filled me with a
sense of achievement, there is now an emptiness; it is in the past,
growing smaller, like a stone circle seen from a distance, and the
space between is empty ground.

July
Since last winter this has been one of the driest years for a long time.
The rivers here are lower than local people have seen them in years;
there is a brown sediment, like coffee grounds, covering still-sub-
merged stones and the Beidog is a trickle of water & rocks. Our water
supply is very low, the cold water runs out when the bath is hot and
we supplement it with buckets of water from the stream.

Today we drove to Swansea through one of the richest cultivated landscapes in Wales. Sue & Joe took the train from Swansea and went to
stay near Lechlade for the weekend, I went on to the Powys regional
meeting at Neuadd Martin hall of residence, where I lectured on John
Cowper Powys. Arriving early, I drove towards the Mumbles,
Swansea Bay a blur through rain. Everywhere we went this weekend,
on any available space even in the remotest rural area, was the fat sleek
smiling face of Guru Maharajji.
   Talked to Gerard Casey about John Cowper Powys and David
Jones. Gerard is one of the deepest men I have ever met, a slow delib-
erate speaker, a spare, powerful man; his few words about Theodore
Powys's last years were more illuminating than anything else said at
the conference.
   After the meeting I feel strong in *my* way – the way these people
would appreciate and understand – and only scornful towards unimaginative petty position-men. How rarely in literary history have the men
of influence & power coincided with the true imaginative writers of the
age, but how strange it is that this lesson, which anyone with the least
knowledge of literary history should know by heart, is always ignored.
Even modernists who know the story of Eliot & Pound, and the story of
Lawrence, are unconscious of being obstacles to the wider recognition
of other writers of genius. Now that a noisier fuss is being made about
David Jones, because of Larkin's crass omission of his work from the
Oxford Book of Modern Verse, we may expect a few more academics to
become aware of *his* existence. Why is English academic and literary
culture so bloody philistine, so stubbornly dismissive? Even Lawrence

had to belittle most of the writers who had influenced him. I loathe the stupid lack of emotional and intellectual generosity (and honesty).

All weekend I felt an impulse to apologize for myself which, at its most acute, is like a desire to say sorry to anybody or everybody for my existence – as if, at death, I might apologize to God for having dared to exist. Then, immediately afterwards, I am conscious of overwhelming someone with force of personality, as when I face an audience diffidently and then this authoritative voice begins to cast a spell.

•

Raymond Williams's *The Country and the City*: *this* is the book I needed, which positively affects my way of seeing and is written out of an experience and concerns which I share to some extent, at the same time as I accept it as a check on some of my speculations. Above all, Williams's way of seeing and of feeling strikes deep, and even in a first reading, I am aware of adjustments I shall have to make in the light of his ideas about true and false history, and about structures of feeling that contract or expand human sympathies.

There is a question Williams doesn't ask, which I feel ought to be considered. In discussing Edward Thomas, for instance, he writes incisively about the limitations of Thomas's structure of feeling, of the true history and the false myth that formed his attitudes. Yet supposing Thomas had had Williams's understanding of social history, which would have changed his structure of feeling, wouldn't that have made him, not just a different poet, but perhaps no poet at all? Williams the critic is able to unravel the contradictions inherent in *his* experience, and in doing so becomes a powerful cultural historian and critic of literary ideas. But perhaps it is his rationality that divests his writing of poetry. He is a critic critics need, one we all need to show us what our prejudices, limitations, and ignorance blind us to.

Isn't a lucid critical and historical perspective more important now than poetry written from a knot of contradictory feelings? Certainly I would rather have one Raymond Williams than any number of poets who falsely imagine Old England, or write in a reactionary spirit of the contrast between country and city, or the old and the new.

August

Wild night after days of intermittent rain & gales. Fell into a shallow
sleep against the rough noise of wind & rain on the windows; woke
in the dark to a continuous loud roaring. At 4.30 we could see the
nant had flooded the drive and was streaming across the garden,
through the French beans & kidney beans, to rejoin its course lower
down. The Beidog was roaring over the waterfall. When we went out
later we could see that the stone bridge had been knocked over, and
there was a large brown lake in the drive. I waded through it and
walked down the road. Sediment & stones on the road over the
bridge, streams flowing everywhere exposing clay & mud. The ponies
were kneeling together in the lee of a hedge; they acknowledged my
presence lethargically, wet & disconsolate. A white moon-faced
bullock followed me with bewildered eyes. Now the sky was broken
with watery blue patches between immense drifts of grey & white
clouds. The grass is flat, slicked down all in one direction, where
water streamed over it, a spectral torrent in the night.

•

Every morning I take Joe on my back and walk with Brutus in the
fields. Joe sits absolutely silent craning his neck round to take in
everything there is to see.

Yesterday we walked beside the Beidog in the field opposite the
garden. I saw that the stream had carried away a large portion of its
bank and brought down a great quantity of rocks & sediment across
the path; for the time being, it ran in two channels, one on either side
of the heap of debris. In several places new banks reveal the cutting
edge of the floods that have made them.

Seeing what a small stream can do in a state of flood, it is easy to
visualise the processes of geological change reshaping a land.

At night a faint gleam on floodwater still standing in the drive: the
moon, just over half full, very bright, with a fine scarf of cloud
blowing across its face: which startled me – as if smoke were streaming from it.

Recognising the mind's limitations makes me realise anything
might happen; the inconceivable is always possible. I don't feel desolate at the *possibility* of total annihilation – No, that is not true, I feel
the possibility of not feeling desolate; only those faced with imminent

death have the right to know what they feel about it. If in truth we are all in that situation all the time, knowing one must die is another matter entirely from feeling one is about to die.

Despite thoughts provoked by reading *The Country and the City*, reading Alyse Gregory's journals, *The Cry of a Gull*, supports my belief that it makes sense to speak of those who live in the universe, with an ever-present sense of the conditions of nature. In her comparative isolation before and after Llewelyn Powys's death, Alyse Gregory *touched* life as many people living in society do not.

If we can't experience a nature unmediated by our social position and the history that has shaped it, there is an unmediated universe; in that sense, there is still a real experience of life and death in nature. In the case of a true elementalist like Alyse Gregory this increases her sense of human responsibility, and of social injustice. Society is then criticised not in comparison with Old England or a Golden Age, but according to its harmony or disharmony with the conditions of life on this planet, and in terms of a philosophy of man's fundamental need for physical, spiritual, and creative fulfilment.

Alan Clodd of Enitharmon Press has accepted the *Giant*.

•

The rare satisfaction of unblocking a stream. Two days ago the drive was still under water. I groped with a fork & a pickaxe in the entrance to the tunnel under the drive. It was stopped fast. Then a big waterlogged sod of grass & reeds came out in my hands, there was a gurgle and swirl of water passing through. Then another sod came loose and I dragged out a long wire mesh heavy with weeds, the water poured through and in minutes the level had fallen in the drive and soon the water had vanished.

Sometimes the impulse to write seems as if it has always derived simply from staring at moving or still water and seeing it as a form of life, totally strange and unexplained.

September
To Harlech with Gillian for an Academi Gymreig conference. We arrived late, missing the talk by Richard Hughes, and walked on the sands. When I sat opposite Mr Hughes at dinner I couldn't think of anything to say to him. I realised only later that he, too, was shy, and

perhaps lonely, and that contact with people interested in writing was important to him.

At first, the contrast between the setting – mountains across the sea, castle rising above us – and the quality of the poetry readings & discussions increased my sourness & disenchantment – I hadn't gone with any real sense of purpose – until I felt completely alienated. Nothing interested me, I had nothing to contribute, and was out of place. Then, talking to individuals – Gill, Cary Archard, Liz Saxon – the depression broke. Sam Adams arrived late on Sunday and, next morning, gave an excellent talk on Geraint Goodwin, which I chaired, and participated enthusiastically in the ensuing discussion. As soon as I could give, everything was transformed for me.

As a result of all the things we talked about, I realised that in the kind of poetry I write the pressure of what is hidden, of underlying forces & tensions, contributes much to whatever power the work has, and is sometimes present even in poems that have nothing to do, overtly, with incidents giving rise to the pressure. So those we love or have loved, hurt or were hurt by, all give something to the poem which may appear to be about the non-human universe. And the felt realisation disturbs me, so that even the familiar landscape seems to tilt and give a sickening lurch, because I contain feelings capable of transforming it, or changing everything.

It is really naive to believe that release of all repressed feelings & desires leads to wisdom & happiness. If some forms of repression are monstrous, others are necessary for life to be creative or even interesting. For me, the voices of the great poets are vibrant with the pressure of what they withhold: as their forms are tense from conflict with formlessness so the shape of their lives depend also on the struggle with chaos.

•

Description is no good if it only paints the surface of things; it's the nature of the thing itself, the life embodied in its particular form, that we respond to when our senses are most alive.

The damp earth is more vital under the warm sun than it has been all summer. At these times it is like the moist breathing skin of a great creature.

Looking up from watching television, I stared full into the face of a hawk sitting on a fence post a few yards from the door. When I went out a little later, a heron flew up from the field and crossed the Beidog. Seen briefly in the dusk, it looked enormous, with the wing-span of a glider, and created a haunting impression so that, for a moment, even though I knew it was a heron, I was prepared to believe it something supernatural. A yellow half-moon hung in the west.

•

Morning, a time indescribably rich with autumn smells.

How much easier it is now to describe a distraught mind or deranged senses than a full sensuous life.

I have seen nothing more assertive of the life in it than the long curved stem of a dog-rose, flexible as a whiplash and sinuous as a snake, with big red thorns shaped like shark fins.

Once through the 'smoke barrier' my senses are more alive than they have been for years, but I still find it difficult to concentrate when writing. For an inveterate smoker to break the habit produces a change of life – mentally, sensuously, and emotionally – that must be inconceivable to one who has never smoked. For me the habit has repressed a sensuousness, even a sensuality, that I find as disturbing as it is exhilarating. All disturbances of the personality are sexual in origin, either for particular reasons or, broadly, because they derive from an interruption in the flow of attraction that carries an individual forward among the objects and people of his world. It seems that man is himself a river of desire.

•

Stinkhorn fungus growing in shade beside the lane. Slime-green cap with a cluster of flies, green, blue & brown – bone white the next morning. Its thick curved stalk thrusts from the broken 'egg', which is like a burst paper bag or wrinkled scrotum. *Phallus impudicus* indeed!

Travelled into town on the bus sitting behind a slim, fair-haired girl with violets on her cream-coloured blouse and a lovely pink and white complexion. Her child, a little blue-eyed blond girl, sat with her face in the wedge between the seats, staring at me. For a time afterwards everything I saw shone with their reflection and the gentle desire she had unknowingly kindled.

Hot days. Everything seen through a fine blue narcotic haze.
Sometimes I think that to render completely one moment of one day
here would exhaust the efforts of a lifetime, and sometimes that all
my experience is a source for nothing real or lasting.

Night. Moonlight shining on the caravan's curved roof, gleaming
on its skull-shaped dome. When in daylight I look down on it from
hillside fields above Hafod Las, it is minute beside the tiny house;
then I think of myself working there, perhaps totally absorbed ...
Often a similar perspective on the town has been comforting, but if
it were habitual all creative effort might be extinguished.

Religious or cosmic awareness breaks in when we move from a
secure, self-centred state to the frightening and exhilarating experience of being peripheral to other forces, other worlds.

•

I woke nervous, was able to eat little all day and felt rather sick. Yet I
hadn't been consciously apprehensive at the prospect of reading with
R.S. Thomas and Raymond Garlick at Theatre y Werin, as part of the
university's centenary celebrations. At the reception in the Great Hall
before the reading, R.S. Thomas cast a gloomy eye over the large, well-
dressed gathering: 'Who wants to read poetry to them?' Raymond
gently indicated the possibility that some would be receptive.

I read first and was soon calm. Then Raymond read. R.S. had the
second half of the evening to himself, and stood in front of us, rather
stooped, turn-up trousers at half-mast, licking his finger to turn the
sheaf of poems held in a trembling hand. More than ever, I noticed
the churchy sing-song of his voice, the plangent liturgical note, with
which he expressed, not so much his religion's traditional plaint, but
a far more personal anguish – indeed, partly the outcome of his conflict as comfortless comforter.

But how personal is it now?

Certainly the poems he read were repetitive, and he lost interest
half way through, showing his boredom in a way that offended some.
John Tripp and Meic Stephens, at least, were still angry afterwards.
Perhaps even anguish can become a habit, a permanent state of
mind, whose repeated sameness of expression may make it seem
insincere. This time, I was aware more of the professional clergy-
man's voice than of the voice vibrant with personal emotion.

But he has a note all his own which will probably be attended to for as long as there are people who care for poetry.

•

Walked the shingle bank to Hurst Castle on a day of flying clouds & blue sky. Looking east towards Southampton, over green, level mud-flats, creeks & masts, at the big chimney of Calshot power station & Fawley flames rising behind a distant line of conifers. Grey-green open sea; shadow of a grey-edged cloud stretching out from the Needles in a long black band, like an oil slick.

Dorset coast to the west: a fragment of white cliffs, round hills rising inland. Nearer, the orange, sand & gravel cliffs of Hordle & Barton curved towards Bournemouth's tower blocks. Vivid orange shingle where water came over or through it. A few big knobbly flints, smooth as bones; strips of dry, brittle seaweed, tinkling crunched shingle occasionally throwing up a pebble that jarred my ankle bone.

Walked past Rat Island & the pillbox, then round the castle under the walls. Ghosts, and ghosts of former selves, but part of the living present. Then Joe with one arm held out ran precariously along the road to meet me, about to pitch on his face when I caught him.

From a Pill-Box on the Solent

On a day of ripped cloud,
Angled light, wind against tide,
I am tempted to begin
The story of my life.

Waves come from far off,
Through the gap they have made,
Between Purbeck and Wight.

Surf booms in the pill-box,
Rattles the shingle,

Folds over it, unfolds,
Laying it bare.

Let it blow sand or salt.
Here at least I tread without fear
Of unsettling dust.

Back in Wales the land is sparer, bleaker, harder than in the south.
Dark rushes lean the same way as dark clouds driven over the ridge;
the big sycamore shakes, all its leaves blown pale side up, as if about
to turn inside out like an umbrella in the gale.

I welcome the austere Welsh uplands – they have a massive, alien
integrity, as though nothing I do or say or think could ever cling to
them or change them into the stuff of consciousness.

For each of us the universe is incorrigibly personal. This is not an
illusion within our necessary and inevitable perspective; yet the rock
casts us off, never once conscious of our clinging, blind to the life
into which we have converted it.

•

First Neruda, now Auden dead.

I was once infatuated with Auden's poetry, then overreacted
against it. Now I read it again, sadly, thinking mainly about post-
graduate days at 133a St Mary's Street and innumerable tipsy
declamations of 'As I walked out one evening', 'In Praise of
Limestone', etc. Auden is inseparable from those days, from the
shouts of fruitsellers in Kingsland Market as I read *The Orators* or
Groeddeck or Homer Lane and waited interminably for a letter from
Vivienne and worried about my psychosomatic illnesses; from
drunken nights with Sandy Tullis at his pub in Milford, and mornings of sickness & self-recrimination. Jim would quote a great deal
from memory; we both relished the poetry and spoke it with excitement, making it part of ourselves and of our friendship. 'The words
of a dead man / Are modified in the guts of the living'.

October

Glyn died yesterday night. A few weeks ago it was discovered that he had cancer, after his doctor had diagnosed measels. It was his fifty-first birthday.

He was very tough, because brought up to use physical effort where Dilwyn now uses machines. Often days have passed when he has been the only person I've seen apart from Sue; always very neighbourly and cheerful. I would see him in his working clothes, striding across the field, swinging a long stick, with two or three sheepdogs bounding round him, or hear his harsh shouted orders to the dogs; or else see him as a family man with his daughter, Elizabeth, laughing so much at something she said or did until it seemed he would fall off our sofa onto the floor.

Disease is terrible when it takes men so tough and full of life.

•

Glyn was buried on a wet, wild day. Our drive was flooded again; black-spotted sycamore leaves were plastered to the path. We sent a wreath but did not go to the funeral. Sue went to work, I lolled about indoors with what felt like the onset of 'flu'. Fetching kindling wood from the shed, when the cortege passed unexpectedly, I hid guiltily behind the house. Our presence at the funeral would have been appreciated and may have been missed, but it would also have caused embarrassment, to us if no one else, at a Welsh service and a Welsh gathering.

It takes something like this to remind me what strangers we are here – often muddled by conflict between the human response and awareness of our ignorance of custom.

November

As I walked in the fields of Pencwmbeidog, strands of black smoke were rising from the village – an enormous flock of small birds. I followed them through binoculars against the dull sky. Then they flew across the sun revealed by a cloudbreak; suddenly, yellow fire and slate-blue cloud. Had there been something awake in me to meet it, this would have been a sign.

•

It becomes increasingly difficult to say 'I', and what it ('I') 'feels' or 'sees' seems to matter less and less.

I haven't begun to write yet.

What is felt, what is seen: these matter, not the I-feeling, I-seeing. It is more than a question of emphasis.

It is what I have remembered and forgotten over and over again: neither self nor world exists separately; each is discovered in the other.

•

Carrying an armful of sweet-smelling hay across the field to feed the ponies, gleam of wintry sunlight in a cold wind on pale golden marsh & bright blue sky between clouds over the mountain: the first time this week I have felt the earth under my feet.

Monday & Tuesday in Cardiff. I got very drunk after eating out with John Ormond & Gwyn Erfyl, and drinking more brandy until the early hours with the Clarkes. When I interviewed John for the HTV book programme next afternoon, I was still sick & shaken. He too was nervous, after hours of lively conversation & long stretches of brilliant monologue, when he read us poems from his book. At one high point of euphoria, gorged on food and swilling red wine bought on Gwyn's expense account, I launched into a long denunciation of television's insult to the 'common man'. Otherwise a not-to-be-forgotten evening virtually obliterated by alcohol.

Wednesday: Tony Harrison came to supper, gave a reading in college, and stayed the night with us. As before, he seemed exhausted, but read and talked beautifully. Afterwards, I read him Tony Conran's translation of 'Rhydcymerau'. I have met few kinder or more intelligent men: he is one of the finest poets of our generation – vigorous, widely allusive, with controlled power & a deep awareness both of personal origins & of the Third World. In some ways, as poets, we are opposites, but have something important in common in the impulse from which we write.

•

First snow, a few hesitant flakes, soft as wood ash, falling slowly in an irregular pattern of steps, as if catching on invisible obstacles in the air. I drove towards a hard white line of mountains, each knobbly shoulder clearly defined.

•

Brilliant morning following a leaden day of rain & flood. Seen from the waterfall, the sun hidden behind the house was reflected in opposite windows, turning them into a cube of shining ice.

Blunt stern of the frosty moon-boat.

December
What is there now for those who love the area I was brought up in? or for our children anywhere in England?

Was there ever a time so obsessed with living for itself?

And yet we conceive and clothe and feed and educate our children, and consume their future like locusts.

We are terrified of a temporary crisis, indifferent to what will live beyond us.

In this country, all creative power without cunning goes to waste – our ideals, loves, talents. All love that is more than a form of egotism links the present with the future as well as with the past.

It is not enough to recover the way back and to find the child in oneself at the expense of those whose lives are to come.

1974

February

I finished my study of David Jones on the day when the curlews began to call, early this year, after a mild winter with catkins in the hedges since late January.

What a time to be absorbed in such a project, during the most insidious & blatantly dishonest Tory electoral campaign I can remember, in weeks of crisis & glib, easy dreams of resolving it – as if more oil will keep the machine on the road for more than another limited period.

Still, *The Anathemata* was written partly during the Second World War.

March

How full of energy & curiosity Joe is, learning more words and delightedly repeating them, word and object inseparable: 'button', 'button', as he pulls at my pyjama buttons, 'catkee, catkee', pointing at catkins in a vase.

Yesterday I dug the garden with a sharp-edged, bright new spade, extending the growing area, now that this crisis, as in war time, makes every piece of earth more precious. Gradually, after weeks of living in an ink haze, my body comes alive again and in mid-afternoon, severing turves and treading manure into trenches, as I feel the length of my arms and legs, I look up and there is a half moon standing high over the house....

Each age has its own awareness of time. Sometimes the mind of the age seems coextensive with the sky, as though all is enclosed by a dome-like structure until even the universe seems to exist within a skull-shaped span.... It is easier to see past ages under the forms they have created, difficult to see those we are making.

•

A soft grey day, sun ghostly behind a low & a high layer of cloud. A strong south-east wind carries rich smells of manure as the tractor of Llwyn Bedw spreads it on the fields, and blows clearings in low cloud so that the silver-grey sky is like water suddenly shelving into depth.

In this place it is as if we are outside history, but that only means we don't know the past and rarely feel it, partly because the present in rural Wales doesn't represent an obvious break with preceding centuries, and partly because our Englishness prevents us from entering either past or present here.

In the south of England, as I felt in Rome, past and present coexist without touching, as if the present were a stratum imposed artificially on the past. Often, one feels for deep ground and there is only emptiness beneath the crust, a void where living connections should be.

Yet I do long to live in the south; the emotional need remains strong. And then I imagine myself living in a history that is both personal and composed of many other lives and times, and forget the oppressive feeling of a stale dusty wind that leaves no fresh air to breathe, and of hollowness under foot.

Then at a turning point such as a birthday, like today, or at many other times, I examine the depth of my life, like a bather feeling for shingle with his toes, and am appalled by its seeming shallowness. It is as though I can sometimes enter the past but cannot bring it into vital relationship with the present, and at other times live in the present but without feeling that it is sustained from beneath.

I am afraid that the way in which I have tried to live is no longer valid, although one hundred or even fifty years ago it would have been. Then I could have lived in touch with the deep life experience contained in place, before places became powerless and our centralized society extracted the last drop from their subterranean streams. The only comfort to set against such emptiness is the unhealthy conviction that much in our society that is confident in its vigour and vitality is merely the activity of parasites on a corpse.

•

Since writing my study of John Cowper Powys I have come to think rather differently of his significance.

I now see his feeling for childhood and for the past, which he recreated by analogy with his own childhood, as all important. It seems to me that he found no way forward that could be expressed in socially relevant terms, and indeed didn't seek it. Since he was long out of touch with English society, it remained futureless for him or with a future that appalled him. His fictional world is based almost entirely on the sensations, impressions, and instinctive animism of boyhood. It is the world of one who was closer than most adults to the earth and to unobtrusive processes of growth and decay.

Glen Cavaliero is especially perceptive about Powys's renewal of the life of the hidden child, but the perception needs to be carried farther. More should be said about the positive aspects of the renewal, but it also needs to be seen in relation to the whole problem of growth into maturity, and the failure of adult life in society, that is *the* problem of modern England.

It is certainly a gross simplification to see Powys as representative of a doomed class, whose life energies could find expression only in the celebration of death. Yet it is only by exploring and confronting this objection that his work can be fully understood.

What I have said about Powys is also true to some extent of David Jones. Each created his world by renewing contact between man and child. This I believe to be essential to all mature development, but the very conditions of modern English society make it extremely difficult, if not impossible, to achieve.

At the simplest level, the fundamental impulse of men like John Cowper Powys and David Jones was to carry right through their lives awareness of that living contact with the natural world which all children seem to have.

It is easy for an intellectual schooled in a materialistic philosophy to deride this impulse or to understand it as, at best, a neurosis ('Only the neurotic look to their beginnings'), but that is itself proof of the divorce between modern systems of thought and the complete human being. On the other hand, it is for the person aware of this impulse in himself to distinguish between the life energies and acquiescence in the death instinct. More than this, to find the creative balance which requires understanding and control of the death instinct as part of the total life force.

Powys's greatness, therefore, can be seen as his refusal to reject or suppress the death instinct – which is not to say he didn't react too far in the opposite direction, in dwelling upon it to the point of morbidity, or that he did achieve perfect balance in a way that is relevant to the present. I don't say that he did *not*, only that this is probably the major problem posed by his work.

All art discloses what the artist is and what he is part of: no aesthetic theory can avoid this conclusion without ignoring some feature of the interaction between man and his world. Once one has realised this, it is possible to see the difference between works that are 'good' because their makers are products of the superficial ideas of their time, and those (which may or may not be 'good') whose makers see the mental construct, the fiction, in which we live for what it is, and are sensitive to the processes by which we create our idea of reality. The former are part of the fiction they reproduce, the latter see it at once from above and from below but are engaged with the larger problem. A superficial artist or writer never really sees anything, least of all himself.

•

Those who are fully alive are up before the sun, though not all who are up before the sun are fully alive. This morning I woke when the sun was already over the ridge, a hot white ball which the naked eye could just bear to look at.

River and falls are the sun's mirror, and yet, seen from the bridge directly in line with them, the dazzling dance and sparkle of white fire is like a new element. Its impressions defeat the mind. Afterwards an image may form, but the reflections are too quick for words; nor may words enact a corresponding quickness.

Both in essence and appearance all life exists outside language; the attempt to capture it thus ends inevitably in despair, for the limits are defined by the reality language itself creates. Yet this is a haunted world.

As I move from the bridge to stand beside the stream, the fire vanishes. The deep pool under the waterfall is yellowy-green with a hint of gold, and where the broken sun burned snakes of bubbles slowly coil and uncoil. We find a bleached snail shell lodged between stones in the bank and Joe clutches it as we walk round the fields. Returning, we stand on the bridge, dazzled. He is as happy as the insensible water looks, a sunny little boy I am aware of as excited noises and exclamations and as a weight on my back, until I see his face mirrored behind mine in the dusty window of a cowshed.

Through sycamores bristling with spiky buds, over daffodils among tattered snowdrops and primroses with cool creamy faces turned full towards the sun, the house against the hazy ridge looks as natural as a stone in a field. I see it through our lives, and in my mind their aura fuses with the curious effect of sunlight shining on a robin high in a tree, reflecting its red breast on the sky immediately behind. The stream will lose its fiery appearance even from the bridge as the day grows older. Earth will be fragrant tonight under a waxing moon. If never quite the same, such days and nights will return, repeating the centuries we have created by transforming them into a language of signs.

April

Old Mrs Wilson said to Mrs Jones the shop that Glyn was needed more 'on the other side', because he was a good man. Dilwyn told me, half believing, wanting confirmation. He is overworked and tired of farming; if it weren't for his mother he would sell up and leave. His dream is to be a policeman. Most of the farmers I talk to are deeply depressed by their economic situation; many speak of being forced to give up and, like Dilwyn, intend to sell their cattle. Then he drives off up the lane on his tractor, too fast, singing loudly above the noise. He is young and healthy, temperamentally boisterous and cheerful, but the work has been blighted as well as becoming harder since Glyn died. He sees him everywhere, he says. I too still see him more clearly than anyone else I once knew.

A Neighbour

I remembered his laugh – once
he almost fell from a chair;
also with one hammerblow
he drove a fencepost in.
Some weeks I saw only him,
with his dogs and stick, old coat
and greasy cap, walking
from the mountain to his fields;
and we talked – we said aye
to everything, with a language
between us, and rare china
civility, out in wind, rain or sun.
He was first to welcome us,

standing in the door saying aye, aye ...

I would have seen him then,
strangely white, thinning the hedge
with a hook, his old coat hung on a branch;
but instead a flock of starlings
turned me aside – a swirl
of black flecks over the valley.
Then, seeing the graveyard,
I did not look again
at the hedge, with white, jagged ends.

May
Looking up from writing in the caravan, I saw a fox in the field
immediately outside the window. It picked its way carefully, as if
stalking, but was clearly unaware of my presence. I told Sue, and later
in the evening we both saw it crossing the field in the same place, long
reddish-brown fox loping along rather disdainfully.

September
In my memories of Sligo, three of us row up the river as it widens
towards Lough Gill, each delighting in the others' company. For now
our world's contracted to this boat, but is less than a water-fly from
the mountain ...

What I remember also are individuals complete in themselves: the
unselfconscious generous friendliness of Seamus Heaney talking
about my poem, 'Elegy for the Labouring Poor', about Hardy and
about the affinities between our feelings for chalk and peat; the
warm, giving nature of Lester Connor, and Michael Longley's
humour and quick wit.

I remember acceptance moving me towards self-acceptance, as if
a gift were something to affirm, not hide.

Giving people open a door on human potentiality, annul the
sadness of the long view and draw one back from it, into the warmth.
Nor is there anything stronger than caring in the conscious world.

•

Tea with Gerard and Mary Casey at Mappowder. Gerard took Joe
for a walk on his shoulders while we called next door on Mrs Lucy
Penny, Mary's mother and a surviving member of the Powys family.
Though old and lame with arthritis, but not at all frail, Mrs Penny
was very kind to us, her eyes in the Powys face (remarkably like
JCP's) shining with warmth and interest. There were portraits of
most of the family – mainly painted by Gertrude – and African landscapes (one on a smooth Chesil stone) by Will Powys in both houses.
Gerard, still carrying Joe, took us into the church. He indicated the
place at the back where Theodore Powys used to spend long hours,
filling the place with an atmosphere of serenity. Gerard was still conscious of Theodore's presence; he said he was the most remarkable
man he had ever known, and the only one JCP was afraid of. It isn't
difficult to visualise Theodore living in the small stone house next to
the church, thinking about the grave on the other side where he now
lies. Perhaps he was a man who sought God with his whole being and
concluded there was none, but found peace in stark acceptance of the
fact. I don't know, it was just a thought that came to me as I stood
behind the pew where he had sat, imagining him motionless there on
just such a mellow September afternoon.

•

Walked across wet and muddy fields to Shroton Lines, rich odours of
decay under hedges and the wind blowing squalls of cold rain, gusts
of warm, drying sun. I climbed Hambledon, finding it steeper than I
remembered, and more difficult, in a wind that almost dislodged me,
then blew from behind, driving me up. On the summit it was blowing
a gale. I crouched behind the barrow to eat cake and plums, looking
across miles of patterned landscape under driven, dark grey clouds.
Descending, I misjudged the gradient of a vallum and involuntarily
ran down it. Then sheltered from more rain under beeches and
horse-chestnuts on the hill's flank, finding a few small conkers; the
rugged, carved hillface looming above. Rain fell slantwise, whitely,
like a fine gauze, across a delicately blue sky, and there was a rainbow
that dissolved even as I turned my head. Walked back to Iwerne along
the road, dark-blue reflections on its wet surface and rain coming and

going while Hambledon grew smaller and less dominating behind.

October
David Jones died on the 28th. I learnt this on the following day when David Parry-Jones rang from Cardiff and asked me to answer a few questions about his life and work for 'Dateline'. There was a fine obituary in *The Times*. Little else so far. It's not news when one of the finest spirits of the age passes. But of course the spirit does not pass.

December
First paperback copies of *Soliloquies of a Chalk Giant*, beautifully done by Alan Clodd, with Sue's delicate tracing of a fossil urchin – the one from Hambledon, I think – on the cover.

I gloated and was, of course, alternately disappointed and proud.

1975

January

Another wet, mild, dull winter. Dad commented with disgust on the 'uncanny' weather over Christmas. So I feel it to be. Without frost and bright, glittering days the year seems out of rhythm. Only occasionally, walking by the Beidog, have I found dead leaves lightly salted with frost. There Joe & I saw goldcrests one day, and on another a dipper – black & white, suddenly gone.

February

Almost all I can see now are relationships, not autonomous persons or things. The writing problem is not at all one of *to whom*? but *who-is-writing-to-whom*? It is inherent in my thinking about poetry, which in turn derives from my problematical relationship as an English poet to society. At times it seems as though there is no real need for the kind of writing I have been able to do so far – no real need in the sense that it is a genuine function of some particular social group. I can analyse my need to write, and find it compounded of impulses that are dark to me, and of those, such as vanity, which are all too clear.

Over the last year or so, I have come to need a specific justification: to know that the 'grounds' are not a vain illusion. Of course, a widely accepted and probably true idea of the Welsh poet has made me acutely aware of how impoverished, how relatively groundless, his English counterpart is; and as an English poet living in a Welsh community I have had to see myself in the light of the comparison.

What I have begun to see more clearly is that a widely held preconception of poetry is no longer valid. Long ago a phrase applied by a journalist to two middle-aged English poets made me react with unthinking hostility: they were 'in mid-career'. Subsequently I came to realise how accurately 'career' describes the conception of their activity held by a number of modern British and American poets, especially those for whom the ironic mode has obviated poetry's claim to social or religious significance. Nor was I only thinking coolly about others, since I have been deeply infected by desire for a career type of success. And I have seen the results in myself, as well as in my reading: the envy, the competitiveness, the paranoia, which is virtually the same as that which seems to be an academic hazard, and perhaps a hazard of all middle-class professions.

For some, therefore, poetry has simply become part of the capitalist bourgeois ethic. Well, not 'simply', of course. For many older significances attach to this one, concealing its bare-faced competitiveness from the poet himself. Poets like Snyder, on the other hand, have returned to what they think of as the poet's tribal function, so that one can't help noticing with irony their source of grants – and, to some extent, recognition – in universities and other establishment institutions. At a different level, the young rebels of English verse are often demanding supplicants at the court of the Arts Council.

What is in question is the function of poetry at a time of total confusion in Western societies. This is one reason why I have written appreciatively of Anthony Conran, since he is aware of the factors negating conventional ideas of poetry when most of us writing it are not. And he is equally aware that the conventional and the rebel against convention are two sides of the same coin. So much then is mere repetition, at best with subtle variations, of the past, which had a function the present does not.

•

A time of expectancy, the baby already five days 'late'. I seem able to forget it, then remember, startled, expecting at any moment to have to act; but the tension, if less than last time, is there nevertheless.

Rain now, after two soft warm days of digging in the garden, hands rough as sandpaper, while the moon came clear of the sycamore and a fine blue mist softened Mynydd Bach. Yesterday evening Joe stood outdoors shouting 'Moon! Moon!'. Earlier today a curlew called briefly, and in shady places celandines are out among daffodils, primroses and wild strawberries.

Some writers are present almost physically in their work; and this may be true of the reticent (like Hardy) and untrue of the confessional. But Yeats who can speak so movingly, so forcefully, of 'the foul rag and bone shop of the heart' or as a 'dying animal', isn't there at all. Sometimes it seems to me that he really did become the golden bird ...

Certainly *his* Ireland gave Yeats what no English poet since Shakespeare has had: not only a nation and its history, but also a folk life with a mythology and a supernatural realm haunting the actual countryside.

One has only to think of Yeats's desire to speak to and for his 'people' – that he should actually desire that as right and natural, let alone achieve it to some degree – and compare it with the desire and aims of modern English poetry to appreciate how decadent the latter is. At least one should die trying to get near that barrier between poet and people, through the defences on this side, which irony and self-deprecation and limited aims have raised.

•

Washed earth from my hands in the running stream, kneeling on stone and looking up at the stone house, moon in a crook formed by sycamore branches. Fire on the hearth indoors, logs perfectly rounded ... After dark now thrushes are still singing. Not yet the full cry of spring but definitely the prelude.

•

Sue woke me at 3.30 on Tuesday morning. First I drove Joe up the hill to leave him with Jenny Roberts, then took Sue to Aberystwyth hospital, with a great white moon burning in the west. Stayed with her until after the child was born at 9am. The head seemed to take a long time being crowned, and Sue was terribly racked; then I looked a long time at the face, purple with eyes closed and squashed Negroid features – again the feeling of utter foreignness, the little creature seeming dead. So purple she was when born, a small ancient all wrinkled from long immersion in the water: Emily Teleri.

On and off all day – out in the garden with Joe in beautiful spring weather, or in the house – I saw the little flat-nosed, purple face and thought vaguely of the drowned face Porius sees in the mountain lake.

Coming back with Joe from the hospital last night, a huge orange moon rose from the hills, and the days have been blue and hazy and alive with singing birds. This morning I saw Dilwyn, whose grand-mother died on the same day that our daughter was born. He was dignified in his sadness, and talked only of the little girl after accept-ing our commiserations. Now Sue and a small hot red-faced Emily are home again, and Joe is delighted, giving her his toys to look at, holding her and eager to do all he can.

After feeding the ponies and before talking to Dilwyn, I had a long talk in the road with John Williams, who had somehow already heard about our child. We talked about Pencwmbeidog, and the legal problems Dilwyn and Mrs Davies are having with the English owner. How absurd to think of this place as an 'edge'. That is a mental state which can occur anywhere, but here we are among people, young and middle-aged and old, dying and newborn, in a community with its own real problems and with old and new values.

Logically, desiring to write but also needing to make a living and acquire a social identity, I should have gone to London, where, paradoxically, I might have made a name – and a living – from writing about the south. I did not go there for various reasons, including obstinacy and fear as well as hostility to metropolitan centralism; and in Wales I have developed an idea of poetry which cannot be separated from imaginative commitment to people and place. For a time I could go on believing that I was being true to that idea, for I was attempting to express it while seeking to return to the place which sustained my imagination.

I see that a writer has to work with what he is and has, and from where he is; and for me this means acknowledging my actual position as a writer dependent on one place but removed from it by social circumstances. If I write of belonging, it is because I know loss; but I can at least avoid sentimentality and false images of rootedness; I can at least try to know England as it is, and therefore to see my kind of feeling for place in its historical and social context.

March

I have never been able to let out more than a fraction of my anger, and have often pretended to a sweet reason that is more harmful than the truth. There can be no approach to the truth unless I admit to the inner violence that has seethed in me for as long as I can remember. I know that destructive impulses are part of creativity, which does not exist without them, while to give way to destructiveness would indeed be merely to destroy.

•

Reading poems from my two collections and from 'Solent Shore', at a reading which I shared with Gill and Roland at Llandrindod Wells, I knew that it is again time to move on; and afterwards, talking to Gill with complete frankness, that I've tried to live up to an unrealistically exacting image of myself in almost every sphere, which is itself a form of vanity. True friendship can occur only between equals; but I have been, too often, either hero-worshipper or supporter, and have rarely looked anyone full in the eyes, hiding nothing, not pretending to be in some respect more or less than I am.

•

Everything except the hooded gorse is white or pale or dark grey. On Good Friday evening the sky cleared, becoming blue and blue-grey, which gave a soft, powdery blue sheen to snowy fields; the sun, flaming orange, touched the mountainside with a faint, fiery reflection. No birdsong, no movement except snow falling and one Breughel magpie drawing its long straight tail across the grey sky. I went to sleep as the full moon rose; woke to the blinding sun.

April
Luminous days with sudden falls of mist. The second stage of growth, almost quick enough to see as grasses push up and leaves unfold. A cuckoo calls as I write.

The Cambridge Poetry Festival has come and gone. Days ago, in a strange house, before my lecture on David Jones, I thought of the relief afterwards, which seemed far off, on the other side of an enormous barrier. And now it is here, the days almost willed out of existence ... So one sleeps out times between crises, which are themselves a kind of dream. Not quite.

I remember the pleasure of looking up in King's College Chapel and unexpectedly seeing Jeff Wainwright crossing towards me, the pleasure of Gill and Dave suddenly materializing at my elbow in a bookshop. I felt outside it all on the first evening, at the reception where I knew no one and everyone seemed to know everyone else, no introductions, a jump-in-if-you-can-or-stand-on-the-edge type of situation. Then Michael Longley arrived, full of good humour and warm friendliness, and, like me, not quite knowing why he was there or sure that he wanted to be. Later I was surprised and grateful to

meet a few younger people – John Matthews and Paul Hills in particular – who knew and liked my writing. After all that I've said about
poet and audience, it's really the known and unknown friends, few as
they be, for whom one writes.

How strange and, at times, alien Cambridge seemed!

Strange and beautiful, but also unreal, as I came on the Backs in
warm spring sunshine, crimson and white blossom on hedges and
trees, yellow willows weeping over the green river, everywhere birds
singing in fairyland.

Not difficult to feel like Jude in Christminster, as I ran my hands
over old rough stone walls, peered in at venerable obscure interiors,
saw workmen renovating the buildings, or in the non-academic parts
of town. But because my position is so different from his, I could see
all more coolly, and see myself, also a cloistered man, admiring the
beauty and wondering what right I had to think it unreal.

It's easy to think of certain places as cultural or intellectual or
artistic centres, and probably inevitable sometimes to wish oneself in
London or Oxford or Cambridge. Real thought begins when one
asks, Centre of what?

May

Yesterday afternoon, at Llanddewi Brefi church, I took part, with
Robert Morgan, R.S. Thomas and Euros Bowen, in a poetry reading
at Moelwyn Merchant's festival. As usual, R.S. Thomas was pleasant
to me, but also ironical at his own expense and, by implication,
everyone else's. He is a shy man, I think, who says what he has to in
his poems, and communicates with difficulty outside them. He
signed a book for me, but said he never knew what to do on such
occasions, and in fact just wrote his name on the inside cover. This
led him to tell a story about an American correspondent who had
sent him a photograph taken from space of the place where he (RS)
lives. He didn't know what to do on that occasion either – did his correspondent expect him to say how wonderful he thought American
technology was? So he simply ignored the picture.

Euros Bowen is a very different kind of man. I had a long talk with
him about poetry. He insisted that Gwenallt – an old friend – was not
a religious but a theological poet, and he evidently thought of himself
as the former. Euros Bowen believes in the poetic imagination, and in
rhythm (not metre) as the measure of a poet's quality. He believes

Christianity is only the truth about life, so the celebration of reality will inevitably be Christian. I found him vivid, forceful and 'profane' in his way of talking. He *wanted* to talk about his poetry, and did so without false modesty, implying comparisons between his work and Dylan Thomas's, and Waldo Williams's, as well as Gwenallt's. Later he read from the pulpit in an incantatory manner. The other poets also read from the pulpit (the two parsons were used to being there), but I couldn't bring myself to do so, and read standing on the steps at the centre of the aisle.

June

Sick again. Depression, acute anxiety. Particularly under stress in college. I want so much to be strong. To *be*, without this other old, tired self. I've been living inside myself, complacently, for so long; then find myself shut in, afraid. Yet it takes this experience to show me how much is wrong all the time.

July

I have forgotten how to speak my feelings – if I ever knew. No doubt that's partly because I try to explain them, and partly from embarrassment – indeed, from shame, from growing suspicion of personal expression as an end in itself. There have been times in these last two months when I could not have written, when again there would have been only a cry ... 'I am poured out like water.'

I went to Swansea, depressed and frightened, to lecture on David Jones. Yet the time passed, once again I made friends, and came back heartened. Retreat leads only to retreat; it is easy to write the truth but very difficult to act sensibly when the urge to retreat is almost overwhelming. Again, though, I have learnt things about myself that I could not have learnt through confidence; and again I know the need to live in and be sustained by a reality greater and stronger than the self.

'The bird a nest, the spider a web, man friendship.'

'Nurture strength of spirit to shield you in sudden misfortune. But do not distress yourself with imaginings. Many fears are born of fatigue & loneliness. Beyond a wholesome discipline, be gentle with yourself. You are a child of the universe, no less than the trees & the stars. *You have a right to be here.*'

September

A fortnight ago, I climbed with Peter Clarke and Gerard and a party of Powys Society members over White Nose and along the cliffs to Chydyok, where Llewelyn Powys once lived.

Bright day with clouds blowing inland, sea blue with purple shadows under white cliffs.

I walked with a clouded, anxious spirit; now and again the day broke in ...

Dipped my fingers covertly in the black water of the small garden pond with an inscription carved round the margin. *Here and now. Here and now. ...*

Returning, Peter and I climbed Glastonbury Tor to the tower of St Michael's; a pack of dogs bayed loudly somewhere in the misty flat land below.

The folly of living within, of making oneself comfortable and secure, complacent until the way out can't be found. The folly of not *seeing*, of letting so many days pass unseen, until even the brightest is dimmed.

Last night a slant, orange half-moon, glimpsed before a storm-cloud swallowed it.

> 'The sap has sunk like lead into your heels and you feel as though you could howl like a winter's wolf. This hopeless despair, by bringing you to the earth, raises you again; it changes your blood, and drives you with vicious kicks forward into a new pasture. It makes a way for you out of your own misery, and creates a new mind out of your unrest: that – with a new beginning. But I can never escape, I can only wait until the mood lets go, and meanwhile the teeth of the mood bite me to the bone, and the black cruelty cuts at the very root of my being .... and so I wait and hope that this mood of God will not last long.'
>
> (T.F. Powys, *Soliloquies of a Hermit*)

Soliloquies of a Hermit contains many great passages, and still I feel there are crucial places where Theodore is not *thinking* hard enough, not carrying his thought through. He is too content with paradoxes and intuitions that a more searching and critical spirit would not have allowed him to rest on.

In my dream I was at Buckler's Hard – that was the name of the place but the dream setting was an abstract of the old muddy shoreline with rows of posts – and a great sea came rolling in flooding the land. I remember escaping with the water at my heels, and going back to save someone – a child – I think, a girl. But the most important thing was the name of the flood; it was called 'The Fisher' and I learnt that it was recurrent in those parts. Waking, I felt the blocked source had been broken, and I had been carried outside myself on the flood. The feeling lasted only a few hours, and afterwards I forgot the details which had been vivid when I woke, and which I made a conscious effort to remember. Since then, as often before, I dream continually of water, of fast-flowing rivers and of stagnant, weed-choked lakes.

•

In Dorchester I bought a copy of *Soliloquies of a Hermit* for £16.75 (TFP received 7d in royalties on two copies sold in six months) and wondered whether in fifty years time anyone would be paying the equivalent for my *Soliloquies* and feeling the same guilty excitement at obtaining a rare, little read book, in which its author had put so much of himself.

•

Tea with Gerard & Mary & Mrs Penny at Mappowder. Gerard asked me to record some of the Giant poems; then we sat in his small room listening to a tape of him reading his 'South Wales Echo'. Peace – the big round apples glowing ruddy in the orchard. Back over Iberton Hill in a blaze of sunlight filling the vale, trees below casting long shadows.

•

Couldn't face going into college for the start of term this morning, and now the pressure is off, temporarily, there is peace again.

I can go no further without professional help – the greater part of the 'holiday' was a nightmare. I got through the much-appreciated day of talking & reading to my parents' friends at Sandy Down – an event I had dreaded almost as much as my lecture on David Jones at the conference in Aberystwyth early in the month – and Emily's christening on Sunday. But every public act – even going into a shop or meeting friends – has been an ordeal since June. When in this state I lose almost all sense of the other.

The dreary monologue begins when I wake; anxiety is habitual, a way of death-in-life.

Yet through this my understanding has been deepened – I know that the other exists, that the world outside me is not the clouded or fearful image in my head.

But as yet I cannot meet it, cannot let go of the false world which is a strained, hideously distorted image of the other – my face mirrored in all things. At Weymouth, at Burton Bradstock, where the turbulent, blue-grey sea pounded on shingle and I ran with Joe in and out of the foam, this false world held its anchor even against the sea. Then in moments of peace I see how much is awry, how loveless the inattentive eye that throws its shadows on the other.

October
It makes a difference to be told authoritatively that this state is cyclical & inherited – therefore not entirely the moral problem as I have interpreted it. Yet in the abyss between this pathology and creative human *being* there are broken or undeveloped connections.

•

On a clear, slightly chilly evening, with a cold, mineral smell of freshly turned earth on my hands, mingling with a sweet smell of decaying vegetation, I walked in the field above the upper waterfall. There I hid in the summer, and sat on stones by the Beidog watching a tiny trout with its face to the current, or reading his sister's moving account of the effect on her of the religious revival in 1904, which Dr Phillips had lent me, together with photographs showing Mynydd Bach black with people, who flocked to an open-air meeting. And there I felt myself poured out. Now the moon was up, the sun going down flaming white, and I lay on the earth to watch, against the sound of tumbling water.

Gerard, more than anyone except Sue, has helped me in this crisis. I have been strangely conscious of his presence since receiving his kind & understanding letter last week – not all the time, but at times distinctly, as if by the power of his concern he were near. He writes that he feels all my poetry is but the prolegomena to something 'greater'. It is what I too want to believe, especially now, after months when I have not thought of myself as a poet or felt myself to be one. There have been times, though, when I have felt the disturbance as an opening of my being to the depths.

•

Donald Allchin, canon & theologian, had a meal with us here the other evening. He left me his typescript study of Ann Griffiths to read – a beautifully written, wholly sympathetic account of her life and work, which assents completely to her faith. In many ways Donald and I are close in our thinking, but not at root. I don't think I have ever loved God, and am not even sure what it means. I know awe, and wonder, and praise to I don't know what, unless life itself. But God? No, I have never consciously loved God. Nor have I contemplated Christ – Redemption and Incarnation – with more than curiosity, wondering at my lack of emotion and at others' overwhelming feelings. It may be that I sometimes call the life principle God, and I pray to the 'lord' whom I knew as the only comforter in my first depression, when a child. But Cross and Resurrection have never entered into my blood-stream. I have some intellectual knowledge of the Christian religion, but have never apprehended it passionately. The awe I feel in churches as in stone circles, in presence of the quiet, the smell of cold stone, the countless prayers, is really a pagan awe.

When I told Donald my intuition about T.F. Powys in Mappowder church, contemplating God's total absence, he was able to include the very absence in God – the God no images can image, who is indeed the absence of all our ways of knowing. Although I can sympathise with this view, and see it as the only possible apprehension of God except as God become man, its danger is that it makes way for a theology so vague that almost any unbelief may be included in Christianity.

> 'Each concrete hour alloted to the person ... is speech for the man who is attentive. Attentive, for no more than that is needed in order to make a beginning with the reading of the signs that are given to you.'

> 'It is not the solitary man who lives the life of monologue, but *he who is incapable of making real in the context of being the community in which, in the context of his destiny, he moves.*'

> 'Being, lived in dialogue, receives even in extreme dereliction a harsh and strengthening sense of reciprocity; *being, lived in monologue, will not, even in the tenderest intimacy, grope out over the outlines of the self.*'

'We do not find meaning lying in things nor do we put it into things, but between us and things it can happen.'

(Martin Buber, *Between Man and Man*)

All Buber's teachings – I suppose all great teachings – are immediately relevant. Tomorrow I have to leave this refuge and go down the hill into town, into college, to meet people, face to face. For as long as I am in it, this is my community. Wherever I am, there is my community too.

'To make a thing is mortal man's pride; but to be conditioned in a common job, *with the unconscious humility of being a part, of participation and partaking,* is the true food of earthly immortality.'

That's not quite the language I would use, but it's the truth I have learnt in the long, at first unconscious, strain between ambition and the need to participate in a common world. Buber speaks of 'our time of *inner loss of community*' and of '*the epidemic sickening of the word in our time,* by which every word is at once covered with the leprosy of routine and changed into a slogan'; but he denies that an artist's work can foster mutuality. I believe in a sharing between the artist and others, and between people brought together by the work.

Some artists may recover or create communion through their work.

•

Out before the sun on a clear, frosty morning, dark ridge in bold outline with radiance pulsing brighter and brighter behind. The risen sun, seen momentarily, Blake's *Glad Day*.

The past week hasn't been without tension, but has been lived with some attentiveness. I fled once – from the queue waiting to hear Yevtushenko read his poems. Walked at Tan-y-bwlch under the moon, which was reflected in puddles under my feet, and on the beach, disturbing oystercatchers which flew away with eerie, piping cries. Came back later for Sue, and listened outside the door hearing the poet's voice lifted in impassioned declamation or sinking to a whisper – a voice that has filled Red Square.

'The coming of truth was necessary, in order that man should cease to live inside himself.'
'What meets our eyes denotes neither a total absence nor a

manifest presence of the divine, but the presence of a God who conceals himself. Everything bears his stamp.'

(Pascal)

A few weeks ago I would have been unable to say I have never loved God; superstition would have prevented me.

I have loved nature and a few people, including some I have never met. Life, too, with the passions which to Pascal are the principal obstacles to our knowing and loving God. Pascal is already well on the near side of an age in which the whole man could live sacramentally. His is a prodigious intelligence, and I know him a man in his terror and wretchedness, and in the force of his intellect. And at times I dislike intensely the man I seem to know. He is called worldly, but his is a mental worldliness. The *Pensées* make me aware not of his attraction to the creatures and the Creation, but of his need to pacify the terror he feels at man's place in it. While this is human, St Augustine is far more human in the sense I appreciate.

Buber is no less an existentialist than Pascal. He is seldom desperate, seldom with the high note of anguish, but what he insists on is little more than an age which knew friendship & neighbourliness would take for granted. He makes it more than that, or rather he shows it to be a sacred encounter, but his insistence shows how far we have fallen from communion.

•

Clear night with a big, bright moon, an owl softly whooing.

When I speak about God I don't know what I am talking about.

•

Country people will remember this as 'the mushroom year'. I shall remember it as the year when I longed for autumn, when my image of the hot sun and a world partially glimpsed, inwardly distorted, were a curse. But I shall not forget the mushrooms, which I found morning after morning, cool and creamy on fat stalks. Seeking them, finding them in colonies, with Joe beside me or on my shoulders, singing out when he saw one, I found peace. I felt their shapes with my fingers, buried my face in their earthy, fungoid smell, and was close to the earth.

126

•

An artist who, in Conrad's sense, descends into himself is always in danger: he may speak or write wisely and still remain a fool in his life; all his pronouncements on love may derive from self-love. He may even know love only through the agony of that immersion in self that is its opposite; he is then like the damned who may be said to know heaven.

November
Robert Gittings finds Thomas Hardy psychologically and emotionally abnormal. Witness his comments on Hardy's fascination with hangings, especially of women.

Can't Gittings feel it to be at least latent in himself? Evidently not.

Whenever someone comments on the abnormality of others, it is interesting to note what norm he is basing his judgments on. I'd back Hardy against his impudent inquisitors any day, especially those whose idea of themselves as reasonable beings makes them critical of his romanticism or class-consciousness, both of which they'd describe as excessive.

•

When a personal life loses touch with a common life there are many ways in which its expression can become meaningless.

Think of William Cobbett, the strong individual in his England, the man made by his binding relationships with a real society. Then think of Edward Thomas, a man who loved the old England which he felt Cobbett represented; think of Thomas's expression of his most elusive, barely utterable awareness. He knows himself superfluous; he writes in the act of falling from a common to a personal world. No, he writes having made the fall, loving an England he never possessed and partly dreamed, and also *between* that dream and the reality to which he was sacrificed.

This morning I read part of Cobbett's ride from Lyndhurst to Beaulieu, but especially his description of St Leonard's, looking across the Solent to towns on the Island. And I thought of the shoreline now, dominated by ESSO, and of what it represents, the economy by which I live, the England in which I have lived.

This very minute is the time of commemoration, Armistice Sunday.

Cobbett's words are in his voice with his body behind them; they are real things, of a time and a place, filled with the matter of an actual social earth, peculiarly personal but with an ingrained commonness. I think that between generations, as between friends, we should give each other real things. Isolation, anguish, nausea – the highest, shrillest note, like a man's voice imitating the gull's cry in his struggle to externalise an inner death: this is a fact of experience. But because I must have it, I want it to be one note among others, an element among elements grounded in love of this earth and this life, in a human commonness that sustains.

1976

January

I should soon be free of extraneous work, reviews all written, lecture invitations turned down.

Last weekend I spent alone, marking essays: the first time in months when I've been free of sick dependency.

I have written so much, thought so much about certain matters, yet when the real poem is written there is maybe an image that carries more of the truth than any of these words.

The sense of having an overview is largely illusory; it is always from below, from an area within the life where self-consciousness cannot reach, that real insight comes.

If only I can care enough to want to write, now that the superficial stimuli which made me ambitious have almost ceased to exist.... Care enough for the love of the thing, feel again the need to discover ...

Floating-Bridge

You look for
a good haul
in green, milky water
where chains slide over reels.

Is it, perhaps, the sludge
of nostalgia, or the unseen
seen too narrowly?

Whatever it is,
the chains go deep.

March

Day after day, year after year, life goes on, the same appetites, the same mistakes; now and then a moment almost filled, the self almost transformed, and if it were, truly, the being made whole by faith and conviction, then days and years would matter less, and time would always be *now*. But of course, it is easier to drift, to live from meal to meal, cigarette to cigarette, sleep to wake and again to sleep, and then again and finally to sleep; easier never to wake.

Sometimes I almost wake, think: it is now, *now*, something is required of me that I wake, and remain awake, always attentive. Then that 'something' is almost visible; I am about to know what it is, I *can* know if I concentrate hard enough, or if – but how? – I empty my mind so that the illumination may fill it.

Perhaps it was there when the wheatfield on Hambledon fell, when I lay down on the moving hill and was no longer afraid. Then again the dust settled, and the world was familiar and stale.

At last that other consciousness returns, and one lives and acts only by effort of will, afraid of dropping the burden of one's self.

Again it is lighter, the self carried, but this time the awareness is duller; when the wheel turns out of half-light the rim does not shine. Anxiety and fear have passed, and almost at once complacency begins to return, but there are moments almost filled, when all could be different.

And it is then, not in the moment of terror or of being transfixed by a single destructive thought, but remembering that time as the mind again begins to secrete its protective complacency, *then* the choice may be made. I do not have to repeat myself; the wheel does not have to go down again; it can be abandoned altogether, like the wheel of an antiquated gun-carriage on an old battlefield. The power it had can be replaced by another, if I choose; if I will to choose.

April

The real is all to do.

•

Knowing damned little about anything except the ground and the act of attention to writing itself is, I think, the main reason for hope that

I may one day come at the real.

And the real is the conviction the poem carries in rightness of rhythm and words together – their necessity, though the creation of a fallible man. It is religious too: the man in relation to all he is not, but is part of, in his apparently separate individuality.

> 'That is the best part of each writer which has nothing private in it. That is the best part of each which he does not know, that which flowed out of his constitution, and not from his too active invention.'
>
> (Emerson)

•

> 'Commitment for the English is really still just a hobby; and they are structurally and psychologically outside what is happening culturally to a great section of humanity, their upbringing, unfortunately brainwashing them into what they do not recognise as a deep foundational complacency.'
>
> (Bobi Jones)

How I resented that when I first read it! I was right, of course, to feel angry on behalf of those to whom it doesn't apply; but not to react personally. When I bristled with antagonism I should have recognised hurt pride, and paused longer to consider how the words apply to me. For they do.

I should require more, far more, of myself – not more strain or tension.

Strain as I know it is a result of resistance, withholding, living with a problem but not living it through, holding on to the most destructive part of egotism as if it were protective, instead of a shell that inhibits growth, armour in which the psyche suffocates.

•

Joe's first day at the village school. He went delighted, with a small satchel full of writing books, pencils & crayons, and came home equally thrilled, with a beautiful abstract expressionist painting and having met a pretty little girl called Sally.

I began again, for the third time, to learn Welsh this week. What a difference, though, when I turn ambitiously from 'Ble mae'r tebot?'

or 'Ydy'r llaeth wrth y drws?' to a bilingual edition of modern Welsh poetry and try to relate the facing pages!

May

As far as Geoffrey Hill and, especially, C.H. Sisson are concerned, my respect and admiration are tempered by occasional moods of visceral anger or cold dislike. The latter is close to Eliot – often in rhythm, as well as in feeling and attitude. The abrasive isolation of one who lives ultimate questions today. Yet generosity of feeling, as distinct from the indifference or sentimentality which may pass itself off for it, remains, for me, the most attractive human quality.

As soon as one admits the necessity for a scrupulous search for truth among words, for affirmations, or negations, or discriminations, which a life has earned, and for the use of those words alone which have been earned, then one has to grant the validity of Sisson and Hill's extreme *care*. Of course the poetry we need doesn't confirm the reader in complacent assumptions, though it may at last enlighten those who have paid an equivalent price in suffering, because they too have lived the questions; then it *may* even comfort and resolve, as it should always excite the depths of feeling and thought.

Easy resolutions, made as one turns aside from evil and suffering, are less acceptable now than at any other time; for there is a degree of evil in this century that not even the most terrible former times have surpassed. This is why I find in Emerson, whose thought continually opens windows in my mind, an optimism belonging to his time, a local optimism, which seems alternately wise and bland. What would he – or Blake, or Whitman – say *now*? The particulars we know seem to me the broken glass cemented onto the high wall surrounding every universal system based on optimism. And of all mythological trees, the tree of the knowledge of good and evil is the only one to remain, and flourish, roots reaching down through all we would continually resurface, the bland coverings of our true face.

> '*The defect of our too great nearness to ourselves.*'

> 'My life is not an apology, but a life. It is for itself, and *not for a spectacle.*'

'People wish to be settled; only as far as they are unsettled, is there any hope for them.'

'All over the wild fields of earth grows the prunella or self-heal.'

'Everybody who is real is open and ready for that which is also real.'

(Emerson)

I would exchange many poems and books describing the English countryside for one sentence from *English Traits*: 'The grass grows dark and rank in the showery England'.

As for self-heal, I found it growing plentifully in the fields round here last autumn, and was moved superstitiously to touch the flower, as if its virtue could fill me.

Come out of that, says Emerson's wise doctor, as a prerequisite of a cure. Yes: but evidently there were states Emerson was not acquainted with, and the advice is too much like telling someone suffering from a 'nervous breakdown' to pull himself together. This robust man sees far into the general human condition, but sees little of the peculiar individuals who comprise it.

June

Midsummer: plateau of the year, time of the yellowhammer's arid, haunting song, of the hay harvest and tractors working late into the night, of foxgloves and dog-roses after the dense cool creamy hawthorn of a few weeks ago. A time when I look down across the lovely patterns of green and pale yellow fields, and across the brilliant blue sea, which at evening shines like a blade, to the softer and darker blue mountains of Lleyn, and of the mid-Wales range from Cader Idris to Plynlimmon. Look down – and find vivid scenes from the past rising in my mind. When I was about Joe's age, for instance, standing gauche and full of peevish discontent, with Mother and Pop Mould, aunty May & aunty Kitty & uncle Tom, and my brothers & cousins too, outside the shop at Park Gate, for a photograph. Driving into Aberystwyth a couple of days ago, I felt inside me, intense & disturbing, the child's gestures, arms lifted, moving restlessly from foot to foot.

This June the most sterile year of my life comes full circle; before me, the most difficult challenge. A poetry, writing of any kind, a life, all entirely without self-pity: that is essential. Only consider the universe in a grass blade or a star; consider human history in the lives of our children & of their children or in the centuries & possibly the millennia to come: how dare any person with much to be thankful for, feel sorry for himself, and expect his blinding self-absorption to be of the least significance?

Last night, after a day of suffocating heat, the red sun appeared to melt. After dark, a red, sickle moon.

July

Storm in the air all night, flickering blue & yellow round the horizon; it came close towards dawn, but rain was still only slight & occasional, not replenishing our spring, briefly laying the grey dust.

A girl of sixteen, killed in a tractor accident, is to be buried in the village churchyard this afternoon, following a chapel service. Dilwyn, who was here this morning to see how his field reseeded with grass & rape is progressing, spoke strongly against chapel, in particular the prolonged recollections & praises of the dead, which he believes only increase sorrow – 'she'll never sit in that chair again; we know that and don't have to *be told*' – and against the two services – 'as if they'd do her any good, poor dap'.

He came again later, bringing us a milkchurn scrubbed clean inside & out & full of water.

•

John D. Rosenberg in *The Darkening Glass* amply illustrates and defines the importance of Ruskin's life and work. But surely Rosenberg overestimates the tranquillity of *Praeterita*. Yes: the undeceived, clearly seeing eyes, the humorous self-knowledge, without hysteria, the serene clarity of recollected ecstasy. Yet the chastely sensual prose is frighteningly hypersensitive; and then the notes to 'Dilecta': 'I think the plague-wind blows every way, everywhere, all round the world'. 'I think the sun's going out'. As it did for Ruskin at intervals during the writing of his autobiography, and afterwards, perhaps permanently. But to make much of these notes may be to cast a shadow known from other sources on the whole book. There is, in fact, too little shadow in *Praeterita*, and too much light. The purity of water & snow, the clarity of light, these are beautiful but also disturbing – so much is seen as if by the eyes of that man fully awake of whom Thoreau and Emerson dreamed. What he sees cannot be looked at fully without fear, because nothing he sees is touched with the darkness of real sleep, of sexual consummation, or the body warmth of a mother's physical love. In such purity and clarity, rendered so lovingly, there is absence of all that bears the individual life, and therefore makes it bearable.

In Ruskin, too much light, but a fine moral and intellectual perception of modern civilisation; in Lawrence, a corrective darkness running to excess. To have a world & human relationships not closed upon themselves, not predatory, but opening upon infinity, is a desire common to both; but Ruskin's idea of culture & society seems to me both nobler and more practical than Lawrence's idea of regeneration, which is still parasitic upon the religion it half rejects, and perhaps only half understands.

Eliot returns us to the seventeenth century, Pound to the Middle Ages and ancient China, David Jones to the Catholic tradition, pre-history, Celtic history and myth, Yeats to a dream of aristocrat and peasant, to Byzantium. Yet it was in the nineteenth century, in George Elliot, Dickens, Ruskin, and others, that the democratic spirit was born to which I feel a deeper and more personal allegiance than I do to the social attitudes of any modernist. Also, it is the *realism* of Romanticism, as Rosenberg cogently defines it, that I have believed in, but without perceiving its source

•

Haunted, grey evening – whitish-grey spirals & eddies continuously, slowly, changing shape under a mass of dark grey cloud; mist in gradual flux hiding & uncovering portions of dark green uplands. Here and there, in uncanny silence, the muted voice of a bird.

Now, when even the most brutal visual images are almost mere films floating detached from realities and incapable of touching the complacent heart and stirring springs of anger and compassion, one image from recent days reached me and still remains: in the Lebanon, a massacre of the old, and of women & children, all running for safety, shot down in flight, foremost a mother with her child held under her, stone dead in the gesture of protectiveness & fearful haste.

•

To Caernarfon yesterday, for a reading with Dei Hughes and Peter Gruffydd in the old County library; Libby Lawrence playing the piano.

The reading, attended mainly by young people, was a warm occasion. To my surprise, Mari Llwyd, Joe's schoolteacher, came with her sister – daughters of the late Kitchener Davies – and it turned out that Peter Gruffydd had been Mari's teacher. It was from Ned Thomas's *The Welsh Extremist* that I first learnt of the long poem 'The Sound of the Wind That's Blowing', as it's called in English translation, that Kitchener Davies wrote when he was dying; a poem which has come to haunt me with its pain and with its terrible tension between the security of the poet's original hedged-in home in the Welsh uplands and forces (symbolized by the wind) that destroy all security.

Apart from me, the reading was a distinctively Welsh occasion, and there and afterwards, in a company crowded into Peter's parents' small council house, I saw another side of Caernarfon.

August
We went down on the fourth for Mother's 70th birthday the following day, and stayed one night at Pulborough. Crossed the Itchen on the floating-bridge from Woolston, under the giant structure of the new bridge, under construction, a series of huge Ts with arms not touching.

Drought was even more evident in the parched fields & dust of the south than it is in Wales. One day we went to the Shallows, at Boldre, and found the river bluish-green with an unhealthy, oily complexion & streamers of greasy brown weed covering the river-bed.

Paintings
for my father

Avon weir pouring
suspended, the race
brushed still, river
and sky, shadow,
sunlight and trees rushing

enclosed, opening
the house on water.

Slow Boldre,
slower Stour:
gold shallows;
dark, Forest pools

or where they run
dammed – white whorl
of an eddy, or flow
barred – green, brown

pass from seclusion
of leaf and earth,
blue oils spreading
contained:

Christchurch fluid
on the wall,
the shore at Keyhaven
where an easel stood.

Returned here via Longleat yesterday. For a moment, despite the
modern road, when the house and its vast grounds came into view
below, through trees, it was all much as it must once have been. The
illusion is momentary – but what can be said for such a monstrously
unnatural playground, except that it is undoubtedly entertaining.

Coming back this time – rowan berries bright orange, massing
haws beginning to redden, and, last night, under a round, faint-
orange moon, moist chill after heat that has the smells & feel of
autumn – I noticed more than ever differences between the two
places, Pennington and Llangwyryfon, and the south of England and
mid-West Wales. First the quiet, and the larger spaces round fewer

people here, spaces which, though of well-worked land & fields that have reverted to the wild, are less tame and domestic, less *humanized*, than southern landscapes. Of course, areas of the chalk feel wild; but their wildness is associated with early man, and provokes awe at *time*, at least as much as at the *otherness* of nature. Here, I don't feel the temporal element as strongly, but rather a nature in which man is small. How different it feels to stand in the garden at Hayford or to walk along pavements, surrounded by houses & a network of roads joining together all the villages & towns & making their amenities accessible, and to stand outside Brynbeidog feeling, quite wrongly in many ways, more isolated, in a world all the fresher for having been less domesticated!

And this feeling, I suppose, is only a faint reflection of what was general in agricultural England before the railways, when Cobbett could lose himself or travel into dangerous country in the south, and meet people who had never even heard of places a few miles from where they had been born, and where they still lived.

> 'The first place an artist should find himself is in prison. The moment he realizes he is a prisoner, he is an artist, and the moment he is an artist, he starts to free himself.'
>
> (Stanley Spencer)

•

Evening: a storm to the south, then rain falling darkly till nightfall.

September
Autumn light is especially lovely now: at Llanddewi Brefi on Saturday, at the church by the river and under the crowns of the hills, at Blaen Cwrt yesterday, as I tried to sketch while waiting for Gill and Dave and Philip Owens – blues and yellows and greens so clear far off.

At the weekend conference on the War Poets at Lampeter I met Edward Thomas's daughter, Myfanwy, who spoke kindly of what I have written about her father. Quite an old woman now, her face is much like her mother's when young, in the only photograph of Helen I have seen. Edward Thomas's great-granddaughter came to my general seminar on Sunday morning.

Meeting and talking to Gerard always makes me want to write, and feel I can. He seems always to attend only to things that really matter, and never speaks a word that doesn't count. I have learnt from him to see that the problem is metaphysical.

•

Crossed to the Island, from Lymington to Yarmouth, Solent pale creamy green, dark green, blue-green. Landmarks from west to east: Hurst Castle, Sway Tower, Lymington church and gasworks, the Burrard memorial, Pylewell House, Fawley, Calshot. At Alum Bay, the rake of the Needles, like chalk galleons. We drove round the Island, and visited Osborne House for the first time, coinciding with numerous coach parties.

Imagine the stillness when there are no visitors, only a few convalescents walking among the cedars, the state rooms' heavy & densely intricate objects, rich as a Pharaoh's tomb but with light through windows that look down over terraces of statuary to the blue Solent and the white tower blocks of Portsmouth ...

Rat Island

1
With first light
The bearings surface.

From Tennyson's memorial
To Sway Tower,
From Jack in the basket
To Fawley,
Point after point
Rises on time.

I mark them,
Borne back
On a freshening wind.

The sea completes the circle.

2
There are no rats;
Except at high spring,
No island.

Only a relic
Of the late defences
Harbouring
Mud-dwellers.

Part of the shore
That curves away,
Keen as a tern's wing.

3
I have stayed long enough
Casting a shadow.

　　Let it be
As it is
When a tern dives
And on the blue sky
In the water, between
The smooth hulls
Of mudbanks,
The wind casts waving lines.

At Ringstead yesterday morning, out in the bay with Stewart, lifting
his lobster pots, off White Nose, seeing the line of cliffs & the front
at Weymouth, the bulk of Portland in misty outline.
　　Until I go back I forget how much has happened to all of us in a
few years, as I forget details of things that do not change, and have to
write memoranda to myself, a kind of notes for my Solent poems. If
the poems are to develop, though, the pressures that will shape them
are the changes themselves.

•

Re-reading Edward Thomas, with an eye less clouded by preconceptions, and William Cooke's biography, two facts are already apparent: that I know all but a handful of the poems less well than I assumed, and that our states of depression/lack of confidence/self-consciousness are of the same family. I almost wrote 'remarkably akin', but there's nothing remarkable in the kinship.

The states are common: common as thwarted or distorted creativity in the individual and in human relationships, and in man's sense of belonging overall.

I still believe the problem was exacerbated for Thomas by his search for traditional sustenance in a nation and a countryside that no longer provided it, and where he willed himself to find 'life', but found, instead, a neither simple nor dream-like 'death'.

The problem he faced, of distinguishing the actual ground loved from false patriotism and false ideals, has been horribly complicated and strained by the sixty years or so since he sacrificed himself.

October

'At Osborne House' last weekend, then days of blankness, strain & trembling ...

After more than two years with few 'poems' written or attempted I don't know what to say or how to say it. Of course I am trying too hard and in the wrong way, caught between a moral objection to 'self-expression' – not fully thought through – and the desire to write from the heart of myself. Haunting the shore without patience, and possibly attempting to work an exhausted obsession, I catch at shadowy intimations and search too strenuously for objects that bear meaning.

Underlying all, fear of impure motivation. The place is focus of so many conflicting emotions – love and hate, anger and remorse, loyalty and betrayal – and is so many related contexts – personal, historical, cultural, geological, social, religious. And if all this is evidence of a rich ground, my agitation is that of a chronic fence-sitter, trying to straddle the personal and the impersonal, relativism and principles of unity, materialism and metaphysics.

Wanting everything, with no singleness of purpose, I find only confusion and chaotic division of aims. Too often, I smooth over the cracks, and the end is self-contempt. Lack of faith. The torment matters to me – every person has his soul to make, his capacity for love to release – but at present it seems inimical to acts of speech and making that transcend the merely personal. But perhaps if I write truly I shall write what I do not want to, find myself forced to say what I would rather leave unsaid or even not know.

I don't think the problem is lack of nerve; it is rather that I find the materials and words impose their limitations. Then I say what I can say and have probably said before, and do not release the pressures or resolve the difficulties. The inner conflict's unappeased: but what seems dishonest is perhaps the result not of loss of nerve or lack of courage, but of formal and expressive limitations. There are times when being kinder to oneself has a wiser object than peace at any price, and when self-torment is a form of evasion as well as an indulgence.

'My own heart let me more have pity on ...'

November

There is far more in 'Solent Shore' than I anticipated, nor is it at all what I expected. At times I have felt capable of saying almost everything I want to say. Then comes retrospection: some poems seem less good than I thought, none is *the* poem.

In the act of writing I want to make the poem more than it probably can be, and, if not to say everything, to make a celebration that is the very essence of the lives and places, and at the same time the quick of myself. When writing in a fever there is delight but also a painful sense of inadequacy: the world each poem attempts to embrace, and the desire to embrace, are both far more than the poem fathoms.

It may well be that I ask too much of poetry, and shall find what is required of me only when I recognise its limitations.

December

> 'Fear is a gleam of hope, the will to live, self-assertion. It is a deeply European feeling, nurtured on self-respect, the sense of one's own worth, rights, needs and desires. A man clings to what is his, and fears to lose it. Fear and hope are bound up with each other. Losing hope, we lose fear as well – there is nothing to be afraid for.'

> 'The death of an artist is never a random event, but a last act of creation that seems to illuminate the whole of his life under a powerful ray of light.'
>
> (Nadezhda Mandelstam)

Hope against Hope is like an axe which, with one blow, brings down the tree of words with all its decadent fruit. Where is the sense of reality or drop of truth? Even the question may be used as an excuse for more profitless self-questioning.

Compare Edvard Munch's *The Scream* with the scream Mrs Mandelstam writes about – it isn't possible to say simply that all who have responded as Munch did to their suffocating bourgeois society are no more than spoilt children; but it must be said that Western artists reacting against their society haven't always thought deeply about the values their reaction may betray. It is essential to distinguish between the terror of despair, the fear that is a craving for meaning in, say, a society given over to commercialism, and the terror experienced in a Reign of Terror.

There is however a danger that Europeans or Americans humbled by Solzhenitsyn, Mandelstam, and those they speak for, may, in their culpably belated awareness of Stalinist totalitarianism and of the real freedoms of the West, come to affirm the reality of all our 'freedoms' and overlook the corruption and brutality of competitive and imperialist systems.

What I come more and more to see – and this questions me – is the reality of good and evil, and that self-pity and self-regard are corrupt. Surely, to 'expect nothing and be ready for anything' is 'the key to sanity' in all circumstances, while vigilance towards humane values is enjoined on all who live where they can be exercised.

I see, above all, the difference between words and fine sentiments that are only mouthed, costing nothing, and those on which a person stands, even if they cost everything. Though *Hope against Hope* isn't a book anyone could read without being made to grow up, it adds little to Buber's lessons. And what it adds is a horrifying and deeply moving account of what happens to many people in a society in which the morality Buber represents is scorned and disregarded.

I have to live my conviction that in every instant, whether alone or acting with others, a person is answerable for all he is and all he believes. And this is true whether the judgement is God's or man's.

Gull on a Post

Gull on a post firm
In the tideway – how I desire
The gifts of both!

Desire against the diktat
Of intellect: be single
You who are neither.

As the useful one
That marks a channel, marks
Degrees of neap and spring;
Apt to bear jetties
Or serve as a mooring;
Common, staked with its like.

Standing ever
Still in one place,
It has a look of permanence.

Riddled with shipworm,
Bored by the gribble,
In a few years it rots.

Desire which tears at the body
Would fly unconstrained
Inland or seaward; settle
At will – but voicing
Always in her cry
Essence of wind and wave,
Bringing to city, moorish
Pool and ploughland,
Reminders of storm and sea.

Those who likened the soul
To a bird, did they ever
Catch the eye of a gull?

Driven to snatch,
Fight for slops in our wake.

Or voice a desolation
Not meant for us,
Not even desolate,
But which we christen.

Folk accustomed to sin,
Violent, significant death,
Who saw even in harbour
Signs terrible and just,
Hear in their cries
Lost souls of the drowned.

Gull stands on a post
In the tideway; I see

No resolution; only
The necessity of flight
Beyond me, firm
Standing only then.

1977

January

Love of a country is a physical experience; one moves in sympathy with contours, and feels textures even without touching them. So it was as we drove back through Sussex admiring frost-hardened arable fields, rough and shapely and varying in rich hues from brown almost to red, and the beautiful country of north Hampshire – Gilbert White's, and Cobbett's, and Edward Thomas's – with its hangars, woods, wooded valleys. Then on across Wiltshire, the more open rolling Downs mottled with snow, and on the border between Gloucestershire and Herefordshire, a nearly full moon rising behind hills in a greeny-blue sky – that 'duck's egg blue' Dad would never fail to point out, for as long as I can remember.

I try not to say in a poem what it is 'about', but to make its meaning implicit, and that, as often as not, is some essential reality of place, outside the generalized consciousness. Most people do not see this, and could not unless I spelled it out syllable by syllable, saying 'I feel', 'I love ...' Which would be alien to me and would probably excite disbelief anyway. After all, the south of England, unlike the north or Scotland or Wales or Ireland, is supposed to be one with the waves emanating from London; and in a sense it is, but the reality I have lived and seen is not.

Every small portion of earth with its living human society and all the forces that have made it just as it is and not like another, is a reality to one who has loved it body and soul. I wish I could make each poem burn with the life in it, and undeniably more real than any discursive statement or shout of anger or pain. What right do I have to damn those who will not see, rather than taking the blame for not making them see?

Certainly one root of this complaint is the knowledge that my position is making me an extreme individualist against my will, whereas in recent years I have desired to speak out of shared experience, giving conscious expression to a common reality. I will not go tamely the way of Edward Thomas's 'superfluous' man, not even up a highly individual cul-de-sac of alienation. The latter is anyway a colourful illusion, since being cut off from others is a common condition which poets

are either tragically unable to break out of, or lack the courage or wit
to see in its true light, or accept as a profitable selling line.

•

A still, grey morning, quite warm with only a few patches of snow
remaining on the mynydd. The wet, winter trees often look almost
black in their nakedness, and now most of the berries have been eaten
the most colourful things apart from an occasional bullfinch are
bright green moss on roadside banks and blue sky seen through
breaks in cloud.

How strange to write 1977!

When I was with Dafydd and Rhiannon one evening after
Christmas I said I still hadn't got used to the fact that we are no longer
in the Sixties and Dafydd said that for him this was true of the Fifties.

Time bewilders me comprehensively.

There's the actuality of present being, the fact of one's live self in
a particular world at a particular time, and this makes death incomprehensible. But others who felt the same are dead, and phases of
one's own life that seemed eternal are so remote that only a gesture
or word or apparently inconsequential moment can be recaptured.

What is the essential person, what is the soul?

Vernon Watkins had an experience after which he could never
again write a poem 'dominated by time'. I don't feel I could ever write
a poem that wasn't.

•

Snow overnight – the first of the New Year – and more light falls in
the morning, between intervals of brilliant sunlight which melted the
snow on branches into countless shining drops almost as bright as
the sun. Joe and I walked with the dogs – open fields a shadowy blue
in the sun, thick white clouds and soft blue sky. A buzzard mewed
plaintively, invisible over the village. Joe told me his dreams. When in
bed he sees the little trout we saw in the stream last summer, and
wolves and other animals on the wall. The wolves seem not to
frighten him, nor does any beast. I can well imagine how colourful
and vivid the pictures are.

Dragons in the Snow

Thaw to the hedgerows
left white crosses on the hill;
      the first thrush sang.

Now a buzzard cries, confirming
      silence under all.

The few bare trees are darker
for the fall that covers
      boundaries,
and in their place reveals
contrasting absolutes.

We are so small,
the boy and I, between
the snowclouds and the snow.

He starts from here,
who talks of dragons
as we walk, the first today
to leave a human sign
beside the marks of sheep and crow.

He warms me
with confiding hand
and fiery talk,
      who also start
upon the ground
of choice, the silence
answering the choice;
happy to be small, and walk,
and hear of dragons in the snow.

Gerard sometimes shakes my confidence in certain things in a way that I find disturbing, but finally stimulating.

I had expected him not only to like 'Birth', but to like it *very much*; but he reacted strongly against it, in the belief that I am bewitched by a theory of impersonality, and the poem is clinical, concerned mainly with natural process in a spirit akin to the scientific. And while I think he has misunderstood it, he may have understood my tendency better than I have.

At any rate, he leaves me with the necessary task of rethinking the whole business of the personal and the impersonal as it affects every aspect of existence, and with the suspicion that I may have confused dislike of the 'confessional' mode with an inadequate idea of the importance of the person. After all, it's personal integrity I admire both in poets who rarely use the first person singular – Eliot, David Jones – and in poets who use it effectively, without illegitimate special pleading – Hardy, Edward Thomas.

I think Gerard's right in insisting that the real issue is whether one accepts a personal Creator, or a universe determined by impersonal forces, or unconsciously combines irreconcilable alternatives.

What Nietzsche in *The Birth of Tragedy* says about the 'I' of the lyric poet rooted in the ground of being probably has some bearing on what I do, almost blindly, when writing with most integrity.

Whatever the truth of the matter, Gerard's letter has halted my growing complacency about some things written recently, and indicates a way of taking my questioning and essential dissatisfaction to a deeper level.

'If I justify myself, mine own mouth shall condemn me.'
(Job 9.20)

•

As I read Dr Phillips's manuscript, 'Mynydd Bach: The Intruders', about the formation of the squatters' settlement at Trefenter and the three Englishmen, including Brackenbury ('Sais Bach') who came during the 19th century to live in the area, I begin to see my surroundings with new eyes and gain a sense of their history.

Sais Bach had Lon Sais named after him. The little Englishman and Englishman's Road! At least one fellow countryman, Augustus

Brackenbury, gentleman, found, in the earlier part of the proud
century, his stature and pretensions harshly measured by a community that did not intend to grant him the position he assumed. The
analogies with the present are as suggestive and instructive as the differences. Perhaps I might have the time and the knowledge one day
to write a book about the historical relationship between the Welsh
and the English, and about their views of each other. But what seems
more essential for me is to write as an English poet living in Wales. I
am inhibited, as yet, by lack of confidence to write of myself as either
Englishman or poet. There's the continuing problem of the first
person singular, and no oblique approach that releases me from inhi-
bition has suggested itself yet.

from **Englishman's Road**
(a poem for radio)

Take a long view from Mynydd Bach: let your eye rise and fall with
ridges that stone walls or bent thorns follow – green dragon backs,
crested like petrified breakers; yet also the walls are always climbing
or in flight.

This is a country of vast spaces: it rolls with hidden hollows to the
mountains of the north, against the sweep of sea –

    preternatural grey,
    the mountains of Llyn
    a chain of islands,
    or blue as spirit flame,
    or a lunula of beaten gold.

Here the buzzard with broad wings spread draws a widening circle,
ringing an intricate pattern of commons and enclosures, white-
washed farms and red-roofed barns.

    At night an irregular pattern of lights reflects the stars.
    Here the western light is always changing, too quick for the eye

though it notes

> grey mystery
> of April, haunted
> by the curlew's salty cry,
> or August
> floating the hills,
> or Winter
> with a hard whiteness
> hammering the ground.

And what the light changes is only a face – face of a work vaster and more laboured than the pyramids; but continuing. For this is settled country, its pattern absorbent, deeply ingrained, but unfinished; without the finality of a coiled fossil, though it too is a work wrought in rock. And here these English words play on a surface through which they cannot shine, to illumine its heart; they can possess the essence of this place no more than the narrow road under the Welsh mountain can translate its name.

> Lon Sais it is called,
> not Englishman's Road.

Clear night of starlight and moonlight; clear cold day when the frost never entirely melts. Icicles on briars & branches hanging in the Beidog where sunlight dances – all the pure things I associate with the word 'soul'; and it is as if the things themselves, even if one does not or cannot conceive of a Creator, look at the person and challenge him, asking: 'In all your labyrinth of sentences and clouded days, where are you true to your nature as sky to sky, stone to stone?' It is essential to regain, with humility, that child-like ability to have the sun present in the word sun.

•

Then a dream casts me back ...

In the dream the emotion of that time, but as if strained through later facts, as she eludes me and I seek, longing, through a strangely altered council estate and village, which I seem to have dreamed of before. And of course John is there, then not there, and I seek him knowing he will know where she is.

When I wake, the village, the common, and the immediate area are in my mind, and I feel, briefly, deep loss ...

Simple, but not simple ...

Never again to belong as then, unselfconsciously, pursuing an end with single emotion, thoughtless of anything beyond the hour and the place. Not broodings on the soul and desire to refine myself to one pure light, like a drop of melting snow, but life lived in the heat of emotion.

But there could be no return unless time were arrested, and I know after a moment's reflection, that without my betrayal there would have been another life, possibly in another place.

February

A phonecall from *The Times Literary Supplement*: Would I be interested in reviewing David Jones's *Letters to Vernon Watkins* for a two page spread on books of Welsh interest? Certainly, with pleasure, but does it matter that I've already reviewed it for *The Anglo-Welsh Review*? The young man with the sophisticated, rather languid voice at the other end of the line has never heard of *The Anglo-Welsh Review*. Nor of Rene Hague's study of David Jones, nor of mine. No doubt they were given to a reviewer who didn't think them worth noticing, or carried off to be sold among the mass of books no one wants to review.

•

Walking beside the flooded Arun, I looked across at the misty, shapely line of the Downs: 'And this, too, has been one of the dark places of the earth'. The river shines long & serpentine on the floor of the broad valley, and the effects of light are beautiful & mysterious while the Downs, at a distance, look more primeval than ever.

A particular smile, gestures, the sounds of voices: nothing more real than these, or better loved; they live in me and remain both part of the tissue of my life and painfully elusive. The deepest meanings are impossible to describe – how one sees the essence of a loved person, in a glance that releases the springs of one's being and fills one with delight at the glory & mystery of existence, which thought alone cannot comprehend.

March
First curlew, and the first lark singing, on a soft, warm morning.

•

First morning in my study (grand word, in contrast to the precious, slowly deteriorating caravan), a fine room with a view! Of Cwm Beidog, where gorse flowers are brightening and the slate roofs of Llwyn Bedw shine after rain, beside the broad field sloping to Mynydd Bach, on which immense slow cloud, with a bright sun break, moves along the ridge.

Here I shall begin by completing a review of Gwyn Williams's *The Land Remembers*, almost in sight of his home at Treweithan.

•

How petty seem most of the things I record when looked back on. Not quite petty, but strange, sometimes to the extent of seeming unreal. Is it that a sloping hand carries one downhill, or indicates the passage of time so that the words appear still to be running on the spot long after the impulse that gave rise to them has been spent? Then, for all their apparent movement, and partial expression and partial recollection of the original urgency, the 'I' often seems a stranger's, and, instead of the one charged image, in which the live person is present and stands by his word, there is stasis – a sepia photograph of the long-dead. It is this experience of never capturing the thing I seek, of never writing words 'graven with an iron pen and lead in the rock for ever', that urges me on to write. Aye, but what a hopeless, ever-pressing pursuit! A pursuit whose hopelessness one admits and yet denies while following it.

It is my life whose flame I want to burn in my words, mine & the people & things I love. I-alone cannot stand firm and at the same time blaze with its essence; it can only be static and self-consuming. Thus, in the genuine poem the 'I' ceases to be the subject and the poem with its own inner necessity takes over, becoming a creative act in which the 'I' vanishes, or becomes implicit, or is reshaped as maker of an utterance it could not foresee.

•

Tiny creamy buds on the blackthorn and a few in flower.
　　Conversation with Joe as we are about to climb a fence:
　　– You know, Dad, I know so many things.
　　– Yes, I'm sure you do. Tell me something you know.
　　– O (pausing to consider) ... I've forgotten.

•

After two cold days with frost in the mornings and a night of strong winds, there were patches of snow on the ridge this morning. Walked to Trefenter in the afternoon – against a high wind blowing rainy mist across the grey-green landscape – and on the way back talked to Fred Jones, Maesbeidog. He was out at 2 in the morning, attending to a sick cow and at that time snow was driving over the house.

Saw Brynbeidog in perspective again, from the gateway above Llwyn Bedw, after keeping for too long to near fields. Now, this window will give a small bright light in the fold under the mountain, infinitely small in the broad hollow between the uplands of central Ceredigion and the mountains of north Wales. It will appear like a low star to our neighbours, as their lights do to us.

Brynbeidog

For ten years the sycamores
have turned about us, the Beidog
has run with leaves, and ice and sun.
I have turned the earth, thrown up
blue chip and horseshoe; from near fields
sheep and bullocks have looked in.

We have shared weathers
with the stone house; kept its silence;
listened under winds lifting slates
for a child's cry; all we have
the given space has shaped, pointing
our lights seen far off
as a spark among scattered sparks.
        The mountain above
has been rock to my drifting mind.

Where all is familiar, around us
the country with its language
gives all things other names;
there is darkness on bright days
and on the stillest a wind
that will not let us settle,
but blows the dust from loved
things not possessed or known.

May
Bright sunlight early on May Day, shadows of new sycamore leaves
moving like small hands on a bank. These red leaves are wrinkled, like
the skin of a newborn baby. I suppose all forms of life are, that
emerge from confinement in a dark & narrow space. I managed at
last to plant the last potatoes, beans & peas after weeks of almost continuous rain.

A storm came up at noon; hailstones whitened the ridge.

Shifted piles of letters & papers from the caravan to my room in the afternoon. As always, the sadness of looking over such things – and something else besides: all the bits & pieces that, in retrospect, compose a life, or – especially with writings – reveal all the false starts & wrong turnings, the apparent lack of direction & of singleness.

> 'It is a most earnest thing to be alive in this world; to die is not sport for a man. Man's life never was a sport to him; it was a stern reality, altogether a serious matter to be alive!'
>
> (Carlyle)

Why should the statement of so plain a truth be so heartening? It is what I have always felt and thought. Yet to find it written is thrilling.

If our world is more complex than Carlyle's, *if* our thought has to be more subtle and tentative, still the life and death issue is as it always was: whether or not we shape our lives earnestly, purposefully, by grounding them upon reality.

•

First cuckoo, faintly, on the first fine day after heavy rain. To think of them coming unerringly through darkening downpour and storm, as the leaves and the gorse and the may have come, regardless of cold and the sodden earth!

Back at college, enjoying it all in a relaxed atmosphere. Towards the end of my leave I was beginning to will myself to write, and so did almost nothing worthwhile. What the things done amount to I can't really tell – not what I expected, of course; nor, perhaps, the kind of 'release' I wanted. I have done what I could. One thing has led to another. More than once, the conviction of being written out has proved groundless.

'The end of Man is an action, and not a Thought.'

•

Week of hot, dry days after rain. Now the earth is parched again, all the water having drained through deep cracks opened by last year's drought. Already heath and forest fires are starting.

Mid-May was even more beautiful than usual, by contrast with the preceding dull weeks – in the colours and freshness of leaves, grass, bluebells, gorse, in the sky and atmosphere, in the new moon gold with reflected light.

Jonathan Raban's recent radio play, *The English Department*, was based on a finals' examiners' meeting in our department. It was a predictable caricature, not of colleagues alone, but of Jonathan's 'life-illusion' as the clever young lecturer whose modern ideas disrupt dull tradition. Not a good play, but his voice brought back those days, when we worked together here, their misery, brittleness, and companionship.

And it brought back earlier days, when we were teenagers in Pennington – when he came to meet me on my Christmas post round, waving a copy of Hopkins's poems; when we talked books endlessly in pubs; and when he was so impressed by my black desperation at eighteen. Nor can I help seeing the logic behind his use of radio and television, and feeling some envy, not of his achievement – our abilities have always been different – but of the communication it makes possible.

•

Dad has the garden in fine shape, with masses of vegetables – early potatoes almost ready to lift – and flowers. He says he feels better than ever and has the time to garden and to paint which he never had before retiring. He is seventy-six this year, nevertheless, and has appointed me his executor.

I saw Jim twice, at The Monkey House, and John, too, on the second evening. Felt rather out of place, however, especially on Saturday evening when Jim and his group were singing. Only a few nights before I had said to Sue that I would be happiest to live in a small place at East Boldre, where Jim and John live now, work at gardening or in a nursery and have a few drinks with them in the evenings.

It must be ten years or more since I was last in the south at this time of year and heard the cuckoo and the woodpigeons in the garden at Hayford. We saw the white and pink candles of chestnuts; the tall cow parsley and creamy hawthorn was nowhere more abundant than in Lower Pennington on the way to Oxey, and along Normandy Lane. Sue went out with the children very early on Saturday morning and found the house near the shore, at the bottom of Tanner's Lane, for sale. She even got the papers from the estate agents – they are asking £20,000 for it and it is in a poor state of repair, with no electricity or drainage. This is a place we have looked at and dreamed of living in one day. I can't believe that will ever be, or think it desirable – but sensible words don't stop wishes, even though I feel and see how much the area has changed in ten years, and how difficult it is for those with a sense of belonging like mine not to feel strangers.

It is one thing to stand near the Community Centre in Lymington and smell the air blowing off the meadow grass at Walhampton across the river, or to see the Island in haze from the Salterns, and quite another to try to live there, by some vision that isn't dominated by commercial success.

It is easier for me, after a couple of drinks, to repeat 'Friend with a Mandolin' to myself, feeling rather sorry for myself in a not unpleasant way, than to see how the life it celebrates could be made actual ever again. Yet I have wanted this, and can still want it, more than anything else. It is too easy, in reaction, to say *all* was a dream, all was a retarded adolescence – and easier because some of it was, and is.

Evening – curlews trilling wildly, a high excited note, over the fields of Hafodlas and a three-quarters moon with the sunlight on it. This, all this – and still I long for the rich English countryside, for bright mustard fields and roadside cow parsley, which are almost absent here. The longing has always been partly physical – for those landscapes – and partly for a real life among my own people. But it could not be had simply, and whatever I have to give cannot be given simply.

June

Pink campions after stitchwort, foxgloves suddenly in flower – or perhaps simply not seen during days of marking & examiners' meetings. Pink and white dog-roses, sweet on delicate sprays, petals quickly scattered. Plentiful sticky blebs of cuckoo-spit on stems of sweet-smelling grass, which is warm to lie on. June dark and cavernous among trees, birds already falling silent.

Yesterday morning I went with Gill to a seminar on Poetry and Politics with R.S. Thomas and Seamus Heaney, which Walford

Davies had organized in the Extra-Mural Department. This after waking up angry and brooding, as often recently – angry with R.S. for his anti-Englishness, resentful of Seamus for not replying to a letter. Meeting them again, especially Seamus, I at once saw the folly of my grudges. Bitterness vanished in an instant, at his warmth and naturalness, his genuineness as a poet. Here was someone talking a language I understand, talking in his way, profoundly, imaginatively, intelligently, but setting me free to talk the same language in my way, without academic constraint, or the strain of either suppressing it or translating it into bloodless and abstract terms. (And who could remain angry with R.S. in the presence of his integrity and of the intensity which affects his voice and makes his hands tremble even when he seems more or less relaxed, as he did on this occasion?)

July

Rain falling hard – a fast patter on the roof and a wet swishing noise among sycamore leaves shaken and turned over by the wind; the mountain a lightly veiled greeny-grey across green fields, and, below, narrow yellow canals and cuttings beside the house, in JCB tracks where John Williams has sliced the bank and moved topsoil off the clay.

In a few hours I shall be leaving for a weekend school at Dyffryn House, where I shall hold seminars and lecture on *Wolf Solent* and *Mr Weston's Good Wine*. The usual anxious prospect: the desire to be among friends and the hope of acquitting myself creditably, countered by the familiar shrinking back.

Wolf Solent thinks Jason Otter has no life-illusion. But how can anyone write poetry without it being inseparable from whatever sustaining idea of himself he has, even if his aim is to strip appearances from every reality?

•

Set out in a downpour on Friday and drove over the Beacons in dense mist. But the weekend, like today, was hot & almost cloudless midsummer. This was especially welcome in the lanes near Dyffryn House, where cow parsley grows high by the roadside and groups of tall overshadowing trees stretch across rich fields. There, on our free afternoon, I walked with Gerard & Mary Casey & Timothy Hyman to the burial chamber of Tinkiswood, where we sat talking in the cool shadowy interior, under stone powdered with pale green & orange lichen, with a view of the Mendips across the invisible Channel. Gill met us on the way back and I walked with her in the fields before my lecture.

On the way back from the school I gave Walter Haydn Davies a lift, and he navigated us across country and then on the Merthyr road to Quaker's Yard, where he visited the old burial ground. Since his wife died, four years ago, he has been a constant attender at conferences, at which, if he were not so dignified and courteous, he would be almost embarrassingly grateful for what he says we give him. And he is to be seen buttonholing fellow participants to talk interestingly about his life and books, and hardly anyone ever declines to buy a copy. Now, as we passed Llantrisant and drove along a narrow road, stopping at traffic lights, he sang, at my request, quite beautifully, in a low clear voice, many verses of the folk song about the Pontypridd collier, who visits every mining community in the Valleys in search of his errant wife. He had had the song from an old farmer – which I suppose indicates how closely the experiences of industry and of agriculture have interacted in that area. And for me, as we drove among traffic in the heat, the song and the singer provided an emotional insight into that life, as no amount of books or even personal reminiscences could have done. My last view of him, in the driving mirror, was of a small man in a smart raincoat worn over his Sunday clothes despite the heat, picking up his suitcase and rolled umbrella and walking off to pay his respects to the Quakers in their burial ground.

•

One evening last week I had a drink with Glen Bard, a lively & likeable young American who is working on David Jones and J.C. Powys at Bangor. We went to The Black Lion, the Aberystwyth pub frequented by younger Welsh nationalists, and I was shocked by the virulence and ugliness of their anti-Englishness. Of course, I am over-sensitive in this respect. But it was the ugliness of the emotions, more than their object, that I found depressing. And this was a strong reminder, not just of the foul-mouthed anger and baseless conceit of our boozy sessions in and around Lymington and Southampton in the early Sixties, but of present deep-seated egotism – that which in me and in most people makes us, when thoroughly known, essentially unlovable in our incorrigible self-love. I saw the ugliness vividly as I drove home on a fine night, between tall grasses, with moths fluttering drunkenly in the narrow path of light. I saw, too, how 'innocent' I have become – of the worst in me and in others – from living such a hermetic existence. I have thought too abstractly of good and evil, but then, at least for a time, I knew evil, not as something Satanic and rather picturesque, but as ugliness and depravity. And I lay awake knowing it rooted in my flesh and in my mind, that will not see, but is often satisfied to think its narrow bounds a generous and expansive world.

•

Hot days, blue sheep's-bit against yellow hawkweed on dry banks, honeysuckle and cool roses. On Saturday we helped Dafydd carry a few loads of hay, Tommy Morgan driving the tractor and Joe and Emily riding back with Sue on the bales, bumping along beside hedgerows, crossing the stream where oak branches brushed against them.

And now at last I am collecting and revising my critical & personal essays written between 1969 and 1975.

•

Walked with Joe to school on a lovely morning, at first in an ill temper, cursing and shouting and waving a stick at the dogs to drive them back home, then relaxing as we strode down Clark's fields to the narrow lane of sun-dried mud and stones that passes his farm and emerges opposite the church. Came back more leisurely, but seeing little through a mental cloud until a scuffling above me, in a thicket of hazels & blackthorn, revealed a number of calves in the shade, some looking down, with that expression of extraordinarily innocent curiosity, their ears sticking out. The light was behind them, breaking through branches & leaves & between their legs, and in the foreground, gnats – particles of gold dust – were dancing. Then I saw keys on the sycamores beside the stream, some yellow & some reddish-gold, and a few scattered on the ground, curved like arms meeting above the head or like pincers. How little I see, half comatose as the days pass! Now a new opening has been made into the field below Pencwmbeidog and immediately above the waterfall, providing a new vista. In places like this, an event that changes the familiar configuration of forms is momentous, and for a time the new opening quickens and excites vision and the new entrance invites exploration. And yet, how little I see! Now there are yellow fields among the green, bales arranged like megaliths on the stubble, and shadows thickening and darkening under trees separating the fields.

Suppose a long vigil some fine evening in July, as the air becomes colder with dew and the slow fading of earth's warm smell, as the sky towards dark becomes almost unbearably pure and then immeasurably deeper with increase of stars; how far would the cleansed eyes see, which are partially blind even to appearances? And would the discipline become a habit of vision, as the mind is habitually in a mist of desires and memories, associations and inchoate or repetitive thoughts, and comes awake only occasionally when a perception of some fraction of the world existing outside it clears its opaque element? Such opacity, not of deep water, but rather of windows blackened by the smoke of habit; and it is often the sweat of physical activity that clears the eyes, and the spirit comes alive, interacting with the world to create a finer relationship.

As a Thousand Years

Not a soul, only
a stubble field, bales
like megaliths; a flight
of trees over the Beidog,
and behind, darker green,
at the back of the sky,
the ridge damming
the sun; then,
for a breath,
there was no sign of us.
Not a soul, only
light flooding this field,
bright as a marigold.

To love, to be awake, to be alive, in this long repetitive dream which is really so brief – that's the hardest discipline.

•

Solent Shore has been accepted by Carcanet, with a letter from Robert Wells, the kindest & most perceptive I have ever had about my poems from a stranger.

•

Lying in bed this morning we saw a fox – red as a fresh horse-chestnut – hunting in long grass in the field. At first I could only see its sharp ears sticking up. Then it leapt into the air, but seemed to miss whatever it had aimed for, and proceeded to cross leisurely to the hedge, looking down & round.

August
South for just under a week, returning a day early, after Joe had knocked in his first upper teeth on a play-horse in Rook's Gardens and with Emily lying very quiet in the back of the car with the onset of measels.

On the way down, we stopped for lunch beside a little-used track near Edge in Gloucestershire, high in the Cotswolds. Close-by there was a peculiar solitary memorial: a tower without roof or doors, part small church & part castle, like a folly. Among knapweed & yellow grasses, looking down into hollows with no building visible except the steep roof of a farmhouse, and looking round at the hills, at rooks riding on the wind, in mist, over trees & limestone walls, I had a sudden relaxing sense of being deep in England, which came also with the fresh wind off cultivated fields, and with the mist that made all seem mysterious and even more secluded than it was.

All along the coast every name is a poem – Sowley, Norleywood, Tanner's Lane, East Boldre, Pylewell, Walhampton, Hordle, Milford. Not impressionistic only, nor in the name alone, but arising variously from each deeply lived-in place. And this reality is everywhere, to be known by the person who lives it, with love but without sentimentality;

who concentrates, but not with a head-in-the-ground blindness to all that has shaped it, and all that continually arrives to affect what is there ...

But even as I write this, I know it is *not* what I have done. Instead, I have seen the places in the poems from a distance that is more than geographical. And I have written this, like so much recently, feeling acutely inhibited, torn between true response and awareness of a love that selects a sense of being 'deep in England' from all that is actually there. So many recent tensions derive from this need to affirm a true and responsible national identity without simplifying the difficulties and confusions, or selecting a version of the past and of locality that excludes all tensions of race & class, & widespread hatred, frustration & demoralization. And yet to say: 'this is what I truly feel; differences of place remain, and are capable of expressing new creative meanings for those who will give themselves to them, but without stiffening in a social & political posture that is hostile to races & peoples humili-ated and exploited by those who think this more peaceful England is their rightful possession'.

After arriving back at Brynbeidog, car unpacked, children in bed: the silence rarely heard except at returning.

Hill Country Rhythms

for Robert Wells

Sometimes I glimpse a rhythm
I am not part of, and those who are
could never see.
    The hawk I disturb
at his kill, leaving bodiless,
bloody wings spread, curves
away and with a sharp turn
follows the fence; and the fence
lining a rounded bank flies
smoothly downhill, then rises

to wind-bowed trees whose shape
the clouds take on, and the ridge
running under them, where
the sky bears round in a curve.
On the mountainside stands
a square white farm, its roof
a cutting edge, but it too
moves with shadow and cloud.
    I glimpse this
with the hawk in view, lose it
to fenceposts and trees holding
a still day down, and wings
dismembered at my feet, while
down the road comes a neighbour
singing loudly, with his herd
big-uddered, slowly swaying.

September
A weekend with Emyr and Elinor Humphreys at the annual Academi Gymreig conference. The love, compassion and acute perceptiveness of the novels are his qualities and Elinor's.

Speaking of Evelyn Waugh, Emyr described 'the black dog' as 'the English disease'. At the time I thought it a neat reversal of Matthew Arnold's generalization about Celtic melancholy, but not without feeling its personal application.

Raymond Williams gave a fine lecture on the growth of the industrial novel. Later I spoke briefly to him, expressing my admiration of *The Country and the City* and his writings on Hardy's 'border country'.

•

Autumn – a thread of gold visible fitfully, hanging in the air.

Walking to Welsh class in the village school on a beautiful evening, from a gate near Pen Gelli – the sea directly under the sun, a shining half circle of watery gold.

This morning, the fox again, crossing the field.

•

> 'A poet-existence in the direction of the religious ... it is the sin of poeticizing instead of being, of standing in relation to the Good and the True through imagination instead of being that, or rather existentially striving to be it.'
>
> (Søren Kierkegaard, *The Sickness unto Death*)

October
How complacently we may speak of the search for God, as if all cultures were our supermarket, when we do not believe that God is our hunter.

November
Coming home tense after a tiring day, I glance in the driving mirror, and see my father's face.

December
End of an exhausting term, the busiest since my first year of teaching. Yesterday evening in the village school we watched the children singing and reciting in Welsh and the older ones performing a Nativity play – wise men with crowns made of cake wrappings or out of crackers, shepherds with tea cloths over their heads but carrying real crooks that were too big for them. The minister introduced the evening with a prayer. Strange coming out of my books & lectures & daily preoccupations to this, not the charm and pleasure of the occasion, but the event it celebrates and each person is asked to assent to. Easy to make the gesture, sitting with head bowed and at the end bitterly regretting my want of a decent voice to join in the singing, but in myself a blankness, a shadowy doubt underlying the passivity – simply the fact of neither properly belonging nor responding to the real cause of the occasion. So many words draw elaborate patterns where there is no fixed centre.

In a Welsh Primary School

for Mari Llwyd

Around me, elements
of this place form a world,
with dragons, flowers,
flying houses on the walls;
shepherds with real crooks
and kings with tinsel crowns.
Here I also come to learn,
and know the same care
Gwion knows, Aled, Ifor
and the rest; and glimpse
through mist between
two languages,
the kindest things of Wales.

Mari, though I stand outside,
may I be numbered still
with all who give you praise.

1978

January

Since yesterday, when I planted the pear & apple-trees that Dad sent for Christmas, it has started to snow. As I drove back from Aberystwyth this afternoon the flakes got bigger and fell more thickly towards Mynydd Bach. Now in the dusk the hillsides are a patchy dull white, divided by hedges, under a heavy sky.

•

The brief freedom of a walk: rain falling & running down roadsides & in ditches, flattening grasses all in one direction; rain dripping from a gate & bushes into grey sky mirrored in small pools of hoof marks, trodden in brown mud. How beautiful rain & standing or running rainwater are in their freshness & nakedness, and damp, rose-like bosses of greeny-grey lichen on a decaying gate.

February

Ice on a pool by the field gate bore me, pale brown pony droppings were frozen together, hard as stones. I can't remember ever having seen so many icicles in the Beidog, hanging from brambles like teats on an udder, and from trailing willow branches, sometimes almost as smoothly round as blown glass. Electric shocks of brilliant white sunlight pulsed on the water. At night, a sharp new moon.

•

Ground hard as a hammerhead & a light dusting of snow on sloping fields where three brown, wall-eyed mountain ponies come to look at me. They are glad of a diversion in the cold bare windy fields, probably hope for food, and are restless between friendly curiosity and fear.

A cartridge case held upright by ice on a pool, like a red funnel. No doubt Dai Morris's, shooting snipe.

Lawrence's kind of critical judgement is repugnant to me. But it unmasks fear, discloses an underlying malaise, sacrifices individual feelings to a cutting, cleansing wind. And this seems to have been inseparable from his release of his powers, while kindness and cow-ardice may corrupt equally, and what seems kindness may be a form of cowardice.

But Lawrence is finally apocalyptic, outside everything except his marriage, alone, or alone with Frieda and the quick of nature, but *in* his vital being. His love of England, his pride, bitter anger, and superb intelligence, were among the forces that made him stand outside, viewing the communal human world as a planet doomed to extinction. I don't believe in that passage, the exploratory being real-izing itself outside community, but feel what Lawrence meant by the destructive old life which most of us, setting out independently, fall back on and repeat.

I quarrel with Lawrence's impatience, his dismissive contempt, and the way in which *his* disconnection affected his view of England and industrial society. But I cannot evade the challenge of his quarrel with England, the force of his vision, the strength and integrity of his feeling, or his real intelligence.

•

Strong wind gusting at night, whistle & shriek, lifting slates which smash on the path. This morning the wind is still quite strong, and cold, and the fields have a swept, wasted, exhausted look. Except the wind, no noise but a sheep's, sheltering with lambs under a thorn hedge, its loud bleat more like a crow's caw, but harsher. There's a greyness about everything under the wind.

•

Emily on her third birthday insists she is two, pushing the small, blue pram I gave her.

March
First curlew on the fifth, a solitary cry from the fields of Hafodlas. I burnt a pile of sticks & rubbish to fine, white ash, and dug again on the second beautiful day, earth a rich dark-brown, soft after a night of frost. It is enough ...

•

How then to break out of the enclosure, introspection?

April

On the flank of Plynlimmon to our right as we climbed, a row of
scarecrows, one in particular standing against the sky, a stark black
cross. The river in its deep cleft ran clear & fast over green stones, a
magnificent sculptor of the rock, which was smoothed or hollowed
into round potholes, made into rounded boulders or square blocks. A
landscape oppressive in its bleakness, beautiful in details of grey rock
& black peat, in vast upsweeping spaces, the only life a few small birds
& many lambs & sheep. As I reached the windy summit before the
others, and saw the country below for the first time, four jets came out
of cloud and swept past, so close it seemed I could almost touch them.

Nowhere except on the sea is the interaction of darkness & light
as visible as it is on the mountains, and tangible, too, for shadows
darkening rocks & rough grass emphasise their texture.

•

Three fine days when Jim was here, and at last, yesterday afternoon,
we planted potatoes, peas & beans. Then this morning – snow. A
dense fall of fine pellets swirling in the wind, lightly covering the
ground in minutes. When I walked out it came on strongly, rattling
against my anorak, quickly becoming a white cloud closing round
me. Turning back down the field, hands & face hurting sharply, I
groped my way almost blind.

•

A large hare with black-tipped ears jumped up from under my
feet in Dilwyn's field, and thudded away, scrambling up the bank &
sliding back again several times before getting over, while the dogs
were oblivious, sniffing in a corner about twenty yards away.

•

Cycled round the village & then to Trefenter via Esgair Hill & Lon

Sais. A wash of white cloud in blue sky. Mountains of Lleyn dimly visible, sea pale blue but silver under the sun, echoed by the dazzling surfaces of a few roofs – hardly more than points in the wide stretch of country between Trefenter and Cardigan Island. Strange to reflect that Sais Bach must sometimes have seen it like this.

Curlews – frustration at my annual failure to catch them in a poem drove me out, to see and hear them again on the higher uplands. I want the impossible – that haunting cry in words. Better just to let it be, relaxing the tension of straining to catch it.

Curlew

The curve of its cry –
A sculpture
Of the long beak:
A spiral carved from bone.

It is raised
    quickening
From the ground,
Is wound high, and again unwound,
    down
To the stalker nodding
In a marshy field.

It is the welling
Of a cold mineral spring,
Salt from the estuary
Dissolved, sharpening
The fresh vein bubbling on stone.

It is an echo
Repeating an echo
That calls you back.

It looses
Words from dust till the live tongue
Cry: This is mine
Not mine, this life
Welling from springs
Under ground, spiralling
Up the long flight of bone.

> 'When Blake said, "Tho' I call them Mine, I know that they are
> not Mine", he meant that when the artist is creatively successful
> the creativity to which the achievement belongs is not his,
> though, while transcending the person he is, it needed his
> devoted and supremely responsible service. The creative power
> and purpose don't reside within his personal self-enclosure; they
> are not his property or in his possession. He serves them, not
> they him. The pride that Blake defends as a virtue is conscious
> and resolute responsibility. It goes with the belief in human cre-
> ativity that is not hubris.'
>
> (F.R. Leavis, *The Living Principle*)

I find Leavis's emphasis on the difference between identity and
selfhood, together with his insistence on the collaborative creativity of
language, especially timely and instructive. It makes me both see that
the hostility to him which even parts of this book provoke has blinded
me to the strength and relevance of his thought. The truth he emphasises is encouraging and sustaining: it implies a clear distinction
between confidence and vanity, and indicates that lack of confidence
apparently arising from personal defeatism may in fact rest on lack
of faith in human creativity. It applies to the isolating and self-enclos-
ing 'romantic' attitudes I have seen and analysed, but whose effects
continue; and it strengthens my resolve to eradicate them, at the same
time as it shows the grounds on which to proceed.

•

Cuckoo on the twenty-eighth, this year with, or perhaps just past, the
curlews at their height. Dafydd says the swallows came a week ago.
This is a late spring, or a late early summer – for there is a time

between the beginning and full growth, when quickening affects every sense, and is so distinctive that it seems to demand another name. Even now only one sycamore has open leaves, and others are at various stages between the thrust of long buds and leaves unfolding. Blackthorn is in flower with the plum, and primroses are still fresh, together with masses of dandelions – brilliant, richly warm, risen suns – at roadsides. I am using every hour to write, with a vigour & confidence not felt for eighteen months, whatever the result. Natural I suppose for it to be either there or not there: part of life's rhythm, and also a kind of visitation that can be encouraged or inhibited.

May

> '*If, as seems possible, civilisations tend to destroy themselves within a century or so of becoming communicative*, then our own may be the most developed civilisation in our Galaxy; but if civilisations last for a million years or more, there may be more than 100,000 communicative civilisations, of which the Earth would qualify, almost inevitably, as the most backward.'
>
> (*The Guardian*, 3/5/78)

•

Robert Wells has sent me a copy of Donald Davie's review of *Solent Shore*. It's perhaps not the generosity alone that's so moving, though that in itself is an uncommon gift, but the generous expression of an attentive & perceptive *reading*; and so of that creative sharing which to me is the supreme value.

•

Welsh class in the evening, after the first sunny day this month. A painful blankness brought back forgotten times at school, when Mari read a story I couldn't follow and we had to answer questions about it in writing. Came out to the smell of earth, and watched the fine horn of the new moon, a blood-red sliver, sinking in cloud at the horizon, clear sky lit by a wide spread of flashing stars.

•

At Heptonstall. Blackened shell of the old church beside the new, ground between them paved with gravestones, almost all old & grey, with many still standing, round & flat-faced, hardly any earth to be seen and a strong impression that grass & other green things are rare in that dark place. I looked half-heartedly for Sylvia Plath's grave, but soon gave up searching; the impulse seemed morbid, with clean greyness under a hot sky & dust & dead centuries underfoot.

Much of the north of England is now a monument to 19th century industry and either derelict or serving other purposes – like the commuter properties of Hebden Bridge – but with a large native & immigrant population making it intensely lived in. Already factories & warehouses & chimneys seem to be acquiring something of that character of a vanished civilisation that barrows & henges have in the south, though this is, at least in part, a sentimental illusion, for where the industries themselves are no longer working, the effects of that system are still ingrained in our society. I see this as a southerner, but with a strong sense that the real & continuing history has been generally excluded from literary & official concepts of Englishness – or simply, that it is all much deeper than many of the images rising from it, let alone what has been admitted by sophisticated consciousness south, and perhaps even north, of the Trent. Yet I see it, inevitably, from the outside, straining to imagine the reality that can't be known except by those who live it.

Night: the mottled face of a smoky orange full moon slowly appears behind Mynydd Bach, and rises clear to the calls of a cuckoo close at hand.

•

Why should any writer now concern himself with place? Given the shadow we are all under, threatening absolute sameness in nonentity; given easy mobility between continents which for some is a way of life, and planetary communications. Yet for the vast majority of people throughout the world the local is still touchstone of the real. It is then a cruel irony that few of them should read writing that finds its roots in place, whose authors and readers often belong with those who are alienated from the reality they seek to sustain them.

•

Cloudy sky like wave-marked white sand with a scattering of blue pools.

Long yellowy-green flowers hang from the sycamores which hum all day with countless flies & bees.

Days of freshness & life beyond words. Waking early I still find the day has been awake long before me, and there's a sense that something is already over. That which is just outside apprehension, but unreachable, where nature is full – leaves shining green, everywhere the glisten of life – is it failure of attention that makes it elusive, or greedy possessiveness, instead of quietly knowing oneself in some sense part of it? Or does it show not just the partial nature of perception, but the individual's inevitable incompleteness? Yet I don't find these days sad; rather, being is continually filling like a spring, when I walk about in the sun or sit and listen. Frustration comes with the effort to articulate what has been seen and felt without any conscious striving to express it: it is the difference between being *in* and looking from the outside.

Then Sue said casually last night, 'But we all must die'. So simple & right, yet at the words – admittedly through a sleepy winey fuddle – something in me, the deep-rooted sense of being this self and no other, but among others equally unique, felt utterly incredulous, and for a time I was strangely awake, disoriented because plucked out of normal half-consciousness, and touched on the quick by unbelief. It is as Emyr says, 'Life comes to life near death'.

June

Making an early morning start – dog-roses in hedges, the night's carnage of hedgehogs and rabbits, a lamb and a badger on the road, a strong smell of ramsons through the car window – we drove to Sussex, where I gave a reading with Robert Wells in the Arts Centre of Christ's Hospital. Afterwards we drank wine with Paul Mills who had organised the reading, and an interesting elderly man who had a wide knowledge of modern poetry. I had been holding forth again about the difficulty of legitimate praise and celebration in the present state of the language, and he said that it was of course up to the poets to renew it, as for example Hopkins and Eliot had done in their time. He insisted too on the responsibility poets have, often without knowing it, since they may deeply affect the lives of others, as his was affected by reading Eliot's poems when they were first published.

Though the ideas weren't novel to me, they came alive when voiced strongly by a stranger to whom poetry mattered. He also regretted that many poets nowadays work as academics. I countered, disclaiming defensiveness, with the conviction that the ivory tower isn't an institution but a state of mind. But inevitably he touched me there too, moving as I often do between college and poetry readings.

·

Over the marsh, two crows harrying a buzzard – as from the beginning, and so to the end.

There's a real sky behind the dirty curtain hung across the mind.

·

An afternoon fishing on the Teifi with Jonathan Raban, who's staying briefly in Pembrokeshire and working on a book on the Middle East. A clouded afternoon, large grey boulders lying scattered on long grass beside the river – evidence of its great force, though now it ran quietly enough, the current moving through long dark pools and racing through weedy shallows. A great relief to be there, after this exhausting & frustrating period: to fish expectantly and to talk again, without competitive edge. No sign of salmon or sewin, but a multitude of small brown trout, live silver & brightly spotted. Under the sky, with fishy smelling hands, out of the narrow mental enclosure of recent days.

July

Rain on & on, almost the whole period of the dog-roses. Many heavy falls & days like today, with mist obscuring even the near fields. The streams pour down from the hills, loud to us at night, and the roads are shallow, quickly flowing river-beds. Days when, after a short walk in the morning, I sit too long indoors, reading T.F. Powys or David Jones, exchanging the Catholic's structured universe for Tinker Jar walking on Madder Hill.

Now, for the first time, I find in David Jones, in *The Dying Gaul*, ideas that I question critically, and expressions for which I feel little sympathy.

There's this, for example:

> 'More and more, throughout the last decades and still more today, any plastic feeling must be looked for not in 'places' – there can hardly be said to be 'places' in that sense: the genii and *numina* of place 'troop to th' infernal jail' in a way Milton never saw. We are all as uprooted as the nation of the Jews and that is why we weep when we remember Sion – the old local Sions with their variants of the form-creating human cultures. We are all of the diaspora now.'

Although I've developed a rather similar belief from a different reading of history, I still can't accept the absoluteness of this. And from experience, standing with my old friends in our common place, and still knowing, from the ground under my feet, what I accepted unconsciously from the beginning, that this place, known in depth, is the ground of our being. The shingle on Hurst Spit, the grass of Pennington and Wainsford Common, the open Forest and the trees, the river-banks at Wainsford, Boldre, Brockenhurst, Queen's Bower, the streets of Southampton – each tangible and distinct, yet belonging within the physical, historical area defined by the reach of our love.

•

Warmth after rain & cold; mushrooms in webbed grass – scent of earth & flowers – birds that should have sung in late June find their voices again for a brief time.

From Gerard, the gift of his well-read, annotated copy of Boehme, which went with him for years about his work in Africa. A sign of the continuity between Gerard and Theodore Powys –

'"this is a book to read ... this book by honest Jacob ... Signature Rerum ... it doesn't matter whether you understand it ... but it is a good book to read...." The small volume in the Everyman edition is brought out lovingly. "Read a little each day ... just a sentence or two ... it doesn't matter whether you understand."'

Another worn Everyman is passed on – the gesture knit in my mind with the edition, beautiful in its plain and useful form, effectively signifying a noble and moving common tradition of living thought.

•

We came back from Devon to find that something has gone: our near horizon of blackthorn, elder & brambles behind the sycamores, over the Beidog. Now a raw, open space shows through, where Dai Jenkins having acquired Mr Morrice's field has stripped and rooted through it with a bulldozer, preparatory to new planting.

Beidog gouged out, straightened, with torn roots sticking through its banks. More change in an hour or so than the flood caused. A scatter of roughly heaped bonfires smoking. Coming in late at night, I see two red eyes burning.

August

How could one commune with spirits or with God, when seeing clearly with the eye is so difficult, mind continually clouding as past & present self-concerns merge, forming different shapes as they constantly come and go?

I talked with Peter Lord in the afternoon, about blankness in Welsh class calling up early experiences at school, when there was no perspective. At Rope Hill, really, as time went on, the most carefree days of my life, or perhaps the happiest, for they surely weren't carefree. But early on, when the red-haired Mr Valentine singled me out to compare unfavourably with Andrew Jack, coldly, dismissively. 'Hooker has no character.' And I sat silent, pale-faced, keeping a stoic forced smile. Past times often come uncalled, revealing that the whole past remains inside one, a single incident bringing all back. I see Rope Hill, wanting in a way to make it live again in words as it does to me – so alive that, curiously, I can feel myself cycling with bare knees towards The Wheel, fearful that my fly buttons might be undone, or watching the Coronation on the Turvilles' snowy television screen, letting Suzanna's hair brush my face ... Perhaps it is intensity of feeling that won't let some days hours minutes die. Yet thought of an after-life demands that it is for all or none, for the dully oppressed and mentally retarded, for all human beings, not only the super-conscious. Though I think too with Keats of life as the valley of soul-making, such a soul need not survive, the belief does not demand it.

•

On Hurst Spit: sea choppy, grey inshore but bright silver far out, with a blistered texture, and green & blue to the west, where Purbeck was clearly visible.

Emily splashed in the water near Queen's Bower, a small bare girl with a green oakleaf stuck to her heel, and the river was a moving still-life (as the limitations of my words must picture it), black & gold & white, reflecting a silver sun, and covered with expanding circles, each with a water-spider at its centre.

•

Thinking, reading Theodore Powys, talking with Jim, I see there's no great writer who does not feel life or God as the element man is borne by, and by which he is broken, driven as if by invisible forces. The ability to convey that element, however conceived, distinguishes the great writer, or artist, from lesser ones. I have always felt this but, seduced by sophisticated theories, have rarely said it, unless indirectly. It's being of the depths that matters – writing that expresses life swayed by its currents, open to the deep influences.

Gerard knows this.

Berdyaev & many others have said it. And Britain has produced many great artists and writers in whose lives and work the element moves, while most of our modern criticism & our general literary consciousness are closed against it, and depict surface patterns with elaborate techniques.

Thus Theodore Powys, one of the great writers of the century, was a profound mystic – a man who should not have existed according to prevailing models of life & literature; a man who lived in a 'corner', but was of the great stream without which there is nothing but forms of death. After long reading I begin only now to see what he meant – and find what can't be imaged or imagined outside the forms he made – a great force that the dance of his creations on its surface reveals. His is a perfect way of saying all that can be said, which discloses an unfathomable power that cannot be caught in worldly forms. For example, Mr Weston isn't God and couldn't possibly be, but is a delightful creation based on 'child man's' traditional literary & biblical images. But something of God may nevertheless attach itself to an old shoe thrown into a ditch, an abandoned roller or a broken chair, or perhaps to simple human beings swayed by His

'moods'. And beyond both these and Mr Weston, but partly mani-
fested by them, there's a sense of the power we may feel but cannot
understand.

> 'In speaking or writing a confession, one is always coming near to
> something ugly in the dark of oneself. I touch the hoof, or the fur,
> or the horns, or the tusks, as I write.
> ... in every confession there is always worse left behind than what
> is said; for we none of us dare to utter the whole of our wickedness.'
> *(Soliloquies of a Hermit)*

I know this is true; and it is said with the authority of one who has
first felt the ugly thing, and then reflected upon it. Almost every sentence could be the text for a long meditation, as when he says:

> 'A star of life with its own colour, its own raiment, and its own
> joys has entered into me to die. But the star has still its desires and
> its longings ... I would like it to live again in some other body ... I
> do not wish to be the grave for the death of a star.... And yet it is
> only when a star is dying in you that you can feel its life ...'

Then I can't help thinking of the almost total obscurity into which
Soliloquies fell for many years, and of its small readership today. We
don't deserve such a man.

•

> Beth yw gwladgarwch? Cadw ty
> Mewn cwmwl tystion.
> (Waldo Williams)

Waldo's words have haunted me since I first read them, in English
('What is love of country? Keeping house / Amid a cloud of witnesses.'), and now do so increasingly in their original Welsh. They
attach themselves to almost every feature of my ground – to the
whole idea of 'keeping house' in the world, but also to this particular
house, our house, but in his Wales, the Wales of his witnesses, which
I look into more deeply from the outside as time passes; and the
cloud moves in my mind with clouds moving along the ridge, and is
also the witnesses of Waldo and his people, yet my witnesses too:
ancestral figures, and spirits I have gathered about me from 'reading'
the south of England. The witnesses are the tradition in whose spirit

the house is kept; but for me, in these words, they are also the witnesses of the Welsh tradition, and of this place – unknown, dark figures in the house I look into, and empty spaces which my ignorance of its interior makes.

The words also touch the heart of David Jones's example, his making of shapes from the very things of which we are made.

And though his images are bodily and Waldo's are spiritual, of the Catholic and the Quaker tradition respectively, the house is our most lived-in dwelling and the things are witnesses.

•

Turned the earth. Made a bonfire of grass & rubbish and watched it smoulder until after dark, fire wearing black patches through the drying cone, and briefly blazing out. Watched for hours, emptied of fret, filled by the motion of smoke quietly rising against the rough grain of furrows in the newly ploughed field, in harmony with mist gradually clouding the distant line of the Wyre valley. Saw again the beauty of light & distinct shadows on the mynydd, red rowan berry clusters against soft blue sky.

•

Walking up the road & across the fields with Emily, picking & eating a few of the first ripe blackberries, I watched her run in front of me. Cloud shadows on a bright, windy day: thoughts across the mind. Of immediate colours & shapes; of the church visible below, which Jim has already visited and I have never entered; of unwritten poems, potential shapes relating curiously but palpably to the shapes, colours & rhythms of this land; of Emily – our children talking or gathering fruit, or running with the delight in being that nothing can cancel, but also towards the world & its threatened end that we with our adult misuses of ourselves have made. Then we sat thoughtless on a bank of warm grass by a quick stream in the sun.

September
Swing of the pendulum after the Academi Gymreig conference at the College of Librarianship, Wales, this weekend, when I heard Dai

Smith and Gwyn Alf Williams lecture, and after talking with Emyr and Elinor Humphreys who came out to tea on Saturday afternoon.

Dai and his professor from the Cardiff history school have a similar manner of address, and both are tremendously effective. They integrate their family and personal histories into the history of industrial south Wales, and Gwyn Alf in particular is an orator – out of the methodist tradition, Emyr says – who moves rapidly from comedy to tragedy, and as rapidly makes connections, so that the relations between areas of experience become clear, with a shock of recognition, as the life among lives, in a continuing history that cannot be reduced to abstractions, is made deeper and more vivid.

I am reminded of much that I had forgotten, and at the same time am led deeper into the history: a real history to set against the mythic pasts which are prevalent in Wales, and, for me, against the imagined isolation I dwell on even with the romanticism I criticise and deny.

•

In living we are all questioned. We are not here to speculate about the meaning of life, but to be questioned by the meaning we carry. It is far easier to be a critic, judging and apportioning blame outside ourselves, without understanding that the true critic is the one most conscious of being questioned by everything to which he attends and applies himself.

•

After lunch at Hayford on Monday I came away with masses of fruit, tomatoes, jam, and two of the beautiful 'Hooker seedlings' which Mother has raised from a pip and on which the future fortunes of the family may depend! Then I drove through Southampton & across the new bridge at Woolston, taking the wrong road and arriving at the quaint preserve of Hamble, with small bi-planes from the training school roaring low overhead. How much they recall that is farther back, from my childhood at Warsash across the water; and Bursledon with yachts contemplating their reflections; the red-brick church at Sarisbury Green, where my parents were married; acres of glasshouses on gravelly soil – of childhood in wartime, Tiger Moths & Sunderlands overhead, beside weedy shingle with its thatch of drab straw & other flotsam.

Sarisbury Green

Between pre-war, redbrick houses
comes a sudden break, yachts
admiring their reflections; then
the redbrick church standing
in a dark pool marked with stones.
Here are the bare bones of my people,
nor is there any thing so mean or dull
it does not bring me to the ground,
not even a strip of pavement
by a bus stop. There I enter
the body of a child, impatiently
straining against the arms
that hold him, his arms outstretched
like a swimmer's, reaching out.

And so through to Pulborough, where I felt a desolate sadness at
Sue's father talking of the old people, his friends & contemporaries,
'dropping out' one after another & of the approaching death he seems
to welcome. Charles is such a good, kind man, ill-used by his nerves
& his forebearance, always just below the surface the child his parents
abandoned in England for long periods, when his father was a bishop
in India, and seem never to have enfolded in love & physical warmth.
There we woke early on a morning of light groundfrost, mist rising
from the Arun snaking under the clear line of the Downs, and came
back under another Battle of Britain sky, vapour-trails smudging
volumes of high blue air, with a touch of cold & a smell of decay.

•

How well Hardy understood and how piercingly he felt what he called
self-unseeing. But the opposite is not self-seeing, for that makes one
a spectator, outside the moment, as I have been in all grey, shallow
times. It can make long phases of life a wasteland. The opposite is

surely a way of being at once self-giving and attentive, of living each moment without possessiveness, appreciating the situation and those who share it.

Theodore Powys has a mystical philosophy of the moment which I don't fully understand, though it seems to involve a sense of the moment being eternal because utterly mortal, breaking man's ever-lasting wanting and getting by his gift of all he is at that instant. But in TFP too there's the melancholy which he calls 'holy', and is akin to the poignant time-consciousness found in an acute form in all the poets and mystics of southern England – Jefferies, Hardy, Edward Thomas – a consciousness pervading their sense of life arising from the feel of the country, its shapes and rhythms, seasonal cycles, and abysms of backward time.

And I too have this, as I don't deny when attempting to under-stand it critically; to distinguish a nerve in the fibre of being from mists rising from the stagnant black pool that gathers in anyone whose life is turned back on himself, because there's no way for his energies to flow through into a shared world, contributing to its present and future. Mortality giving rise to melancholy, not our per-sonal mortality alone, but the beauty which in all things is inseparable from their dying nature: this is close to the heart of life. But it's a morbid melancholy that feeds on our failure as a people to relate cre-atively to one another, and to give meaning to our history. I see this too, in different degrees, in these writers and in myself. From this, in part, comes the feeling that I write from an end, voicing degeneration not generation, disintegration not integration; therefore the need to understand it and to see clearly what if anything can be done.

I think of fragments, of myself, my writings & notes as fragments. Then I think too that the great writers offer fragments – as David Jones does – of a broken order, or else sound the deep break in their rhythms and images. And seeing this darkly, a new light begins to creep out of much that I have thought, written or tried to write; a light that once again suggests a new perspective on trials & efforts conceived too narrowly, with a mistaken sense of the personal.

Person/place/society/nation/world/cosmos: not to look only at one broken link, but at the whole unbinding.

•

With Emily on my shoulders, her voice just above & behind me, commenting eagerly on John Ty Nant's yellow digger working in Dai Jenkins's field, our long shadow descends in front of us, with the shape of her small head far away from her words in my ear.

New term approaching. It seems hardly credible that this will be my fourteenth year in the department. I could despair; at times I have despaired. Is it really true, as I was led to say to Gill & Dave the other evening, that I am wasting my life here? Compromising; propping up a system I don't believe in; having a vision of what our relationships & common endeavour could be, but without power to realize it, without energy or courage to stand out for change, doing my best with things as they are, patching a few wounds?

Yes, there is some truth in this, and it has been a strange combination of sympathy, failure of nerve, and awareness of my own weaknesses that has stopped me from ever writing much of this down. Also living imaginatively in other concerns while living for most of each year practically in these things.

Fear is our curse, the curse of a small institution in this corner of Wales, but also throughout the world, certainly the white world, today. Fear. I know fear, but not the fear that makes academics stand off from their students, assuming and therefore creating a division between them. Academic man! And often enough I, supporting this system, wear his grey, pedantic, fault-finding mask.

October

Four weeks into term with almost no time to make a note or develop a thought. Again the sense comes of having let the wrong things matter: a self-criticism, but not only; anxiety over academicism, but not exclusively. The insignificance of English departments in the world at large – yet for most of us living in institutions their mental horizons or even their physical walls can so easily come to define the bounds of space. And within these, often with equal ease, having ideas about literature replaces a response to living words. At times I find myself loathing even the word 'literature', which gives too much of a sense of libraries crammed with books about books, showcases of an industry, and ever more clever ways of making smart talk about what to any real writer was his life's struggle to create from the depths – and these too are clumsy words.

I know too well what contributed to Ivor Gurney's madness: wanting the whole order, the poet giving and receiving in his own country, voicing its essence and in return being honoured, not I think in any official way but by being accepted as one who belongs. Not having this was a state of utter unnaturalness which cut his brain as deeply as Lear's was cut by his daughters' ingratitude. They were both men obsessed: there was the root of their madness, but to me Gurney's need is infinitely saner, truer to what is fine in human nature, than most ideas hanging like dense stale clouds where our 'talking heads' gather. And did he really want more than a place in his country, to feel that the way in which he used himself was useful, and so to be free to walk and to create, coming in from the stars to the golden fire-light & music & companionship which fill his poems?

November
Consider the ironies. Someone who is obviously not a specialist reviewing *Solent Shore* in *The Lymington Times* fails to hear a hint of musicality, and a professional writing in the *TLS* hasn't the slightest idea of its structural or unifying principles, and seems to me to have read some other book. What a fool I was to think it might mean something in the locality; almost as much of a fool to think that more than a few people anywhere would bother to regard it with care. This is of course what has to be gone through, demanding everything of myself and receiving, for the most part, carelessness & indifference.

•

A fearful battering of hailstones on the roof one night; ridge & hollows white in the morning. Then cold, hard days of perfect clarity, the peaks of Llyn dark as slate across the bay & Snowdon shining white, due north. Last night, snow; a thin covering over all the high ground this morning & Joe's voice wild with excitement, waking me as I tried to get farther under the blankets: 'Not snowballs today, Dad, snowmen!'

At times, all things are clear. In the quiet of the night, having given myself fully talking with students & colleagues, I see the utter waste of bitterness, the folly of querulous introspection. As when one looks another person full in the face and feels both lives, looking and looked at, seeing and being seen, knowing the primary concerns underlying all evasions. Times when all the trivia of ill will towards others & deadly repetition in oneself has been swept away, cleaned out; when all one really lives for and is sustained by stands out in bold relief. When consciousness is a state of simple prayer, quietly naming all that really matters, people and things seen in stark forms, not called up by complicated thoughts, but simply emerging.

December
Yet I see this too, as if the cold beauty of the new moon with the old moon in its arms warned me: that a too zealous criticism of 'waste', which sees its opposite in figures of stark, 'clean', wintry things, may pare a man to the bone. This is also the danger, and in part the significance, of my poems set in Wales. A development of the problem of 'I' and 'world': while I do not give myself, the 'I' is stark, almost no more than an eye, so that the 'world' which it does not engage with, to find confirmation and release, is stripped to an almost equal starkness. Yet this is no more the whole truth about my life here than the wintry figures express what I seek. Both however reveal a common danger. That alienation which I have criticised and for long resisted is more my experience than I have ever admitted.

•

My first impression of Raymond Williams was wrong, merely a reflection of my defensiveness, as I realised after a seminar on *Border Country* with him & a small group of colleagues and students in my room in college.

He is a kind man, communicative & unassuming: not one of those who live in a cupboard. Introducing the seminar, I quoted the passage from the novel that struck me with such force when I first read it: 'The valley as landscape had been taken, but its work forgotten. The visitor sees beauty; the inhabitant a place where he works and has his friends'.

This was much in Raymond Williams's mind; he had recently been back to the place with a film crew, filming from above to get the external image, when across the 'scene' came a train, loaded with car bodies ... A complicated irony in view of what he went on to, in *Second Generation*: an example of new connections crossing an attempt to exclude even the old; and as personal experience, hard to bear.

The confinement of Margiad Evans's *A Ray of Darkness* is terrible: it seems to me just the space of the crazed ego, terribly lucid even as to egotism, but the worse for that, because accepting and even glorying in it. And while it sickens me, I fear it: not just as the end I could come to, but as the place where, without knowing it, I may already be.

•

I haven't done Margiad Evans justice. She was a real writer – I don't question that. But also *A Ray of Darkness* has a frightening kind of honesty. She wrote completely from the state she was in. And if her spirituality is distortion of spirit, that too is an unusually honest reflection of the state many of us are in; it is certainly uncomfortably like mine.

Then she could write, 'The only abiding and bitter resentment I have felt against my life was there being no place for me in that home country I had moulded out of my heart'. This moves in my mind with Ivor Gurney's:

> To make the time's greatest song, and be given
> Dust on the covers for all the pain striven.
> To cast out a shout of love to a far
> Country, long loved, and be given bare
> Silence, and cold unhonouring there.
> 'This is enough to break the heart
> Of David the King ...'

1979

January

Our neighbour, old Mr Morrice of Pen Gelli, died early in the week. He was here to greet us when we first arrived, leaning on the fence and interrupting the unpacking we were anxious to get on with; and afterwards he was often in his field, with a sack over his shoulders, or coming in with a gift of coins for the children. He was always kind, and he allowed us as a very special favour to have his beloved field dug up for our water pipe to pass through it. He would tell us in his difficult English that we were 'good neighbours', and he was more interested than anybody except Mrs Crease (who was born in the house) in any alterations we made to Brynbeidog. Neighbourliness was to him very near the heart of life.

•

Days of glorious sunlight, everything hard & clean. This light has fallen on the page, or worked as an image in my mind, as I have read Simone Weil's *The Need for Roots*. Her light of truth: but in any circumstances, however grey the days, the pure light informing her life & thought would shine with the same clarity. *There* is seeing clearly. Among so much touching so many things – as it must, for her thought is all of a piece and constitutes a vision – her analysis of France's demoralization in 1940, and of its historical causes, illuminates our condition in Britain today.

She is a demonstration of the fact that there can be no fearless, clear thinking except by the mind rooted in spiritual principles.

•

The pathos of the artist; the phrase seemed to come without forethought as, driving to college yesterday, I turned by the sea. What it refers to is the essential incompleteness of every work of art and even body of work. Even if metaphysical considerations don't arise, the 'world' is so much more than any person's reflections.

Almost immediately after the words rose in my mind I found myself thinking of medieval artists, who worked in and on cathedrals, each contributing to a universal design. Modern artists are necessarily much more individual, and what they make is fragmentary. Pathos, in the sense I have in mind, belongs to the condition of all people, because of our essential incompleteness, but much more to the extreme individualist who is vain about his singularity and thinks his work significant.

•

Half moon & morning star. Clear & frosty, but with a slight breeze, and not cold. I climbed the fields above the house before the sun came over the ridge. Maesbeidog with its dark roof & long barn on high ground on the other side of the valley. Behind it, a sudden jump for the eye, to the range of mountains bearing north & east from Plynlimmon, nearer ones clear, with a little snow, those farther off more snowy, but cloudier – all with that indescribable sense which combines distance, vast mass & arrested movement, elusive colouring of grey & white & blue, and comes alive with a leap as soon as the mountains are seen.

It is more than a widening of the physical horizon, just as walking away from Brynbeidog and seeing it against ridge & sky is literally like coming out of my skull; so this horizon expands with sudden leaps as I climb. Then, returning, with even more dramatic suddenness, the sun whose light was on the farther mountains, starts up behind me and its reflections strike back like shocks from frozen ground under my feet, and it throws my shadow in a long line almost to the fence. Turning to face the sun, not quite blinding when viewed aslant, part of the disc appears as a dark curve within pulsing whiteness. Below, ten miles away, the small mound of Pen Dinas hid all but a few houses on the edges of town; where I might have been sitting at my desk, oblivious to the sea just across the road.

•

No possibility of going into work today. Snow: our first fall of a few inches, in a period when, widely in the rest of Britain, heavy falls have added to the general misery. At last, now the Public Service people are on strike, Mr Callaghan speaks feelingly of our all being one nation, members of one community, which extreme action on behalf of sectional interests threatens. Essentially true, but how can this be authentically said or acted on in a society where in fact money rules, where many doing communal work are poorly paid while others, who are serving only themselves, gain immeasurably in material terms from our unprincipled system?

•

Yesterday we lifted a dead sheep from the stream, thinking it one of Dai Jenkins, and today the crows are at it, and buzzards, and a kite down from the mountain, circling close by the house, over the snowy field.

•

Thinking of the past, of a sense of belonging, has always stopped me at a certain point. Not that what I had then was unreal, or not a good foundation, but that turning upon it is no answer to the problems of adult existence. As a man, I start from the disintegration of our human image.

Intellectually, even without any colouring of feeling and need, I'm having to consider the truth of the claim that we owe what survives of true values and personal qualities to the remnants of Christianity working in us. But it is hard, probably impossible, to understand why an event in one nation's history, many centuries ago, when one man was crucified, should have been the source of such light. Then it seems to me that only two conclusions are possible. Either people throughout the centuries, among them the finest spirits, have been deceived, or the man was God. If he was not – is not – the teachings and the heroic life-story alone would hardly have survived, burning with a more than natural intensity. Scepticism may still suggest the primacy of man's need to believe, and locate the intensity in what he has consequently made for himself in the form of God; but scepticism has no authority, and if honest, is sceptical of itself.

> 'I am without a belief -; a belief is too easy a road to God.'
> (T.F. Powys)

> 'One cannot arrive at God, to him there are ultimately no "ways"; one can only go out from God; he is not merely at the end; he is at the beginning.'
> (Nicolas Berdyaev)

> 'I am the way, the truth and the life.'

191

February

Thrush singing after the thaw.

Dogs wildly chasing the scent of a hare.

A large flock of geese – several hundreds – fly overhead in their wavering, irregular V.

•

Now again I feel the danger of going down as the sap rises. 'My work! my work!' – again that sickening emphasis, something good made rotten by brooding on it.

So I get out in the east wind at dusk and try to stamp my bitterness & anxiety into the earth, thrust it down with a stick. I lean on a stout tree swaying throughout its length in the wind, and feel its resilience & a new rhythm independent of my thoughts, rather like a ship on a swell. Then there is this to fall back on, to keep the mind from gnawing at its splintered bones – this other movement, & the half-light & the wind ...

The problem is not only obsession with work, but also excessive concentration on light: the emasculating ideal. I felt recently that I was divorcing myself from earth & darkness, and again, despite warnings, seeking an inhuman ideal, some stark but essentially incomplete perfection.

Then, reading Jung's *Answer to Job* – on the whole, a rather vain, empty book – I found this:

> The encounter between conscious and unconscious has to ensure that the light which shines in the darkness is not only comprehended by the darkness, but comprehends it.

And I could see and feel it – simply that the glory of physical light would not be without darkness, and that, concentrating on light, I have encouraged in myself a destructive division. The old divorce, by which, for example, sex and vice become identified, and the whole pressure is thrown on consciousness, as if it were the sole artist responsible for shaping a person, which it whittles down like a bone or a stick.

The way of light seems to burn people up – so that some shine (like Simone Weil, perhaps) and others destroy. But for those who are neither saints nor devils, but more ordinary human beings who cannot bear extremes, the way is the way of half-light, where darkness and light are interdependent. This need not lead to a dull vegetative state, but can be as real and necessary as the cooperation of opposites in nature. So I felt anyway, walking across darkening fields, as if there were more depth as well as security in the dusk, which seemed with the wind almost to carry me.

Nor is this again merely to turn back and look for a safe perch on the fence between belief and unbelief, or, as it seems to me Jung does, to talk about powers such as love and fear of God without feeling them, or without a hint of their force in his words. (How could he write so blandly about such a terrible, beautiful and mysterious utterance as *The Book of Job*!) Rather it is to acknowledge a fuller power and a deeper mystery than that of light or darkness alone – even if what I need to keep up my spirits is simply to walk more often in the dusk and the wind!

•

It's not Ruskin's stormcloud I see, but a spiritless, exhausted greyness, & overall a language almost dead – alive enough in the sense that we still speak it, but in which all words of value sound mockingly vacuous.

•

Eisteddfod in Tabor vestry last night, the village children singing & reciting & the adjudicators giving lengthy assessments after each event and awarding coloured ribbons. A full house despite snow & cold.

How strange to me these occasions are, partly because they are almost entirely in Welsh, but more because of the kind of community spirit they express. Sometimes they seem cruel, when a small child is brought forward and kept at the front, if only for a short time, though overcome by shyness & tears. But in fact this rarely happens, and most of the children are completely at home among their little group & on the stage, and enjoy themselves, while only one or two show off. Over & over again the same songs are sung & the same poems recited – and for me there are periods requiring great patience, especially when the adjudicators are holding the stage – but the point is that each child is known, and his or her performance is attended to with affection & interest, as well as indulgently. All are applauded, those who perform with special charm or accomplishment most loudly, but somehow the award of applause & honours is done so as not to encourage the unpleasant side of competitiveness – indeed, this is entirely absent. And for most of the audience, no doubt, this is something they have done themselves – and will do again into the small hours, long after those of us with little children have left – and their parents and the people before *them* have done, so that this is a living tradition, and an enjoyable way of training the arts of public life which are valued highly in such communities.

Then, sitting on a cold hard wooden bench, with a chilly draught blowing about us every time the door behind opened, I experienced another kind of moment, when I caught, or imagined I caught, the eye of a girl sitting on the far side of the hall, and with the look & the wooden benches & the whole feel of the draughty high-ceilinged place, I was taken back to Confirmation classes in Pennington church many years ago, to that time of intensely romantic feelings & unselfconscious belonging, as if there could be no other time & no other world. Such instants are not memories; they have the feel of the very time and are momentary re-entries into it, when the whole interim has not occurred – we are as we were then, because the time lives in us, independent of memory, and needs only a similar sensation to wake it from long inner sleep.

•

Still hardly any signs of spring, though last weekend Joe & Emily & I saw, with great excitement, two hares standing on their hindlegs boxing, and snowdrop tips are whitening very slowly under the sycamores, while the Beidog is frozen from bank to bank & under the waterfall branches are spiked all over with icicles. The hard fields are a pale, exhausted yellow and the variable east wind blows almost all the time, making my jaw ache not unpleasantly when I walk out.

•

Finished typing out what may possibly be the final contents of *Englishman's Road*. Already it seems to belong to the past, and I want

to go on, dissatisfied, and stimulated by several ideas; also by reading
Frances Bellerby again.

Beidog

Sunlight and shallow water,
rock, stones with red marks
like cuts of a rusty axe,
dark under hazel and alder,
broken white on blackened steps
and below the falls a cold pale green –
how shall I celebrate this,
        always present
under our sleep and thoughts,
where we do not see ourselves
        reflected
or know the language of memory
gathered from its fall?

Beidog running dark
        between us
and our neighbours, down
from Mynydd Bach –
this is the stream I wish to praise
        and the small mountain.

I am not of you, tongue
through whom Taliesin descends the ages
gifted with praise, who know
that praise turns dust to light.
        In my tongue,
of all arts
this is the most difficult.

I could never adequately express the beauty I find in time, in the seasons, or the months whose names are poems.

I don't say Simone Weil was not attached – *The Need for Roots* & her moving sense of friendship show how much she was. But her attachments were based on detachment, on her uncompromising following of Christ. For me, much that she saw as illusion is real. So, because of my strongest instincts, if for no worthier causes, I find Berdyaev's idea of the person far more congenial – the person as necessary & important in relation to God. Yet what Simone Weil says of necessity, frightening though it is, rings true. No one could have lived the necessity of her time more honestly & more courageously, and she was not determined by it, but by her adherence to absolute truth.

•

A glimpse of snowy crags in half-light as I drove to Dolgellau yesterday evening. My reading in the Literary Institute coincided with a debate on Devolution (in the pub where I had a drink beforehand, a man kept repeating 'Jobs for the boys', possibly in response to the 'Yes to the Assembly' sticker on my lapel), and my audience was consequently quite small. After the reading, I had coffee with one of the organizers & with the chairman, Dr Edmunds, & their wives. My host, a retired bank manager, was an expert on Thomas Taylor the Platonist, and was thrilled that I had heard of Taylor. His mother, he told us, had been a monoglot Welsh-speaker, her only reading the Psalms: 'she was a happy woman'. Dr Edmunds, a retired GP & the only Englishman in the audience, was deeply read in 17th century English literature, the Metaphysicals & Thomas Browne & Jeremy Taylor, whose works he had collected while in practice. For another retired bank manager, the reading was his first excursion from home after a severe stroke last year. He was delighted when I mentioned Trefenter – strong family connections, as there seem to be everywhere in Wales.

Where else but in Wales ...? I was their one English speaker of the year. It was a great honour, not only to be invited, but to be listened to in a way that freed me from inhibitions. It was a bare, cold room – but I really had no sense of that – with a picture of the Queen on one wall, and a picture of the Duke of Edinburgh, who should have been beside her, on the floor under the table. 'The communists must have had a meeting here,' said an old lady with a twinkle in her eye, and went on to tell me that her brother & husband – both miners & both dead – had been poets in the strict metres & chaired bards.

March
Catkins out in misty rain & a lark singing. Snow again early in the week, a surprise in the morning – the first things I saw through the window were two black lambs in a white field.

•

Curlew on the fourth. Frogspawn hanging in clouds in clear water, or scattered like glass eyes on the ground. Birdsong quickening.

Sleepless one night, I came downstairs well before dawn, and saw the patterns of stars magnificently illuminated, with the Plough appearing almost to touch the ridge. Something to turn to in a strained day: a clear image with vast spaces round it; for the shut-in mind, a releasing if momentary flight.

After giving a talk to the Alun Lewis Society, Emyr Humphreys stayed with us two nights ago, and we stopped up late. His & Elinor's sense of not belonging – how well he put it, lightly & seriously enough for comfort; how they will often sit up in bed at night anxiously asking themselves what kind of people they are, and where their 'place' is. Of course, he accepts the writer's alienation as a fact. I could see its effects in his books, but foolishly didn't realize how clearly he sees it. But this is naturally a feature of his honesty, and contributes to his freedom from the indulgences of alienation, not understood, but romanticized.

•

Shifted loads of wet topsoil over the weekend; trees black in rain. How in resting between bouts of hard physical work the external world is *there*, distinctly itself, with no daydreaming cloud to obscure it!

Wind Blew Once

Wind blew once till it seemed
the earth would be skinned from the fields,
the hard roots bared.
    Then it was again
a quiet October,
red berries on grey rock
and blue sky, with a buzzard crying.

I scythed half-moons in long grass,
with nettle-burn stinging my arms,
bringing the blood's rhythm back.
    At night
in our room we lay in an angle
between two streams,
with sounds of water meeting,
    and by day
the roads ran farther,
joined and formed a pattern
at the edge of vast, cloudy hills.

    The house was small
against the mountain; from above,
a stone on a steep broad step
of falling fields; but around us
the walls formed a deep channel,
with marks of other lives, holding
its way from worked moorland
to this Autumn with an open sky.

At Builth Wells, standing on the river bank outside the Wyeside Arts
Centre, on the spot where I fished every day for a week, in rain, during
my first visit to Wales as a boy. I passed the Park Hotel, where the pretty
blond girl, newly wed, whom I saw on the stairs with her husband – he
with the corduroy jacket – became one of my two imaginary sisters;

one slight & fair, the other tall & dark. It was here that Mother thought it time I knew about homosexuals & their danger to boys, and I thought she meant my friend David, because he'd told me – uncleanly, mockingly, inaccurately – almost everything I knew about sex! That was a time of intense hostility to Dad, nervous hatred, perhaps, of his nervous temperament, and with a strong physical dislike. Will Joe feel that for me, and if he does, will I know? Perhaps all sons have to, in becoming themselves – which is also knowing their fathers in themselves, themselves in their fathers, the best & the worst.

April

Easter. South on Thursday afternoon, through intermittent rain-storms, with a brilliant bow in Herefordshire, almost too bright to look at: a double bridge with a magnificent inner arch, always travelling just ahead. Full moon over Salisbury Plain, huge when first seen, rising behind a hill, along the funnel of a narrow road climbing between hedges. Night more than day separates the towns & villages of Gloucestershire & Wiltshire; seen far off, they are first a glow, then a crown of lights, set far apart in a great darkness, despite the moon. Travelling quickly, we still have a sense now & then of what this country would have been like to a traveller before the car.

On Sunday we walked near Norleywood, from the small pond along the edge of heath into a spacious oakwood with a soft floor of new grass & dead leaves, and on the northern edge a view of Forest distances, the sweep of Beaulieu Plain. Looking at houses round the heath, at Norleywood, East Boldre & East End, I was thinking all the time: if only we could live here! Almost everywhere we went, that was my refrain. And to Jim the area is 'arsehole of the universe', where money rules and there's no community.

At St Nicholas's, Brockenhurst, we saw the grave of Brusher Mills. My grandfather, as a boy, knew him. (And *he* 'ached' for the south all his years in Yorkshire, Mother said.)

The arrest of feeling in childhood or adolescence has occurred again & again in Englishmen with attachments similar to mine. Can such love be carried through? I suppose the presence of a world depends on whether it is shared & with whom. Or perhaps its 'creation' can precede its discovery & inhabitation.

To Pulborough for Charles's 80th birthday. Early morning: magnolia blossoms opening outside the window, mist over the Wild Brooks & the Downs, with here & there a tree's dark crown rising above it. A late spring but with blue election posters well out in the south.

May
Snow on the second, like icing sugar on molehills. This morning, a very fine ice on the pond, with the first cuckoo, curlews crying and a glimpse of a swallow.

•

I have been nearly desperate to get away, to go *back*, in the weeks since Easter; at times an unreasoning cry: 'I want to go home', beyond the long argument with all its questions & qualifications, just an intense physical yearning. More than ever, at a gesture – washing a plate, picking up a book, digging, or merely stooping or turning my head – some particular place has risen in my mind.

Then, waking one morning last week – the seed of a poem, circles broken, thought fresh as the light. Still no time to write, but the freshness continues; less, but with a change of light. Later, at the weekend, cycling with Joe & Emily on the road between Maesbeidog & Lledrod, the sweep & flight & curve of the green fields & slopes were live as Hambledon.

•

The vastness of this hill country, shades of light & dark; grace of curves & ridges, bare slopes & slopes crested with a row of trees. Here & there the ballooning shape of a sycamore standing out against angles & lines, near a house or ruin. From Mynydd Bach: a varied green foreground of patterned enclosures, then a mass of dark-blue mountains and far across the sea the fine, pale blue profile of Llyn. Indescribable, unless colour, shape & movement could be caught simultaneously, and with the heart's leap, the mind's instant release from mental space.

And this is both a cloud country and a country of massed stone.

June

After a particularly bad-tempered start to the day, I looked up from washing dishes, and there in mid-field was Dilwyn counting his sheep with gestures of his long crook as his dog rounded them up. I thought 'shepherd'. But this was Dilwyn.

A goldfinch settled on a post, and behind him, over the ridge, the back of the sky was slate-coloured cloud, with lighter cumulus slowly moving across. This was as much of the world as the window framed, that could be taken in at a glance.

Shepherd

Others have died or left;
he has grown louder, bigger,
filling the fields which he keeps
with an old skill.

I picture him through glass,
framed in the window,
against the mountain:

tall, strongly made,
ruddy from wind and sun,
a man who strides, sings,
waves a stick, then shouts
at his dogs with a voice
they will hear in the village.

And he turns, walks
through the frame, as he has
since he came as a boy
and stood with his father
saying aye, aye ...

Almost the end of term, with all marking & the final examiners' meeting over; and I am tired, and less than enthralled by academic work.

What is it about even the word 'academic' that makes me shy away, and even want to deny that it applies to me? Isn't it a profession with scope for creative activities & contacts, for being of use to others & for being stimulated & helped to develop oneself, & with more freedom than most? It is. Then it should be a particular honour to work in the University of Wales. So it is, though I have felt it intermittently. Then again, it is my good fortune that this university, unlike more fashionable & socially prestigious ones, has many students who need encouragement to believe in themselves, and are much as I was. I should be, and believe I am, beyond the bourgeois reaction against bourgeois values, that thinks all steady work & ideas of personal & social responsibility deadening or a 'cop-out', and that 'real' life occurs only among peasants or industrial workers or in a revolution.

But still the pull south; and still my pull away from the customary goals of an academic career, feeling not only the incompatibility but also the potential enmity between academic ambition and the cast of spirit writing poetry demands. This at a time when, with 'Englishman's Road' probably completed & with criticism written & to write, I feel less certain than ever of a poetic direction & energy to pursue it.

This is Britain 1979, or have we slipped into a dream of the 1930s? It is easy to satirize, of course. This is a great time for phrase-makers & verbal terrorists, for the killers of language as for the killers of people. What is not easy is to think and feel communally instead of as a desperate or complacent solitary ego, or even as a family man or a member of a profession or class; to know one's human image cast down with the general breaking of our ties.

July

I read at the Apollo Theatre, Newport, on Saturday at the invitation of the Isle of Wight Poetry Society. Brian Hinton met us at Yarmouth, and, with enthusiastic talk & gestures, drove us in his noisy old mini to Cowes. There we had a meal with Olga and Edward Watts, in their house with a view across the Solent, where we later spent the night.

Lights across the water, lines of white & orange lights from west of Fawley across the mouth of Southampton Water towards

Portsmouth, with red lights marking out the tall chimney at Calshot (which, years ago, my brother David helped to build, as he and Tony worked for a time on the construction of Fawley) and a ghostly haze of pale smoke above all the chimneys, against the darkness. Most haunting of all, a single green light travelling up-channel some way out from the shore at Cowes.

I felt the reading & discussion was one of my best. It was the first within Solent shore, and therefore required a different introduction from a reading in Wales. As I read poems set just across the water the initial sensations or experiences from which they had arisen came vividly into my mind.

Next morning, after we had walked on the front, in a fresh breeze & with waves lifting glistening straps of kelp below the stone wall, Edward drove us back to Yarmouth via Carisbrooke & narrow lanes which gave fine views of the Island & the mainland.

So, once again, a quickening: all seen & felt more acutely than I might otherwise have done. Above all the essences & differences of places: Purbeck, a shadowy outline far beyond Hurst, as we wound along the river; dark-green oakwoods of the Forest shore, across pale mud-flats; Sway Tower standing out clearly. Lymington church & the Burrard memorial. Later a chalk track on Salisbury Plain, hot in the sun, & brilliant chalkland flowers – poppy, cranesbill, knapweed crowned with one or two red & black cinnabar moths. After the smooth hills, Gloucestershire & Herefordshire, inscribed with more intricate histories; the distinct shapes of the Malverns, the Brecon Beacons clearer than usual.

Back here on Sunday evening, I remembered the green light moving up the Solent the night before & the morning on the seafront at Cowes & on the ferry – all the marks & the shadowed waters; remembered how it felt to be within that world, & my unconsciousness when I actually lived there – this against the loneliness of being here, despite all our friends around, & against the strange unhomeliness of this beautiful & familiar land. For a brief time, there was a rather cold foreignness about even the garden & the house. (In the morning, on the seafront, I suddenly thought, and in a moment of exaltation said to Sue, as we looked across the water: 'I have made a mark on this'.) Now I could still see the mainland shore & the green light on the darkness as the sun set golden red behind the sycamores and its rays caught a large fox slowly crossing the field by its usual way.

Behind the Lights

Last night, I looked from the Island.
    Then I was again
behind the lights, living there
blindly, where the mainland
long shore shone, with breaks
at Forest and river mouths,
a ghostly smoke round chimneys;
till suddenly, a green light
on black water cut across my view.

Tonight, I return
to another darkness, the house
strangely cold; behind me
the long road back to Wales.
It will be dark in an hour
but now the sun setting
picks out a fox in the field
above the house, cutting across my view.
There he goes gingerly,
a lordly fox, golden red.
    Tired, I see
a green light on black water.
Better to follow the fox,
from sunlight into shadow,
on his cold way home.

Edward Watts had a letter for me from David Gascoyne, with whom we were to have stayed before he received an invitation to Rome. It is a very friendly & apologetic letter, in which he says he is keen that there should be solidarity among poets and is touchingly self-effacing about his own poems in commenting on mine.

On the whole, I find his *Paris Journal* moving & profoundly sympathetic, especially towards the end, with the outbreak of war, when his suffering & spiritual intensity, & of course the quality of his poetry & prose, cancel out the danger of pretentiousness, which he himself was aware of in his 'call' to a prophetic role. I find his & Lawrence Durrell's way of writing about the 'English Death' less sympathetic, not because I doubt that for them it was a real experience, but because their way of apprehending and presenting it betrays the bourgeois bohemian expatriate – the very type to think superciliously about 'provincial' England and never see the things of value in our common life.

•

On Sunday morning at Church Hanborough, on ancestral ground, I quickly found Wastie graves in the churchyard, one of a girl who died at the age of 17 in 1881. A church service was being held, the door of the church was open, and as we walked past the vicar could be seen standing in the aisle & in a loud voice apparently upbraiding his congregation ... There were horse-chestnut trees around the graveyard – in season, conkers will thud on the tombstones – and a notice on the gate about keeping the sheep in. My grandmother's people worked in the fields around. Kim Taplin told me that models of hay-wagons, like the one we used to have, are still made in the area. She also told me there are still plenty of Wasties thereabouts.

•

A coffee cup full of harebells stands on the table in front of me. The children picked the flowers at Sue's suggestion, as a comfort because I cannot write.

Now I wonder if among all the words I have spent in these note-books the only thing of value I have ever grasped is that each person has a life to make.

To *make*, with the effect of being there for others, and of use. Perhaps this is largely Keats's soul-making, except that I think too of all past lives, whether obscure or in history's eye, all who achieved a finally simple, irreducible shape, because they meant something, lived their meaning, and are as definite as names cut in stone. This is no doubt one reason why I can't bear to hear the dead mocked or spoken of lightly. There is also the fact that in dismissing anyone –

thoughtlessly denying what life to every being is – we dismiss ourselves.

With this sense of other lives goes my feeling of the otherness of other times, their unapproachable quality, their integrity as of a finished artifact, or say an imperfect one that can be worked no further, as a dead poet's flawed poem is finished and cannot be revised.

•

At Kilpeck I felt tired, looking at the figures but receiving little from them, and when Gill spoke of the shiver she had from putting her fingers in the stone stoup which had survived from the earlier church, I could only mouth a suitable response. But a more alive reaction *can* come after the event, when something that was merely looked at is seen & felt. Joe, in his Roman soldier's outfit from the Christmas play, ran with Emily about the castle at Skenfrith, and Emily shouted at almost every sight, 'Look at this, Dad! Look what I've found!' I see this afterwards, and all of us picnicking in a short, heavy shower by the river, laughing at the rain & at a joke of Dave's.

At Kilpeck, though, I thought more of Geoffrey Hill's master-mason pestering on 'tympanum and chancel-arch his moody testament' & of 'tendrils of the stony vine' than of what I was looking at. I tried to see the church in the context of that country, its hills & fields, feeling – though faintly, and again because of words (from Domesday Book, inscribed on a plaque inside) – some sense of the peasants working at the time of its foundation, but also of all the labouring generations, all the lives without a stone to mark them.

Then at Hay, at our unexpected arrival, Anne Stevenson & Michael Farley welcomed us warmly in their flat near the Poetry Bookshop, in a pleasant sunlit room with a comfortable disorder of books, cats, a friendly black dog & a boxful of kittens. I talked with Anne mainly about Frances Bellerby, whose posthumous papers she has. She spoke also of being glad to be out of Oxford, away from the metropolitan literary world generally, and of how these places inhibited or even stopped her writing, whereas the rawer, more abrasive climate & contacts in Scotland had stimulated her, as she felt this border country would.

In the evening, stopping to eat our supper in the corner of a barley field, with the great cliffs of the Black Mountains above us, the cloud broke for me, and I saw the beauty of that country. And Gill said,

'Now we are really where Kilvert trod'; and I hadn't given him a thought since the morning, coming down the Golden Valley.

•

Climbing slowly up the last slope of Hafod Ithel with Emily, we suddenly saw Joe, where his voice could be heard shouting to us, standing on the white stone which marks the highest point, lifting his arms in triumph, a small, distinct figure against a massive blue sky with swirls of cloud.

We rested in warmth on the hillside, with the hills above Tregaron just visible through misty rain, but the northern mountains dark blue through a finer haze, yellow hayfields among shades of green & brown & greeny-grey, all fresh under cloud shadows & in a warm, gusty wind. Though I picture these things, my recent image of this place, narrowly defined in terms of my pinched, arid self, has broken. I now feel that, if patient & attentive, a sense of presence could return.

August

To the Island again, for Mother's birthday. Carisbrooke Castle in rich, hilly country & the Roman villa at Brading, as much like a Mediterranean site as possible – sheltered, fertile, warm, with a strip of bright blue sea. We sat on a sandy, shingly beach near Bembridge, and while Sue & the children paddled, Mother told me about Dad's unhappy childhood, how brutal in opposing his artistic interests his father had been – and he of all those boys is the nervous one, with many fears. Dad was entirely without confidence in himself before their marriage, and only gained professional confidence in his early forties, when he got an advisory job with the Ministry. Before we set out for the Island, on the green by Lymington churchyard, Mother had warned me against 'the canker of bitterness'. I know it, and still need to be told.

One evening with Jim at The Wheel, getting drunk. Then I fished alone at Walhampton before six the next morning, facing the rising sun & its burning reflection with half closed eyes; at first with a mist like fine dust & a track of ripples & bubbles shining through. Lymington across the water – warm red of old brick buildings on the hill. It was here that Penny once said, 'you love this place', and I realised it for the first time.

September

Shapely Hambledon, at once dynamic & massively still, with a mild blue sky & warm breeze, a broad country of trees & fields & hills spreading out far round. Climbing, looking down, I was absolutely certain that I would never be able to make anything corresponding to its beautiful appearance, let alone what it is or the feelings it evokes. With this came a sense of the gap we never cross – or I at any rate can't cross – between expression and the truth of experience, words and life. Life is 'in here' as well as 'out there', but I can only feel its great power, touch its hem so to speak, and say to someone else, 'Look!' I can feel it sweeping on, but can not hold it in any form.

Wind and Shadow

1

Day of brief rainbows
and stormy cloud.

Rain drips like dark juice
from blackberries, runs red
from hips and haws.

Where my clogged shoes
take me, wet and happy,
across the fields, under
long, skating shadows,
Hambledon darkens and gleams.

2

Ploughed fields with a scud
of white flint run high,
break at the edge.

Red fruit and yellow leaves,
beeches turning gold,

fall short.
Over the brow I can hear
continual dull thunder.

From my feet,
grass soaked dark as iron,
rounded like a planet,
the hill abruptly starts
its motionless ascent.

3
I let the wind carry me,
half asleep, like a child
who dreams of flying.

It echoes in the cave
of my head, putting out
all but a dim light.

Under my feet
which scarcely touch,
the hill flies up.

4
In the centre of the hill
I crouch.

Brilliant in shivered rays
against black cloud
a cold light falls
but does not settle.
All boundaries are open
to a race of shadows.

Against wind and shadow
the pattern holds,
ring within ring

like a banded shell.

The earth against my back
feels motionless.

In the shelter of the barrow
I rest with eyes still.

Again the rings encircle me.

Yesterday, at her big redbrick house high above Aberystwyth, I had
lunch with Gweno Lewis and her brother, formerly a master at
Price's, Fareham, (where my brothers went to school, though not in
his time). She told me Alun Lewis was a manic depressive – which I
already knew – but that he'd said to her, standing by the tall window
beside us, 'you don't come between me and the light'. Slightly boozy
after wine & drambuie & much talk, it came through to me with a
shock that *he had stood there* ... But of course.

I sometimes think that if one could stop this absorption in or
assertion of self, completely stop it, and look and listen, the dead
could be seen and heard...

•

Early one morning this week, I finished reading a collection of
Frances Bellerby's short stories, and with her inner voice and her
evocation of the Spirit in all living things in my mind, took up Alun
Lewis's *Letters from India*.

It was like listening to the same voice.

I was aware of their differences, but saw at once that perhaps in
all of us the unique spirit is the same.

Maybe it lives in us, rather than being ours. Selves are lonely, conscious of being unique & vulnerable, while the spirit is common,
though rarely able to find expression. Obviously we are all made of
the same human stuff, and perhaps that's what I've come on again,

rather than any mystical intuition. But to live in the knowledge that we are kin in our inmost places as well as of one body would be to come alight.

October

First real cold, with a sharp wind. An impression of sudden bareness about hedges & fields, and darkly sodden sycamore leaves in the dogs' bowl.

With Charles last Saturday. He was very weak. Once when we were alone he quoted 'My life is light, waiting for the death wind' and cried briefly, excusing it as a 'hiccup'. Later, when Sue was there, he cried more, but always caught himself. This is partly the misery of extreme physical weakness. But we hear now that he is stronger, and has been cheered by being able to go out by himself in the car. On reflection it seems odd that I have never felt anything but affection for him despite his snobbery.

He is a good & lovable man; if I see what wounds and limits him, I see what wounds and limits me, too, and, in various degrees, every person I've ever known.

November

Looking away from the sun, I have a clear view of a red concrete-mixer approaching the Vicarage & Vicarage Hill, with the mast of Blaenplwyf tall & dark behind it, then of St Ursula's & the school, and instantly see the village to be more compact than I've ever realized, and a real, known place.

Only a few steps out and I know how little of our life here I have caught, how very little of the life around us. With a greater gift I would have brought home more, to inform a shape, but words at their strongest & most sensitive are a net with great tears. Any lived minute is immensely more than its most subtle verbal evocation.

Last night, as I was driving back in rain & darkness from a Literature Committee meeting in Cardiff, past signs to Aberdare & Aberfan, through Merthyr & over the Beacons, I thought of Alun Lewis, and of the history and continuing life of Wales, that even the bravest & best writers are only able to reflect a little, do a little of the honour it deserves, express a little of its tragedy & humane values.

I was with Gweno a few days ago. When he was depressed, Alun Lewis woke in chaos, everything whirling in darkness, without sense or order. And nothing was done to help him, again & again she came back to this.

With what courage he went on writing, searching, as his life in India became less & less bearable!

I have known enough of being stopped and silenced to know how brave he was; and for some, writing may make the experience worse, by increasing mental pressure, and spiritual and emotional intensity, when the exhausted self wants desperately to sleep. And others by their effort may come through.

Where Alun Lewis was, all was against him; but I think it our fashionable morbid romanticism to see his death as inevitable, and him as a victim of a death-wish. In other circumstances, destructive energies might well have fed his art to the point where it dissolved their darkness.

Hail now falling makes a visible impression on the field where it strikes innumerable grass blades shining in the sun. Dilwyn arrives as the hail strengthens to a hard, steady fall, and walks up the field – Brynbeidog field, though never ours – slightly bent with a bale of hay on his back to feed the cattle, and as he nears them, shouting all the while, the hail becomes violent, he throws them the hay and runs for cover under a tree in the hedge.

•

With what ferocious dismissiveness my thoughts will often glance off public words & public faces, now when there's little to admire in the public world; when our common language seems incapable of alternatives to the forces ruining us. And I risk making this an excuse for an innate intolerance & lack of charity, a trait of my father & grandfather, but more vicious in me. Until one day the word 'love' tastes bad in my mouth, and I have to will charity, breaking the habit of contempt, and at last start learning to deserve to love.

And this *has* to be, even though our world could end at any time in a meaningless nuclear glare, or run slowly to death, as we kill nature.

It has to be, because contempt of what's out there in the common world – a government of hard-faced ideologues who believe the free play of market forces can lead to anything but destruction of our few remaining common graces, and the general failure of those in all spheres of power to imagine a humane corporate future – my contempt of this only poisons me and so infects those closest to me. Anger & contempt come back like spit against the wind.

•

Played a tape of my radio poem, 'Englishman's Road', and read from 'Under Mynydd Bach' to friends and neighbours at Argoed. As on the Island, I felt the exhilarating strangeness of sharing the place through the poems. And again I have moving proof of what this means to others, so that I know that in this respect I can do something useful.

Faith in people and faith in poetry are one and the same, because poetry is a deep need of all. It speaks the best of us; speaks our love to the world.

•

Walked with Jim & the children from Balmer Lawn towards Queen's Bower. River banks treacherous, with slippery clay under damp leaves. Water in shallows & narrows all sunlight, with a muscular current & ever-changing patterns – the texture of the silversmith's work – where a fallen branch broke the surface. Deep black pools with a gleam of gold far down. Where moisture dripped from trees, small circles expanded on still, black pools, like the marks of summer water-spiders. It was utterly still where we walked, with oak leaves spiralling down singly, light through the trees an arc of steady beams, and a faint woodsmoke mist.

Jim showed me that the holly leaf is like a crown when held with spines upwards. Hence one reason, perhaps, for 'the holly bears the crown'.

We pulled long, dead creepers from trees, and everywhere by the river knots of snake-like, slippery roots were exposed. I was here with J. I walked along these banks with a fishing rod as a boy, the first misery in me, black as stagnant water. I know how deep I go in the Forest, and felt, as we talked and picked our way with care, that for me poetry comes from reaching down in particular places, with all

my senses – today the rich sweet smell of decay was all round us –
and through my whole life, and through the history bedded there.

What we saw was surely much as the Conqueror's Forest had
been, and once again it was Rufus I thought of, redbeard & blood-
stained acts & dreams, bracken colour & reds among yellows, golds
& browns.

Something to come for, confirming the richest ground.

December

According to a newcomer to the village, who is a spiritualist, this is a
'heavy' area. The life going on in these hills since ancient times is still
going on, and we – it's not clear whether she means only newcomers
or descendants of the old people as well – are totally insignificant in
the place occupied by that real life. She feels an oppressive but not
hostile atmosphere, a strong presence that simply disregards us,
without malice. I have kept the word *heavy*, turning it over in my
mind, weighing it against the feel of the surrounding land. But even
as she said it, I thought too of the assertion of new life – our lives, the
lives of every generation – against the possessiveness of the dead,
their holding on. I think such assertion not only necessary, but part
of our relation with the dead. Or so it could be.

•

To Sussex on Christmas Eve, where we all went to church at
Stopham the following morning. I walked back alone afterwards, the
day utterly clear, freezing hard, with rime furring grass & hedges. But
the next morning was warm, ground hard & frosty only from the cold
of Christmas Day. While the sun came up behind Chanctonbury, I
walked the chalk path intricately patterned with shoe & hoof marks
down to the Arun, and thought of red fire in darkness, light &
warmth at the heart of elemental, black cold. I realized obvious facts
for the first time: that Birth is affirmed at the dead of the year, Death
in its first vital freshness.

To the Rufus Stone in rain & fierce gusting wind. Giant beeches, tops
swaying, the elastic movement transmitted even to their trunks where
we put our hands. Several Orlandos had been at work: DAVE
LOVES LISA – STEVE LOVES CAROL. Some beeches had been

felled, and quartered, chipped like rough carvings, wet facets gleaming orange. But those standing, when the eye travels up them, whip
sight into space like an immensely powerful catapult. Looking up, it
was possible to imagine what it must have been like to climb the
rigging in rough seas. Whether or not Rufus was killed here, where
we played hide & seek among hollies, oaks & beeches, on moss &
roots, the place was well chosen for his fall; where, for all their clearings, the deep, ancient woods have a rather sinister, 'dark'
atmosphere.

1980

January

Evening, New Year's Day, sawing logs in the cold, under a blue sky, I was startled by the full moon, a large curve appearing over the hedge-bank at the top of Morrice's field. Once up, white through sycamore boughs, the full depth of space was about it. A beautiful night followed, frost hard & sparkling, sky vast & cloudless & utterly still, with many stars. There's no new word under the moon to say how it transfigures all, and draws the spirit out, delighted & wondering.

February

Driving down to Aberystwyth this morning, I felt friendlier towards the town than at almost any time since my early days here. This winter has made the change: seeing friends such as Greg Hill and David Annwn, getting to know Gweno, and also, I suppose, simply acknowledging the beauty of the changing sea. I think I could never be at home here, but the truth is that, day after day, I am – to the point of taking the place for granted and only occasionally noticing things in a dramatic light, or the peculiarity of some permanent feature which I have always overlooked.

Now I find Time increasingly becomes the growth or ailing of loved ones, as I notice with regret that in a few months Emily has advanced a whole stage, and in less than that time the threat to my father's sight has occurred.

Earlier, time had a different rhythm – day after day after day: childhood & youth are a false eternity, which in my case lasted longer than the usual span. But I have always been slow, which is not such a bad thing in all respects, perhaps. Now I think more of death, but rather assume there will be time to get to know it, and time to prepare.

But at times fear drops into my mind's slowly turning pool, and violently breaks the movement of gathering death to the centre and gradually absorbing it. This is inevitable, and just. For no one can so order life that stones won't unexpectedly fall – when even such metaphors will be instantly shivered.

•

Mary Casey's funeral service will be now, rain tapping on the church windows at Mappowder and more water and mud than usual on the narrow winding lane, if the weather is as it is here.

Mary was a strange person to me; I was rather afraid of her. To begin with, she was physically striking, tall & thin, with high cheekbones & her white hair swept back & somehow rather feathery – the 'Red Indian' look of the Powyses, which is one of their faces, evident in some pictures of JCP for example.

In lectures we attended I would see her sitting bolt upright, her head nodding with what seemed an extraordinary inner tension; and this too alarmed me, as I inferred, no doubt quite wrongly, a barely controllable panic, like mine when similarly hemmed in, and I would find myself looking at her, covertly.

We never spoke much; I was shy of her, as she too was probably shy. But if so, then with the Powys assurance, as Sue calls it, the confidence in being unusual, from a remarkable family. And I felt her integrity to be frightening.

She impressed me as being so integral, with her religious faith & her love of nature, and because she was so rooted, strong but not stern, neither frivolous nor earnest, perhaps even with the gaiety of assurance, I couldn't understand her; she really did have, for me, an unknown kind of being.

Much more than Gerard with his knowledge of Kierkegaard's 'anatomy of melancholy' (*The Sickness unto Death*) & of *dis*integration. He once said to me: 'Mary has more poetry in her little finger than I have in my whole body'. Which was certainly an exaggeration, although her poems are, I think, exceptional.

And now her ashes will lie in the same place where Theodore Powys is 'at rest'. Gerard in his beautiful card writes that, as Mary left the house for the hospital, she quoted Theodore's words to him about death always being a mercy; which Gerard now thinks of all the time. I had sent him my 'Emily' poem, which arrived on the day Mary died.

Emily

The season is late; our long shadow
with two clothes peg heads notched
one above the other lies flat across the field;
and from above me, breaking
the quiet of sleepy baas and caws,
an excited voice exclaims
at a sudden vision:
    a yellow digger
uprooting bushes, changing the stream's
meanders to a straighter course.

Now our single track divides,
a dark fork in dew-grey grass,
and a small girl in a red frock,
sun yellowing her fair hair, runs
away from me with a bunch
of corn marigolds, campion,
harebells and a magpie feather
crushed in her fist.

Away she runs through a drift
of thistledown, seeds
stuck to her bare wet legs;
runs away laughing, shouting
for me to catch her –
but I know now that I never will;
    never, my darling;
but run with care, run lightly
with the light about you,
run to the gate through moist soft grass,
webs and bright blades all about you,
    hint of a rainbow
in the silver shower at your heels.

•

Frogspawn in the pond, rising in opaque clouds from a rusty-orange bed, in clear water. And I think: like mushroom clouds/like freshwater corals, fancifully taking the visual image. Then think truly of the strange hidden life, invisible all winter, that has come again to reproduce itself.

Outside almost all day, I relaxed as I dug holes and put in posts for Joe & Owen's Robinson Crusoe stockade, coming close to earth & water & sun. But first I was embarrassed and angry with myself, after ringing the Head of English at a College in Southampton to enquire about posts advertised in his department. Somehow I did it badly, giving the impression (to myself at least) that I might be interested in applying only if the work demanded less time than my current work. The episode touched a nerve. He was decent enough, giving me the information I asked for, but I saw myself in his eyes as a curious, rather importunate, & perhaps condescending stranger. Not only *Solent Shore*, but my fifteen years of teaching, and everything I have thought, felt and written about Southampton simply didn't exist – I was just a rather awkward stranger on the phone. And of course I'm a good deal less to almost everyone in what I still think of, sentimentally, as 'my' city. Later I thought of Brother Elwin's cruel, acute, 'you think you're special, don't you, Hooker'. In my mind, all the specialness of my relation to the south, the unity I want of life & work & place; in their eyes, irrelevance & possibly conceit. And if that is their view, I can't simply say that it's entirely without foundation.

Later I felt angry, not only with myself, but that I should be embarrassed, and turned against myself; that what has been natural & worthwhile should have become complex, difficult, even suspect to me: a love whose innocence I can no longer trust.

I won't apply.

•

As it got dark, I walked about Cambridge, through busy streets & under a bone-white glimmer of old stone buildings & dusky stone figures. Then sat for some time opposite King's, watching Venus & a new moon rise above the Chapel roof.

Students came and went on their bikes, with soft lights loud or intimate voices, and I felt nostalgic for that life, as I never knew it, but also detached, with a strong sense of the roles we all play – as for example a tall young man with a shock of red hair comes full-tilt down a narrow alley, deliberately riding at, and swerving round, two of his friends, and rides off with loud, laughing sarcasms, all with a swing of confidence. And this is a gesture expressing the part of student, confident in his world, that has been performed by young people countless times through the ages. It is at once spontaneous and one among many expressions of a form of life.

So too the faces in the streets, all different but many with the same kind of intelligence & sophistication, like a family resemblance.

Everywhere a few styles, from the young chef reading a paperback in the Wimpey to the student striding along plucking a guitar. Cambridge seemed to be a city of two extremes, each with its possibilities, but one desperately limited and the other at least confident of having its way.

I met Peter Robinson & Clive Wilmer at The Eagle – its waxen ceiling signed all over by American airmen – and Glen Cavaliero kindly gave us all a meal at his home. We had a lively time talking mainly about Geoffrey Hill and *Tenebrae*, differing amicably in our views of whether or not Hill should come out with his beliefs, or, if he has none, whether his worrying at the Christian paradoxes is more than escapist repetition, but sharing our admiration of his 'Platonic England' poems.

Afterwards, at my reading, an elderly Hungarian lady participated with loud comments, beginning with a eulogy of my 'handsome' appearance and a prolonged discourse on the difference it makes to one's response to poetry if one likes the poet's looks! I think it was all more embarrassing for others than for me, since I was intent on reading, and could control her to some extent by answering her comments, while they could only squirm. And in fact I didn't find the interruptions too disturbing, and despite all the good-humoured talk it's one of her sayings I remember best, in abrupt response to my figure of speech about not tempting the gods: *There is only one God.*

•

All my life, since I first became conscious of the possibility of grief, fear of showing emotion has twisted and cramped me.

Not to escape grief, but to root out the habit of referring everything to the self-image. That is what I mean by seeing clearly, by being grounded in reality and relating to a centre, by everything I look for over & over again. I want the true selflessness by which one is most a person.

If only it could be as it was at my fear of witnessing birth, when I simply said to myself, *this* is the wrong way to think, and it changed at once!

March

In Trefecca last night I was guest reader at a creative writing weekend led by Gill & Phil Owens. Many of the sixth and fifth formers, who were attentive and appreciative, and eager to write, spoke of indifference and even discouragement from English teachers, not only towards their creative efforts, but towards literature itself. It is terrible to see this life in them, this hunger for guidance and encouragement, met by cynicism and defeat. Of course there are many exceptions; but with our large number of schools & children, universities & students, there are far too few quickening influences. And how can we hope for their increase now, when in some schools – their annual equipment grant exhausted – children are writing on paper bags and have few books to read, while in many homes books are thought 'useless'?

This was Howel Harris's Trefecca. Looking through a book about him, I chanced on this:

> *Life* and *power* were also the criteria by which Harris judged words, his own or anyone else's; but to him their creative quality was neither inherent in the words nor yet came from himself; it was the present power of the living God.

Words were alive in Sharon, a young West Indian girl, who felt passionately the deprivation of never having lived in one place for long, as well as the educational deprivations which others too felt, but who spoke with verve and imagination. In others, less quick in that way, the same openness – it is hope, creative hope, which is fully alive despite everything opposed to it. Surely nothing could be worse than killing or injuring this.

•

The man whom God has created in his image ... is the man who is formed out of earth. Darwin and Feuerbach could not speak any more strongly. Man's origin is in a piece of earth. His bond with the earth belongs to his essential being.

(Dietrich Bonhoeffer)

•

Alun Lewis Society party, with John Tripp reading & with songs & poems from others. A slight girl, not pretty but with long fair hair & a jumper almost down to her knees, bowed over her guitar, singing old ballads in a soft, earnest, rather plaintive voice. It is all in the word 'sorrow', vowels round as moons & full of sadness.

With his warmth, honesty and directness, John brought me back from days of lust & distraction when my life has been mere time-wasting & a sour dream.

When I drove home the night was black & bitterly cold, with brilliant stars in cold blackness. I saw the extent of my self-image & its horror. How I persistently relate everything to myself and have nothing beyond me. This imprisonment is not reality, nor a true dream, but a feverish half-sleep.

But I thought more of what caring is: that when all is referred to a stiff brittle defensive self, for which even 'love' doesn't really *see* others, but is counted to the credit of its own assumed largesse & generosity, caring never in fact reaches the other.

Only when there is a beyond self can care really occur. Then all have their reality by virtue of that which is beyond all, but is God *and* man, creator of man's true image.

These perceptions may be self-lacerating, but though I derive them from the only source I can know, it isn't the same case now as when I was little more than a child, and felt myself to be the only sinner in the world. Now I can see that the personal truth has a wide application, because our culture encourages and helps to create the self-image.

•

Anne Stevenson showed me Frances Bellerby's diaries: ink a little faded in old ledgers, the dead woman's intensities & notations, her immediacies.

On the way back from Hay I remembered the moment of 'Jim Insole & Iris Woodford at Taddiford Gap', when, all those years ago, from the top deck, I saw them get off the bus, so live with the salt & the sun on their bodies, completely absorbed in each other, going down to swim in the sea. This moment has come back often in the last year: an image that opens that whole world in its time, mine as well as theirs, where all is as it was, with the very gulls, and the sea might pour through. And is now one of two images that seem to want to start a novel. The other is also Jim, grey & exhausted, poking a stick into grey sand on Avon Beach, and asking, Why live? while I search desperately for something helpful to say. But the figures are not only ourselves; they stir with independent life when I look at them. They're true to that world, but not slaves of memory with all its mists & gaps.

My touchstone for *everything* companionable, & imaginatively & intellectually alive, was given me outside school & university, particularly with John & Jim, in a few years from about the time when I was sixteen. Good to feel the rock of that; not just ourselves, but the same life struggling for expression in many others. This is what I have to be true to, and can keep me true, when doubt & even loathing of all the *letters* of my professional work set in.

April
On April Fools Day we made a detour, in rain, to Uffington Castle. The white horse (or dragon) images the superbly dynamic, shapely hill flanks & curves. More than any other man-made thing, it is the spirit of the chalk.

I could barely stand on the greasy paths, which Joe called 'rivers of milk'.

From there we went for the first time to Wayland's Smithy, approaching the circle of grey beeches in misty rain. Close-to, the pitted sarsans are monumental, and their greeny-grey surface is the same colour as the trees. We stooped inside the chambers. Outside, tiny red & white thorn buds & unfolding bramble leaves hedged fields of new green corn.

A strong dungy smell of Wiltshire came through the car windows.

•

On the Downs above Amberley. Floods stood in broad blue pools below, and cloud shadows made darker pools, emphasising contours & colours with their movements. A glider high above us turned gracefully between light & dark. Sea & Arundle Castle to the south.

After lunch Charles surprised and upset himself when reminiscing quite cheerfully about his experiences in the First World War. A bomb had gone off under a party of fifty men; only twenty survived, and he had the job of clearing up.

Occasionally, observing the richness of Sussex with its secluded cottages & well-kept gardens & villages, I was struck by our widespread terrible contrasts, and thought of holiday cottages set on fire in Wales, and the millions of people out of work, and wondered what the men at Shotton would make of all this. Yet I would live in the south if I could.

•

Near the Knightwood Oak – brimstones fluttering among the trees – we came upon an oak & a beech that have grown together. 'Inosculation', a helpful notice tells us the process is called. Such notices are common in the woods now, making the Forest a great outdoor natural history museum. The trees that had grown together were like J.C. Powys's Portland rock – with a marked suggestion of sexual union about the trunks, wood of their wood, male oak & female beech.

•

On Easter Sunday, I walked with Jim along the shore from Pitts Deep, hardly aware that we were trespassing on private beaches. He surprised me by saying he only really notices the place when he is with me. But of course, it is the place between us.

We saw marks of erosion: here & there a stripped, white tree, lost with a fall of gravel & soil; concrete sea defences from the last war, heaved up in slabs or collapsed, and rows of old posts, split & partly eaten away, more beautiful than any outdoor sculpture.

Later we went to Boldre and walked through the woods and by the river. Below a bridge, wind & current eddies were shaped like Catherine wheels & galaxies.

Prospect of Boldre Church

Raised above oaks
Above a full river.

Once the living
Of William Gilpin.
Now his quiet mansion.

He hopes to rise
In God's good time.

Dim, coloured light
Stains the sanctuary,
The lettered stones
Charged with patience.

Things that seem misplaced
Catch the eye
Irresistibly,
Even as it bends:

H.M.S. Hood;
The Book of Remembrance,
Names illuminated
Of the able-bodied.

The head inclined to bow
Remains unshocked,
But cold; observes

St Nicholas
Overlooking benches
Carved with her crest;
Pictures the sea

Outside the frame: colder
For fires quenched in a flash,
For steel made a harrow

Useless on the ocean bed;

Even here, enclosed
Above oaks above
A full river, the sea
Open, spirited shipless.

As we drove back to Wales, the lowering sun was a red ball coming &
going in ash-coloured cloud.

While Joe & Emily were oblivious, playing in the back, we listened
to a radio programme about the Bomb, our lack of 'preparation', the
commitment of several governments, with next to no public discussion, to making these islands an arsenal.

I remembered the marches, the slogans, the music.

Will it start again?

A feeling of impotence is widespread. Apathy hides anxiety; but
anger is growing too. Astrologers reckon 1982 as a time of catastrophe.

All I can feel now, as twenty years ago, is rage: rage against all that
makes us feel impotent, and against the people & ideas in whose
name the unthinkable might be done – the Thatchers & Carters &
Russian leaders, the former now moralists on their high horses, who
only yesterday were in Vietnam, with the acquiescence of the British
government. But neither rage nor any other emotion is equal to the
possibility.

We can't afford the imaginative luxury of Jefferies's *After London*
– one woman living in the south-east said that she and all but one of
her friends had agreed, in the event of nuclear attack, to move *towards*
the centre of maximum radiation.

> '*There is no longer any faith that makes the deferment of the nuclear
> war very urgent.* So that a particular Welsh experience of this
> century, the crisis that the Welsh Nationalist Party evokes and was
> organized to avert, takes on universal reference and significance.
> Civilization must be more than an abstraction. It must be a local
> habitation and a name. Here, its name is Wales.'

(Saunders Lewis, 'Welsh Literature and Nationalism', 1965)

How could I have read this before and not felt the shock of the first sentence? I must have read it in a dream.

No. I don't see things as Saunders Lewis does, but nuclear war has been at the back of all my thinking about place and centering. It is the ultimate power of absolute reduction; a light wasting all, against which all things stand out with their particular identities made immeasurably sharper and dearer. A nothing concentrating all into 'the actually loved and known'.

Does the hatred in Saunders Lewis's poems, the bitter contempt of common people in 'The Deluge 1939' and 'A Scene in a Cafe', arise from love of Wales and of what the people *should* be? Is it hatred that respects people more than the pity of a liberal or a socialist does? Does Lewis respect them more because he acknowledges their dignity and worth in possessing will and the capacity to choose and to create, which he believes they have denied? He was what a leader of moral force might be, because of his ideal of man and culture. But I understand why Dai Smith should feel antagonistic to him; as I would, had they been *my* people he describes savagely and contemptuously. I would have hated him for that. But I can appreciate Emyr Humphreys and David Jones's unqualified love and admiration for him too.

•

In a period of about ten days the whole temper of nature has changed, even here, near the bare uplands, where spring comes late. Greenness wells up in fields, with the first waves of the flood of wild flowers, gorse daily a hotter, more golden yellow, and blackthorns all white. How long this winter has seemed! Earth sodden for so long, and now the change is a rapid quickening which promises greater depth & sweetness, days of sticky warmth & the cuckoo. Never enough of this!

May

Certainly I never dreamt what Kathleen Raine's 'politics of first principles' could mean in practice. This was a shock in reading *Dai Greatcoat*. Not so much David Jones's enthusiasm for *Mein Kampf*, which in any case is an innocent reflection of his views on cultural decadence, as is his enthusiasm for Spengler. Nor even his occasional virulence about 'leftish' idealisms, or his admiration for Chamberlain. These surprised me more than they should, and were initially more upsetting than they should have been. Retrospective anger? or superiority? God forbid! How could I, or anyone, afford such reactions? In fact, it is *my* moralizing that he judges.

No, what has disturbed me most is his not being, as I thought he was, *in the common place*.

Perhaps these letters are an erroneous guide here. But his friends in the years after 1918 seem all to have been 'upper' class; which unfortunately coincided with his hatred of the ersatz & the utile, which are associated mainly with people with whom he seems never to come into close contact, such as industrial workers and shopkeepers. In this respect, his attitudes are just another version of the boring & facile disdain of the other Modernists for the actual people, and idealization of a mythic 'People'.

Again, it is the reality of 'these islands' that is in question. How can it be truly represented when everything & everyone after 'The Break' – in effect, since the Industrial Revolution – and therefore almost everything we have and are now, are outside his love? For that's what it amounts to, say what one will (and I have) about his *inclusion* of the modern world in *The Anathemata*. But even in writing this I can't believe it. For he did love the men in the trenches; he loved them and the world they made – that re-creation of an earlier culture – but hated the actual world they came from, and went back to. David Jones was lovable because he was capable of love. Yes. But his People were an abstraction, and the actual people, in a class society and a culture in which as an artist he was completely isolated, were outside his love.

Now I rub up against his Catholicism too: the feel of that exclusive rightness again – not at all the same feel as being 'saved', but rather of belonging to the authoritarian establishment – I can't describe just what it is, but an assurance, a shared, rather smug assurance I'm outside of. There's something in David Jones's strictures on Protestantism, combined with his love of the sacerdotal, that brings back those boy 'saints' of dear old Brother Nicholas, at St Peter's, and the tone of self-satisfied unimaginative conservatism. Perhaps that's all it is: not the Church's inner life, that essential *body*, which I've never really understood, but its reflection of bourgeois attitudes.

•

In these weeks of long hot days, new leaves wetly fresh but earth like cracked rock, with a surface of grey dust, and streams a trickle, I have turned again to some of Jefferies's essays, 'The Pageant of Summer', 'Hours of Spring', etc.

First the marvellous quick detail, the poignant note; but now I notice how his essays are made too, thought growing out of natural description & evocation, with poetic echoes & repetitions, and recognise how much I owe to his ways of writing and seeing.

Now, though, I am not satisfied with Jefferies's 'mysticism', which seems to me either to bring him to the otherness of nature, with the inevitable sadness & even desperation of knowing himself apart, but with no searching into what man who is not wholly part of nature *is*, or to fly into a futurism that doesn't differ essentially from visions of the mechanically-minded, like H.G. Wells.

For Jefferies, life wasn't *now*. His grasping for a new idea, a kind of future greater life, is fully understandable in a dying man. But then also, for him, his life, human life, wasn't now, because the life of nature was too present, with an insistent quickness that shut him out, left him behind, the watcher hopelessly trying to note it all, knowing he couldn't, and therefore feeling a defeated being, slower, duller, less *quick*.

And now, for me, this is no longer enough. For all his intelligence, Jefferies is somehow asking the wrong questions, looking in the wrong place.

I understand his looking ahead – but perhaps the fullness of life for which he looks to the new idea is in the old idea he has lost, which wasn't alive for him: not immortality of the soul, but resurrection, that infinitely greater life in the body.

And if he taught me how to see, and was himself catching stray beams from the end of a tradition he did not understand, and thinking them his own ...

I have at least to go back through Romanticism, from which Jefferies's vision came, to find the source of its light.

•

How differently Dad and I see certain things. I had been learning more about Sway Tower and when I mentioned it to him, he dismissed it as an eyesore, a thing which should have never been built. But I could never say all that it means to me: a lifemark of course, but always fascinating & curiously beautiful in itself. Yet I thought as we drove away from Hayford that my poems are his waterscapes with a tanker & Fawley flame, or his landscapes with Sway Tower above the trees!

•

Last night, just before falling asleep, I had a vivid memory of the old men I used to meet or see walking on the Common or about the village when I was a boy, and even later: Mr Bullard & Mr Hancock, farmer Smith & farmer Pardy, Archie Fugget looking for his cows ('ave you seed she?'), the shellshocked Colonel on his bicycle, muttering to himself, Mr Swimmings, preaching to no one in the open air, or perhaps just to me, because I could never walk or cycle past him, but stopped to share his sermons with beasts & birds. My father will be a 'character' like them for other boys now. As in time I might be, somewhere if not there. Yet, in my lifetime, such continuities have never seemed less likely than they do now. The Eighties have begun with such a narrow 'opening', as if we could hardly pass through, but move like people sick with anxiety, forcing one step after another towards an ever narrowing time.

June

At last, with a few hours free from marking, I cycled towards Lledrod & on to the Garth, speeding back downhill to the village. Dog-roses in the hedges, as I always seem to find them, with a few petals already scattered. Where a hazel nut was forming on its twig, curiosity made me pick it and pull it apart. With a stab of guilt, I suddenly realised the immense *patience* of nature, not as measured against man, but the force even the most patient human being has little of – a sense of trees & grass & all green things continually coming back, their waves mounting year after year since the beginning, rising – so far – through all our destructiveness, the evil I felt then in myself: one small careless act, but behind it that other force, grossly insensitive & stupid. So far always this great strength & patience; for us, the terrible pathos of its vulnerability.

•

Landmark – lifemark
A landmark is by definition a communal & usually a historical sign. It is a connection between those who live in sight of it and past generations; a feature identifying the place. For the individual, it is always a lifemark too, gathering and contributing to personal associations, helping to form his identity; a part of his world. But a landmark's personal significance becomes greatly intensified when it represents loss of shared meaning, once the world it is part of is no longer common. This process affects the self-feeling itself, with the romantic 'I am I' born of breaking cultural & communal forms; lifemarks are then symbols of the self, held onto with desperate intensity, private, no longer marking a land.

To date, at least in *Solent Shore*, perhaps I have held a balance: raising other voices from the place/writing my autobiography into it, like figures concealed in landscape drawings, but belonging with the land's shapes & forms: making the signs mark a land & a life. Now I have somehow to avoid turning everything into lifemarks alone.

•

There's something about the self-feeling I need to affirm – its numinous quality, which reading *The Idea of the Holy* has made me realise.

Rudolf Otto writes of that in ourselves which is wholly other. I remember the trances of childhood, that peculiar dream which, usually in class, I would wake into. Or was it a feeling that everything apart from this was a dream? It's so difficult – probably impossible – to recall meanings that were felt. But then everything would feel, and look, *strange*.

I associate the feeling with both a rushing in the ears and silence, as if I were viewing everything round me from under an element like water, but without water's suffocating & distorting effects. The strangeness was that I should be *me*, just this person in these circumstances, in this time & place, and that every other person & thing should be their selves.

Could the self-feeling and its general recognition be easily separated? Not easily, but perhaps I felt most my own unique particularity – but not as a particle – while in those periods of perhaps a few minutes, or less, because the feeling could become frightening, when I would switch back in (like deciding to wake from an unpleasant dream), the other people & things were less uniquely individual, more a world strangely composed of just these and no others.

However it may be experienced, I don't think this kind of recognition is uncommon. Surely all people when young live in a far more mysterious & unpredictable reality than the condition we later think of as real. This feeling may not be what Otto meant, but it isn't just a rudimentary megalomania, with everyone & everything existing only for oneself; nor is it that we are all the stuff of a dream. Rather, we are all another life.

Two 'implications are clear. That the experience is to be valued because it is common, and discovers a common uniqueness; and that in feeling wholly other, not as discrete atom or alienated ego, but deep in the life we all are, I found the source of what is most valid in my poetry. The feeling which I think all real poems recover, giving back the strange familiarity of ourselves & our world.

Now, reading Belinda Humfrey's *Recollections of the Powys Brothers*, I see how they helped me to recover this; which is much the same as saying that, for me, and others, the Powyses – and especially John Cowper – have been life-giving. Each in his way communicates a vital self-feeling – 'extraordinary' & 'remarkable' are words that occur again & again in the memoirs. Yes. But each being uniquely himself activates that common gift – the otherness of *our* selves, and releases our life-current. And of course there's also the fact that, English though they were, they were free of our various class vices – meanness, self-righteousness, envy, superciliousness.

It is as if I have been assimilated to their 'myth', and were somehow linked to them through the chalk long before I knew of their existence; as though my life were interwoven with theirs, although I never met them. At any rate, there's no doubt that at a critical period for me they confirmed and released more than my sense of place. They've been life-giving for many because, in our society, in this pinched, desperate century, they had more than other writers of the largeness & generosity of life.

•

In recent weeks Sway Tower, or Peterson's Folly, has become unusually present to me, in truth more pressing than anything here, and in the same way as the Cerne Giant did, as if it wanted to 'speak'. Even when reading about the Bomb the image of the tower far at the back of my mind formed a ghostly association with the structure in the American desert where the first A-bomb was detonated. Yet the tower isn't sinister to me – quite the contrary – though I realise why it might appear so – derelict, empty, with its rough texture & faintly skull-like summit. Because I had just found out that the mysterious Peterson was a spiritualist, I even let myself imagine that his spirit was trying to contact me, through the tower haunting my mind, as I drifted to sleep last night.

There *is* something beyond reason about the kind of power some things or images acquire: as indeed Peterson may have known, so that by having such an unusual, widely visible & dominating landmark built he was deliberately investing his spirit in a body that would survive to haunt others long after his death. And it is said that the tower has as many stairs as there are days of the year, and as many windows as weeks of the year, so that as well as dominating space it freezes time in a symbolic form. Add to this its phallic shape, and its vaguely 'Indian' look, which, as a flicker on the inner eye, raises for me the shadowy image of a cobra enchanted by music, risen on its tail ...

And these are, quite possibly, all my fancies, and Mr Peterson had the single prosaic object of proving the strength & durability of concrete. As he did, so that his tower of Portland cement has the poetry of historical fact in the area, as well as being a 'finger of God', with all the personal & archetypal potency it has for me.

•

While we sat long over our evening meal with Gill & Dave, Peter & Maggie, two big hares chased each other in circles through the dusk, in the field across the stream.

In the morning, after a late midsummer night, I walked with Joe upstream to the source of the Beidog. There were hay rattle & sorrel in fields of long meadow grass we edged round, and tall yellow flags here & there beside the water. Within a quarter of a mile of the house we were in country I had never been in before, following the stream in shadow, between banks of crumbling clay rising high above us, but

with roots & branches forming a low roof to crawl under. Joe, who
had been here recently on an expedition with friends, commandingly
led the way. Then we climbed the more open hillside, past several
ruins, space opening on a cloudy patchy summery blue, with a
margin of bright sea & far shadowy mountains, Pen Dinas small
below. Finally we came to a disused sheepwash and found Pantamlwg
quite close-by, and crossed the source as we walked to the road.

July
The midsummer is again a cage – no fault of the season, though it
has a particular quality of silence when most birds have stopped
singing, and the full growth is already darker & just a little worn. No,
it is still being unable to move, and the feeling – based on plenty of
hard evidence – that we may never be able to, at least to similar work.
Even moving back into town has proved impossible so far, a move
which – though desirable for the children & also for ourselves – I
can't but see as a defeat; and loss of a place I love, but where I've
come increasingly to feel we don't belong, because in such areas the
Welsh-speaking community does still belong. Even if we were eventually to sell Brynbeidog to a fellow non-Welsh commuter it wouldn't
alter the fact of our unease. After making a premature move in my
mind last summer, I failed with the Welsh language, but even if I
hadn't, the feeling of being out of place wouldn't have gone. And only
in part because of a prior attachment: our unease hasn't been wholly
due to our looking away, but is in the nature of people with our circumstances 'settling' in such places. It is also true that we owe to
being here a debt we could never repay.

•

> I wrote about mud and soil and grass and trees. But I felt the soil
> of Hiroshima was mixed with the bones of the dead, and the
> young trees and grass growing out of the ground were – if I can
> speak metaphorically, the eyes of the dead, looking at the people
> who had survived.
>
> (The *hibakusha* poet, quoted in Robert Jay Lifton, *Death in Life*)

All power to Lifton. To begin with, his book is hard to bear, and must have been harder to write. But in the end it wasn't morbid curiosity, or a dutiful feeling that this *has* to be read, that carried me through, but absorption, arising from the need to know as much as possible about the meaning of the event. What it meant for those who experienced it. But also what it means to us, for it has changed something in all succeeding lives, in the conditions of life itself.

The annihilation & suffering had a qualitative difference – something new, of man's own doing, entered the world on August 6th 1945. I have always vaguely felt this, but feel now that any faith, any philosophy, any way of ordering & making sense of experience, of being human, has somehow to comprehend what was *done* and what was *suffered* then. Above all, what happened mustn't be complacently accepted: which is what, on the whole, has been done. The moving words of the *hibakusha* poet exemplify one way of trying to live creatively with the experience, but it is only open to a *hibakusha*. Others have no right to call on natural things – the old healers – or be familiar with those dead. We have to look at the mechanical process – the continuing process – and understand how it could leave human minds & hands for such a destiny. Inhuman but humanly contrived – how can there be such a connection? Such disconnections between human faculties preceding the event?

•

Low heavy sky at dusk; feathery grasses on the bank outside the window gather a dark purple from the light. Looking out, some slight unease, but inside, the usual mental sleep, a familiar lit room, a world fitting the television screen. Then outside, by the waterfall, Beidog running full, I see the house with its small lights through thick foliage, suddenly isolated & small. This is the most haunted spot in darkness & especially at dusk – where the Irish tinker, Patrick Manion, lived years ago, under the trees, but also an ancient crossing, and for long on a path at the boundary of the common lands. Above it the great outlasting presence of Mynydd Bach, misty against leaden cloud, but with immense solidity & *weight*. Not to be humanized; simply there.

Then this morning the cloud broke, without a storm, and the light was fresh and the air sweet.

•

When I was in my room in College a few days ago, a porter, a Welshman, came in to collect some sacks that had been left there and showed surprise at my having a picture of Gwenallt on the wall. I explained why and we talked about the man and his remarkable face. 'They don't make faces like that any more,' he said. Later I recalled a similar remark which an old Dorset countryman made about Theodore Powys, and Edward Thomas expressing much the same sentiment about the old men of his time. Perhaps people always feel this about the great elders. I know I do, even though I expect contemporaries to live – if humankind survives – to belie my feelings, and though I see the myth to which such feelings belong.

•

Lucy Penny is very frail & almost completely blind now, but so warm & welcoming, with a look of radiant attentiveness – her beautiful face full of light – that seemed to pierce me, even though I knew she could hardly see. Gerard was calm & still, containing his grief. In the morning he played me a tape of his reading of Mary's poems and talked about her devotion to Plotinus. Mary had been cremated, and her poetry is full of imagery of spiritual fire, and of fire consuming bones. It might seem a morbid coincidence that linked this reading with Elsa Corbluth's, which I had heard in Bridport in the morning. Elsa had read her poem about the death of her daughter in a fire in a hostel in London. But I didn't even make the connection at the time, but was only certain of the absolute necessity of poetry.

Gerard & Lucy had scattered Mary's ashes on the sea at Chesil Beach, where the three of them together had once scattered John Cowper's ashes.

With Gerard, and in my small room at night, with everything simple & clean (and many books in the bookcase with dedications from one Powys to another or by their ancestors), I felt completely at peace. Peace was outside me, a presence in the house, which I could share. Most of the family are there in photographs or in Gertrude's portraits. One in particular, a painting of Llewelyn, seemed to come alive out of the frame as, opening the bathroom door, I unexpectedly caught its reflection in the mirror. There was also a strong painting by Gertrude of Durdle Door from Bats Head. As I came away afterwards, everything I usually am and do seemed to belong to a more superficial level, and I had a sense of depths beyond me – but not apart from everyday living – which are all that matter.

•

First copies of *Englishman's Road*. And it makes me want to write, seeing what I have not achieved, but finding in some poems indications of a stronger & deeper way. I do know more the kind of thing I want to aim at now, and feel that, given time, there will be the energy I've sometimes feared comes only with one's blindness, so that *seeing* more, a poet can only make a theory of poetry, and poems that make the right theoretical gestures, but are lifeless. The truth is that as long as a man remains a poet it is impossible to see too much, for he is then always in the process. If he could see all, it would be finished, with no potential for growth, no uncertainty of growth. But a real poetry is never finished, not only because it goes on living & revealing more & different things to its readers, but also because it stimulates new poets, who grow from it in the sense that we all grow from poetic tradition.

August
Hiroshima Day
   'The sky was serene, the air was flooded with glittering morning light.'
   'I am become Death, the shatterer of worlds.'

•

Rain beats steadily into sodden fields, drips continually onto my windowsill. Thunderstorm far out at sea, the atmosphere close.
   Broken sleep last night. Winifrid rang in the evening to tell us Charles is much worse. We expected him to die in the night, and Sue felt he had, as she woke feeling drained. It would be a mercy now.
   When a death occurs or is pending, how one realises the waste of one's everyday life, all its sleep or half-sleep, wrapped up in selfish & trivial aims & desires. But to live always awake, clear-eyed, without an insomniac's habitual fatigue! How?

•

To Pulborough on Friday, where I left Sue for a few days and went on with the children to Hayford. Charles is bed-ridden and almost certainly in his last weeks.

One morning we went by ferry to Hurst, where there were yellow horned poppies under the castle walls, and impoverished Herb Robert, apparently with nothing but shingle to root in. On another, glorious morning we walked from Puttles Bridge along the edge of the open Forest, by Oberwater, gold & darkly shadowed.

In that rare sun, in the mellow cloudless afternoon of the same day, we walked with Mother to Pennington Common, and came back through Yaldhurst, where there is a sense of ancient occupation under corn & in the hedgebanks, & below tall oaks & beeches & pines. There C. and I once saw the sun's brand fire-red on a pine's bark, and I went with J. to gather holly years before. This sense was always there for me, though I know it is now my childhood & youth too.

Another morning, in rain that later became a downpour, with the sea grey & choppy, we drove to Lepe and, after walking on the windy shore, sat in a cafe, rain streaming down the windows. Mother talked about her childhood, as she often does when we are out alone together now. When she was young and her mother died, the nurse gave her the dead baby to hold, 'like a doll'. That night she stayed with a friend whose father was station master at Swanwick, and steam from the trains whooshed up right in front of her bedroom window. Bishopstone, I now realise, was her mother's place, though the Moulds also came from Salisbury & thereabouts.

•

Two visits to Pennington Marshes on glorious fresh late August mornings of sunlight & cloud. At Oxey, by the stile under the oak tree, an autumnal smell of oakleaves mingling with a smell of salt & mud. The Island stood in bold, dark outline across a saltern filled with water, Tennyson's memorial a stub on the high Down. Tide out. Nests of bladder-wrack loosely wound round old posts, mud & bright green patches of seaweed beyond a brilliant silver – light glittering in water. I could walk or stand on the wall for hours.

Sky, water, light, the mud a shining mirror. In that place I seem almost to understand things I don't approach anywhere else.

On Saturday afternoon Tony & I walked round the Common in

rain and talked about our concern over Mother. Sharing this, all my frustration & irritation at once vanished. On Sunday, a fine, blowy day, we took her to Hurst shingle-spit; all clean & clear & fresh, with a little spray in our faces & sharp cloud shadows dark on the face of the sea. Then back to Wales after lunch, the Forest in sunlight & shadow; always passing through where I want now more than ever to stay ...

There's so much I can't say, either because I don't know how or because I am afraid, but between us almost everything was at last spoken. That walk in the rain is a touchstone. Remember when life is an introspective dream, or the gap between self and others fills with trivial, monstrous fantasies. What peculiar selves many of us grow, with such suspicions & fears & hideous ego-dreams, grossly warping our spirit which would naturally be so different if it could. All the worry I give way to, bringing me to the edge of dread – this isn't love for anyone's sake, but a selfish anxiety to protect my world.

September
Light, blue as woodsmoke on the mountainside & in all hollows under it. White sun & mild blue sky, windblown grass blades shining and the stream's dazzling loops at the field's edge. A tiny yellow hazel leaf, almost closed like a hand, dances wildly on an invisible gossamer.

Seeing doesn't have to mean the tyranny of the eye, but is a crucial part of being in the world. Even on such a morning, even trying to concentrate, I cannot take more than a few steps knowing where I am, being just here in a world vaster than I could ever know, even with finest attentiveness, but revert to a half dream, dim shapes changing monotonously into one another – fantasies, ambitions, resentments, now & again a start of clearer thought: the muddy, waywardly lit stream of normal consciousness. More and more, I see the distorted shapes we make of ourselves, beating up against others, succumbing to external images & pressures, suffering conflicting desires ...

Brynbeidog may be standing in a hundred years, the Beidog flowing as I saw it just now, through sycamore branches which the wind blew towards me, turning over dulled leaves, as I looked across at the white wall and the kitchen window by the coal bunkers, where Joe's bike was leaning, one wheel on a heap of stones and the saddle tilted back – used and ready for use, fitting exactly into his life now, as all this belongs to our lives. At such moments I can feel that everything may be saved, somehow existing for ever in a way totally beyond my understanding, which can hold even a precious detail only with difficulty; that there is something other than time, though time is what it saves. I can doubt it too, seeing the river flow, and think it wishful, the natural human desire to hold on to everything, certainly for the sake of love, but also to preserve the world each is the centre of.

To me, there's no more haunting passage than this from *Mr Weston's Good Wine*:

> But even with death defeated in one manner or another, modest death still has his set duties to perform, and immortality, viewed in passion or solitude, can only be but the patches of sunlight seen upon a dull, hot summer's day, when thin, soft clouds are above. But these patches should at least console us a little for the loss of ourselves.

What Theodorian irony – sad & gentle, mordant & poignantly stoic – in that last sentence! I can't do it justice; perhaps there is really no undertone, only gentle mockery of his own acceptance of the unbearable, which is acceptance all the same.

I come near despair when all things seem only unique, infinitely precious to those who love them, but entirely mortal, themselves only in and because of time. Yet I live more in hope, or perhaps in a relative unconsciousness of time as destroyer, carried along without facing the fact of death. In any case, I am more than ever sure that the purpose of true art is transfiguration – as Berdyaev says, but I'm not sure that he meant what I mean. Marvellous as much of his thought is, it is rarely particular enough for me. Berdyaev generalises creativity; he often excites me, but seldom offers anything I can *grasp*, though the fault is no doubt my poor understanding of conceptual thought.

Art transfigures; it works in the human sphere in a way that is analogous to the Christian resurrection, in a spirit that would lose nothing, but keep all that is individual in its essential being. Various though its manifestations are, art springs from the essential human need to present what we love, and reveal it so that we take its timely self out of time ... I am beginning to see only now, vaguely, what has long been an instinctive belief, the very mould of my feeling, which first drew me to a poet such as Frances Bellerby, a religious thinker such as Berdyaev.

Love can't be against time, because what we love exists, as we do, in and because of time; but is inevitably against the nature of time to pass over and lose its creatures and things. We are all in a sense responsible for not letting each other go or losing the dead. But the artist has a special responsibility – not to fix the objects of his love photographically; to reveal them, then, *sub specie aeternitatis*? Certainly to *reveal* in the light of a love that perceives and values their essential being; that sees and does not fantastically transform.

But I mustn't be hypocritical about 'the dead'. We do let each other go, all the time. I care far more about the frog I've just mangled and killed with the fly-mow than about the masses I've never known. Even major symbolists can produce facile rhetoric in respect of The Dead. It's terribly hard really to admit the existence of another person as fully as one's own, easy to make high-sounding noises. The eye of the creature looking up at me, with a childlike innocent watch-fulness; one useless leg stretched out and its beautiful body, yellow as a wet autumn leaf, twisted and torn. Just a bloody mess with no sense to it. Nothing to do but kill it as quickly as possible, and curse the machine and myself.

•

The greatest error of historical Christianity is linked with the fatally limiting idea that the revelation is finished, and that nothing more is to be expected, that the building of the Church is com-pleted and the roof laid on it.

(Nicolas Berdyaev)

It is the image, above all, that makes this so effective. Especially in Europe, where the Church has been so long-established, with ancient buildings that can make what they stand for seem 'finished', at the same time as they inspire awe. At best they connect believers, and even, to some degree, agnostics, with the past, as members of a com-munity that is at once historical and timeless. At worst the very completeness of their ancient forms, which are aesthetically pleasing, make people feel that what they house belongs entirely to the past. They are historically full but spiritually empty, with a perfect finish and no present life.

Some things are little on the outside, and rough and common, but I remember the time when the dust of the streets were as precious

as Gold to my infant eyes, and now they are more precious to the
eye of reason.

(Thomas Traherne)

•

New term tomorrow. This summer I've done what I set out to do,
completing 'Poetry of Place' – but not a line of poetry since last
September. Several times the impulse to write has come, and I've put
it off. Now again I feel the need, and have no time. This postpone-
ment is a dangerous game.

Now, determined to sell Brynbeidog, we're almost certain to leave
here within the next few months. Yesterday afternoon I raked up
weeds, carried them to the compost heap; the same as when we first
came here, the same autumn smells, the same fine weather, all as in
that glorious period. Ironically free of work pressing to be done for
the first time for many months, this morning, with a half moon in the
sky, I walked round the near fields, my gumboots washed with dew,
shining like blackberries.

October

A few weeks into term, with little time for anything but academic
work. So far I'm reasonably content to be used & to use myself in this
way. Then comes a moment's pause and I realise the other need, and
how exhausting the pressure of teaching is.

Last weekend, at Gregynog, I met and read with Derek Walcott.
He is a generous & marvellously vital man, and if in much of his
writing he is too wordy for me, letting his images come so close one
on another that they often wash over each other, his energy makes me
long to write.

One day Sue remarked that Joe has an innate sense of failure. This
morning he and I greatly enjoyed ourselves gathering wood and
cutting it up into logs, and he was full of confidence. But I've seen in
him the feeling that I know so well, and wonder what can be done
now, before it becomes the devil it can be.

November

South by myself for two beautifully sunny days, when I took Mother and Dad to see his paintings 'centered' & 'hung on the line', as he always proudly says, at a Private View of the Bournemouth Arts Society's annual exhibition at the Russell-Cotes, and went next day to Southampton to submit his canvases at the Art Gallery.

To Bolderwood with Mother in the morning, where we walked among tall Douglas Firs to the Earl of Radnor's stone. On our way through Rhinefield we saw a deer with its great head-piece of branching antlers, apparently top-heavy, though part of such graceful movement, cross the road and vanish through the trees. The turning beeches were a startling, almost blinding, fire of yellow, orange, red.

Having arranged with Jim to meet in the evening, he rang up, slurred, at ten to eight thinking it was ten to nine, and I went out to find him being turned away from The Musketeers, looking like a tramp & conspicuously drunk. We staggered about on the Common for an hour or so, shouting at each other and then I went home, shaken, while he went on to The Wheel. The following morning he rang from Brockenhurst, where he had gone on a train from Sway, hoping to get a drink in the buffet. We walked by Oberwater, the river stately in its slow progress of oakleaves, with deep, clear reflections of sky & trees, and acorns falling explosively through the stillness or thudding on the ground, so that we went half-flinching. I don't think he remembered details of the previous evening, and only referred to it by saying that he had been drinking all day with Ike Keeping who has a bar in his house at East Boldre and this usually has ill effects. It was a splendid morning of free talk, sunlight & laughter.

•

Arriving at College on another fine, cold day, almost the first thing I see is DIM CROESO I CARLO in bold white letters on a wall of the Arts Centre and a party of workmen scraping away at them – the Prince is due to visit tomorrow. Minutes later, walking past Michael Munday's room, which is next to mine, Michael is vivid in my mind, as he has often been, his hands paper-thin, too weak to undo a shirt button to show his latest operation scar. At last this is coming home to me – incomprehensible, irreducible fact. It is hard to write or speak of without feeling somehow heartless, insulting his great dignity & his quiet, patient waiting.

•

Olive Schreiner in *The Story of an African Farm* risks everything as few writers ever do, incorporating the furthest reaches of her experience, her relentless questioning mind, and poetic sensibility. Few novels can ever have incorporated so much of their author & his or her sense of life. I leave it knowing I have touched something real. And thinking about that extreme intensity which I've only met in writing by women – Emily Brontë, Emily Dickinson, George Eliot, Frances Bellerby & others: intensity of thought that cannot be separated from intensity of spirit & feeling, but is utterly clear, hard up against reality & unyielding, showing how it is without seeking refuge in should, might or ought to be. To some extent, this is an intensity born of their subjection – life as known only by the humiliated, shut out from the dream existence of all whose social power gives them the illusion of mastery or even god-like control of life itself, and who consequently know nothing of its real conditions. But there is then something frightening about the unforgiving feminist intelligence, won from perceptions of the oppressed but without their knowledge of suffering or sense of kinship with all who suffer. There's nothing more frightening now, however, than the dream of our masters (and mistresses) with their actual power to affect life & death.

•

Winter sunlight in Winchester, where I was appointed creative writing fellow at the School of Art for a year – with joy. Then the anxiety of selling Brynbeidog and making the move, together with worry over the extra difficulties I'll be causing my colleagues. But all outweighed by excitement at the prospect of really getting to know Winchester and feeling a way back into the south, and of much more freedom & flexibility.

Delight at going & regret at leaving. However we may be, I will always feel grief at not holding to Wales, as I have at not returning to the south. This must be, with love of people & place, with any divided life, which in fact owes much to its divisions. I accept these feelings which could not be otherwise. Certainly, if I am really to write, to move on, the coming year will be critical.

Then on the morning of our return to Wales, there was snow, an overnight fall mottling the hills & a heavier fall at breakfast time. The daylight moon of recent days, always high over the chalk country, was now a snow moon, like a flake of the far mountains in their hard, pure whiteness under a clear sky & dazzling sun.

December

Ridge black against dawn. Venus bright above it in a clear sky of cold, pure blue. Later the house with its white walls & slate roof was naked in sunlight & dew – as I have often seen it and loved it, and forgotten again; with light filling it.

It is the same moving away as walking out; perspective broadens. Already I can see Cardiganshire again, reaching further north & south, while months ago I was virtually confined to near fields, unable to imagine more than the ridge enclosed. So under Mynydd Bach was intensely my living space; I could not grasp imaginatively anything beyond it. But now as we prepare to leave, Wales begins to grow around me again, regaining the coherence it has always had – the life that is much more other & more various than any image – but I failed in my narrowness to see; just as, fifteen years ago, I began to see past my confined space in Southampton, towards the south of England as a whole.

•

We left Brynbeidog after lunch on the twenty-first in response to a call from Winifrid and drove to Pulborough three days earlier than we had originally intended. It was dark from Hereford on, or rather night-time, for there was an enormous full moon and the sky was a mild, milky blue. We arrived to find Charles had died some four hours earlier, having been given an injection in the morning and lain in a deep death-like sleep all day. The undertakers came shortly after us, but at least we had been able to see him.

When we say the dead feel close to us we may mean that they become in their absence a focus of intense concentration, more than they were when living, and so more real than ever to us. I can admit this now, at Hayford, writing in cold blood, a week after Charles's death, but could not have done earlier. We had talked so much about death & dying, especially about his hopes and doubts of an after-life, that

the break feels abrupt & absolute – in a conversation for ever interrupted, looking for a completion it could never have. He would have
appreciated the irony.

•

On the Downs above North Stoke, fields strewn with great flints and
bleak in spite of the flowing, curving lines. No berries & little old
man's beard, just dead things not worth gathering. Battlements of
Arundle Castle some miles to the south, mysterious & imposing
under a cloud-banked sun. I was rebuked by a tenant of the Duke
when walking with Joe off the path up a field edge to look at an earth-
work, which turned out to be a dewpond. An apologetic response
turned away wrath, but as usual the incident lodged deeper in me
than it should. Yet was salutary too, breaking through that mist in
which the world seems composed according to my susceptibilities.

•

Service of thanksgiving for Charles at Stopham church, where we were
on Christmas Day, but now, with the tree still lit, the church was full.
Up at the front, with the coffin in the aisle beside me, I was too sensi-
tized to be wholly there for more than part of the time. I associate
Charles with the shingle-bank in Chichester Harbour where he used to
watch birds, rather than with any other resting place. Afterwards we
went in a limousine to Worthing Crematorium, where in a spotless
chapel, with an organist playing discreetly, yellow automatic curtains
closed silently, tastefully, around the coffin. The limousine whispered
back under the darkened line of the Downs, in a soft dream world of
lights coming & going on the roads.

Leaving

Against the wall
a boy's bike leans
waiting for its rider.

I look from the stream
through a sycamore –
breakfast things on the table
wait in place;
vapour trails shine
like ruts in the sky
on airways far to the south.

Sun on the ridge.
The house filled with light.

> *For the first time*
> *it is hollow, echoing,*
> *the living room*
> *cavernous.*

As I walk away
the Beidog winds, gleaming –
joining field to field.

I climb and the sea rises,
silver, a planet's rim;
peak climbs on peak
blue and far,

the house settles –
smaller, deeper, in place.

> *Do we simply*
> *pack ourselves away?*
> *The hearth's a black hole*
> *where you knelt.*

After days of storm,
fallen slates, fields
grey with exhaustion,

buzzards come, and a kite
picking red slivers,

a ewe shelters lambs
at the lattice of a thorn.

> *Floors skinned,*
> *picture shapes on walls,*
> *in each doorway*
> *a shock of cold.*

Under hills clouded,
bent backed,

I crumble black earth
through fingers
caked with earth:
ground worked
over and over, where
we too grow round
with windbreak sycamores.

> *Just now*
> *I put out my hand*
> *for a table, which this morning*
> *I broke up and burnt,*
>
> *and nearly fell,*
> *nearly leant on its rim.*

Midsummer silence falls,
the dry lanes smell
of dog-roses and dust.

Foxgloves snake from hedgerows,
a buzzard circles mewing
round and round.

I lie down, dash
the stream in my face,
look up at the slate roof
tilted against the ridge.

Bare flesh-coloured boards.
Briefly
in childless quiet
the house waits.

Index